THE EGOTISTS

THE EGOTISTS

Sixteen Surprising Interviews

Oriana Fallaci

HENRY REGNERY COMPANY
Chicago

Interviews with Anna Magnani, Jeanne Moreau, Duchess of Alba, Federico Fellini, and Alfred Hitchcock appeared in *Gli Antipatici,* published by Rizzoli Editore, Milano, 1963; with Sean Connery, Geraldine Chaplin, Mary Hemingway, El Cordobés, and Sammy Davis, Jr., appeared in *Limelighters,* published by Michael Joseph, Ltd., London, 1968. The remaining interviews were published in either *L'Europeo* or *Look.*

Translations: Interviews with Mary Hemingway, English translation copyright © 1966, with Dean Martin and Hugh Hefner, English translation copyright © 1967, and with Ingrid Bergman and Nguyen Cao Ky, English translation copyright © 1968, by Oriana Fallaci, Rizzoli Press; with Norman Mailer and H. Rap Brown, English translation copyright © 1968, by Mihaly Csikszentmihalyi; remaining interviews (translated by Pamela Swinglehurst), English translation copyright © 1968, by Michael Joseph, Ltd., London.

Photographs: Norman Mailer (D. J. Davis); remainder, courtesy of Rizzoli Editore.

To François Pelou

FOREWORD

Most of this book was published in Italy under the title *Gli Antipatici*. Now the word *antipatico*, along with the word *simpatico*, which is its opposite, is perhaps the most untranslatable in the Italian language. In fact, it is to be found, with the same meaning, in only two other languages: Spanish and French. In English it doesn't really exist. Some people think its equivalent is the word antipathetic (and its opposite, sympathetic). Antipathetic means adverse, unfavorable, contrary: nothing to do with its sense in Italian. So, what does *antipatico* mean?

The New Dictionary of the Italian Language explains it like this: "Unpleasant, disagreeable, annoying, unbearable, intolerable, odious, boring, tiresome, disliked, dull, or someone who suscitates *antipatia*." The Etymological Dictionary of the Italian Language describes the noun *antipatia* like this: "From the Latin word antipatia which comes from the Greek word antipatheia which means state of not-feeling, general adverse feeling." Yet, when the Italians say *antipatico—antipatici* in the plural—they mean none of these things. Actually they mean much less. Or much more. Just as *simpatico* is someone you like on sight, so *antipatico* is someone that you dislike on sight. Should I be forced to choose a translation for *antipatico*, I would say "unlikable"; for *simpatico*, I would say "likable."

Or, to cut a long story short, *simpatico* is someone with whom you agree to have dinner, even if you are not hungry; *antipatico* is someone with whom you won't go to dinner, even if you are starving. *Simpatico* is someone for whom you would

vii

jump into the river, in winter, to save from drowning; *anti-patico* is someone you would calmly observe drowning in the river, someone you would refuse to help, even if it is a very hot day in summer and you are dreaming of having a nice swim.

Many of the characters who figure in this book are my friends. Or almost friends. Or possible friends. Those who are not my friends, or almost friends, or possible friends, are my enemies. Or almost enemies. Or possible enemies, who have, however, sportingly shared the distress of a difficult encounter, so earning my grateful respect. I do not therefore consider them *antipatici* in the precise etymological sense generally applied to the word. I consider them *antipatici* in another sense. Everywhere people are talking about them, discussing them, their doings, their loves, their bullfights, their poems, their goals, their music, their meetings, their movies, their millions, their misfortunes. And their celebrity is so vast, so clamorous, so exasperating that it obsesses us, plagues us, suffocates us to the point where we exclaim: "God, what bores! God, what *antipatici!*" I am explaining this, before anything else, not to beg anyone's forgiveness for a title for which I need beg nobody's forgiveness, but to make myself clear both to the reader and to the *antipatici* themselves, who are nearly always *simpaticissimi*. I am explaining it, moreover, to forestall a question that will be on the tip of many tongues: why, among the *antipatici*, I have not included myself. I have not because I am not famous, and consequently I am not *antipatica*. I can be a bore, it's true. But when I'm a bore, it's not because I make people talk about myself, about my loves, my bullfights, my poems, my goals, my music, my meetings, my movies, my millions, my misfortunes. I'm a bore when I report what bores others are, as these interviews show.

There are sixteen interviews with the *antipatici*, and they have been selected from a series published in many magazines, all over the world, during recent years. Rather than interviews, however, they are conversations recorded on a tape recorder, then transposed into written dialogue. Rather than conversations, I would add, they are monologues provoked by my questions or opinions. I have always thought that letting people talk and faithfully reporting what they say would contribute considerably to written profiles. And in fact this was what started the idea of the interviews, which, beginning with my first interview with Ingrid Bergman, went on for months and then for years—not to my great delight, however. If getting famous people to talk is exhausting, getting them to talk in front of a machine that is recording every pause and every breath is, in 50 per cent of the cases, fraught with tension. At first the presence of a microphone used to embarrass me, too. Knowing it was there was like feeling spied upon, judged, and ridiculed. It wasn't uncommon for the subject to grow pale or to mutter haltingly, to the serious detriment of both syntax and common sense. If he didn't mutter haltingly, he would fall silent. If he didn't fall silent, he would drown the microphone in a chaos of words, and, as the tape wound inexorably on, I would be consumed with the thought of afterward. Afterward came the worst moment: when I would listen to the silences and torrents of talk and have to transpose them into normal conversations, profiles. Listening to someone talk isn't at all like listening to their words played over on a machine. What you hear when you have a face before you is never what you hear when you have before you a winding tape. At times a flashing glance or a movement of the hands will make the most stupid remark meaningful, but without the hands, the flashing glance, the remark is left in all its disconcerting stupidity. On the other hand, a disagreeable nose, a humble attitude, can at times detract from the value of the richest remark, and without the attitude, the nose, the remark acquires once more its full reassuring richness. I realized this when I realized another important thing: that reported remarks are not enough to give an idea of who is speaking, the shape of their features, the clothes they wear, the gestures they make, in short, the complete profile.

To complete the profile, and not from some urge to appear malicious at any price, I have prefaced each interview with an introduction, sometimes short and sometimes long, relating what led up to the interview, how it took place, and how it concluded. It also relates things not always directly connected with the interview that, inevitably, contain some judgment on the subject. This will not please the devotees of objective journalism, for whom any judgment is lack of objectivity, but I can't say that this bothers me much. As I have said many other times and will always say, I don't believe in objectivity. Objectivity is hypocrisy, presumption, since it starts from the supposition that the person who is providing a piece of news or a profile has discovered Truth with a capital T. In fact, when one writes a profile, there exists, there can only exist, the honesty of the person who furnishes the piece of news or the profile. With this honesty I have written my prefaces.

With the same honesty I want to say that my *antipatici* were not warned about this. When I left them, I had no thought of collecting the interviews in a book, and consequently I didn't tell them that in the book I would be relating what the microphone could neither see nor hear. And so it is very likely that they will not much care for the idea and will withdraw their friendship where they had given it, deny me their friendship where they were thinking of giving it, redouble their enmity where it already existed. Even more likely, they will loudly protest they have been betrayed. I am very sorry, but, apart from the idea of betraying them, I feel myself positively cleansed by the betrayal. My conscience is as clear as the conscience of a babe. I never felt quite happy when I read over these interviews in the magazines, because I always realized that I hadn't said everything about the people I met. Now that I have said it all, including what I had kept back—if I had been keeping anything back—I feel as if a weight has been lifted from my heart. I feel fresh and clean, ready to fly up to paradise—in the event that one of them challenges me to a duel and is quicker on the draw than I am.

ORIANA FALLACI

CONTENTS

THE EGOTISTS

NORMAN MAILER

Why Do People Dislike America?

If one were to give human semblance to the America of today, this hated and often misunderstood country, I would choose Norman Mailer to be the model. I would choose him as he is now, in the middle of his forty-sixth year, in the midst of a maturity full of pain, full of tragedy. This body is heavy, massive like the country that gave him birth. From this body hang two short arms, like those of a child yet bulging with muscle, ending in thick worker's wrists, and from those wrists emerge two tiny hands, well cared for, distinctly bourgeois. When he spreads them in front of him—a customary gesture—you are not sure whether he wants to pick a fight or whether he is asking for mercy. The face? Well, the face is noble and vulgar all at the same time. Underneath a dome of gray curls his expanding brow is marked by a thousand anxieties, sins, half-formed thoughts. The nose is misshapen by blows, the mouth a chasm that swallows alcohol and regurgitates incomprehensible words slurred by faulty or extravagant diction. At times, like America itself, he says beautiful things to which nobody pays attention because of the way they are said. The most significant detail is the eyes—one large and one small, because of a drooping eyelid. The large one is good, patient; the small one is wicked and aggressive. One tries to catch America—Mailer's stare—and one doesn't know which eye to choose, which eye to respond to. As a result one cannot reach a moral decision about him. But the practical dilemma remains: Should one be his friend or his enemy? Most people consider him an enemy; to be his friend is anything but easy.

There are times, for instance, when he is drunk, when he can exasperate you to the point that you forget his intelligence, the fact that he is one of the best known writers of the world; you turn your back to him, wish that he were lost. He is almost always drunk in the evenings, till the lights of dawn. At such times he

1

becomes the typical cowboy of the Westerns: ready to fire his guns
at the drop of a hat, getting into a rage at the least provocation,
the most innocent remark. Drinking and getting mad are part of
his personality, at least the personality he has assumed for himself. He likes to be tough, a no-nonsense kind of a guy—let them
send one missile to Cuba, and I'll unleash the war. Drinking for
him is not a habit, but a well-figured-out challenge. "I am a very
lonely man, and I'm very quiet when I don't drink. When I do, I
become alert, critical, my intelligence becomes sharper, I can
think more and better. Like Jekyll and Hyde. Of course I don't
write when I'm drunk: to write one should feel healthy, like a
man who is about to take a woman to bed, but I am getting ready
for that feeling while I drink. In other words, I store in the back
of my mind the things I will write later when I am sober." Before,
he used to drug himself with marijuana as well. "Marijuana has
been like love to me, like the kind for the sake of which people fall
in love. There is wisdom in love; as long as it lasts, you think you
understand everything. Well, marijuana was to me like a beautiful
woman who suddenly walks into your room, a rose in her hand,
trailing a perfume, sensitive, wise. Then she left me. It wasn't I
who left her, but the other way around. And it was very painful."
And he likes to be discussed, to amaze people. The man is obviously
not a saint. Just think of the knife he slipped into his second wife,
Adele. It began with a party, during which he had drunk much
and become very aggressive. He had an argument in the street with
the fighter Donoghue, who had been the guest of honor; then he
returned home and without a word plunged a knife into his wife
twice, close to the heart. He missed it by sheer chance, or good
luck. Then he wrote a poem:

> So long
>   as
>   you
>   use
>   a knife,
> there's
>   some
>   love
>   left.

So far he has had four wives. First was Bea Silverman, an intellectual he met at a concert. Then Adele Morales, a Peruvian painter he had known in the Village. Then it was Lady Jean Campbell's turn, the daughter of the Duke of Argyll, whom he used to call the "best lightweight ever exported by Great Britain." Finally Beverly Bentley, an actress, who is presently in charge. He has had at least one child from each, six all told. "The fact is that there isn't anything more pleasant than a good marriage, nor anything less pleasant than a bad one. And when the meanness that feeds the good as well as the bad marriage takes over, then the marriage blows up. Mine have all blown up"—after frightful arguments, blows exchanged, dishes thrown. Still women are his great passion, the fame of a great lover surrounds him. He claims in this respect to have an "infernal talent." The wicked eye reflects a bloody, adolescent America, barbaric and sad—the ugly America of skyscrapers, gangsters, drive-ins, Vietnam, insanity, Hemingwayan rhetoric. The taint of insanity has been following him for years. He himself admits to have been influenced by Hemingway, although, he claims, only on a literary level: "His style was so magnetic, an adult style. I write differently, but I've learned so much from him. The man was a great cobbler, he taught everybody how to make shoes. It makes me cry to think that I've never known him." Let us now look into his good eye.

In the good eye throbs America the beautiful, the brave, the free—America of the spanning bridges and the Constitution, of the revolutionary ferments and ceaseless renewal. And this Mailer is a well-bred Christian gentleman, shy to the point that one may suspect that he drinks to overcome his shyness toward himself and others. This is the Mailer who loves his children with a passion, his parents with respect, his wives with generosity, his friends with loyalty; he is the one who writes such books as *The Naked and the Dead, Barbary Shore, The Deer Park, An American Dream, The Presidential Papers, Cannibals and Christians;* the Mailer who believes in culture, who studies engineering at Harvard for four years, who seeks God by arguing theology with priests (he was born Jewish), who wears out his brains fighting and thinking, who raises himself to his feet to denounce, at the top of his voice, President Johnson, the Asian war, the CIA, the specter of a new witch hunt. If he is not quite a saint, he is close to being a hero. With some hesitations and a change in scale one would be tempted to call him the American Sartre, even though he lacks Sartre's discipline, the sense of sacrifice, the depth that comes from being born among cathedrals instead of supermarkets. He shares with Sartre the guts, the flexibility of mind, and the clear political choice with which it is beside the point either to agree or to disagree. "Marxism is the mold of my intellectual life. I am not a Marxist to the extent that I believe in dialectical materialism, but I am a Marxist in that I reason dialectically—so it's more exact to say that I have gone beyond Marxism. To each historical moment there corresponds a philosophy on which historians will agree five centuries later, the *geist* of that period. Marxism was the *geist* of Victorian times; now that they are ended, we need to go beyond Marxism. How? If I had Marx's mental equipment, his ability to apply himself, to spend ten years in a library, if I weren't such a romantic, a half-intellectual, if I hadn't spent my time drinking and working at half my capacity . . ." There is no doubt that the importance of this man is out of the ordinary. Like America, which we reproach for not being perfect, better than we are, we cannot forgive him a heavy body, short arms, dainty hands, a broken nose, confused ideas; we should like him to know more and be able to teach us more.

The incredible interview that follows was almost impossible to get. For two weeks I ran after him with a glass in my hands; with his wife, a handsome, difficult blond; with the court that often surrounds him to agree with everything he says, a court made up mostly of half-wits, as usually happens to such men; and with his good friend and former brother-in-law, Mickey Knox, married to Adele's sister. Finally Mickey convinced Mailer that he should see me during the day—sober, that is—and he set the meeting as one sets the date for a boxing match. First round at Mickey's house. The second at his. Mailer's home is in Brooklyn, where he was born; it's an old town house overlooking the East River. Beyond the river is Manhattan, its lights burning in millions of bulbs, its skyscraper profile making one forget domes and the nostalgia for trees. On the left, the Statue of Liberty hangs between a green sea and a purple sky. It's a great responsibility to live in such a setting, while a helicopter rattles overhead, jets streak above the clouds, white ships plow the water, raising wings of foam. The house itself is built like a ship. There are no wooden or stone steps inside, to reach the studio where Mailer works, right under the roof. One has to climb up rope ladders like those sailors use to reach the top of the mast; one risks one's neck. More than a workroom, it's a mystic temple that one conquers through hardship and danger. This, then, is why he can only work when sober; drunk he could never get up there. At the start of the climb there is also a trapeze, a rope one crosses like a rope-walker. The walls are covered with thousands of books, including treatises on mathematics, physics, biology, astronomy, medicine, philosophy; to be born among supermarkets rather than cathedrals is not enough to quench the spirit of Man. In one corner of the living room is a strange construction that seems to be a toy but isn't: it's a model of a city of the future. Streets, houses, offices, theaters, schools, and hospitals are not built on the surface but hang from suspended bridges, imaginatively distributed on different levels and in various directions. Imagine a huge Christmas tree of steel and concrete, with bridges instead of branches, buildings instead of needles, electronic elevators running up and down the trunk. The visitor's astonishment is answered by Mailer with a satanic chuckle: "See the results of four years of engineering at Harvard. But if we have to give up trees and live in a world of damned computers, this is the solution"—transform a town into a green tree.

It's a spring evening. There is no one else in the house. Beverly is playing a part in the stage version of *The Deer Park*, the children have gone out with the grandparents so as not to disturb our boxing match. Mailer is drinking a glass of water, pure tap water. There is a program on TV, about why Europeans don't like America anymore. Mailer speaks with a voice that is understandable at last, and his good eye is very beautiful. Quietly I turn on the tape recorder.

ORIANA FALLACI: *The problem I want to talk about is a difficult one, but we have to deal with it. The fact is, we Europeans used to love you Americans. When you came to liberate us twenty years ago, we looked up to you as if you were angels. And now many of us don't love you anymore; indeed, some hate you. Today the United States might be the most hated country in the world.*

NORMAN MAILER: You used to love us because love is hope, and we Americans were your hope. And also, perhaps, because twenty years ago we were a better people, although not as good as you believed then—the seeds of the present ugliness were already there. The soldiers with whom I fought in the Pacific, for example, were a little better than the ones who are fighting now in Vietnam, but not by much. We were quite brutal even then. One could write a novel about Vietnam along the lines of *The Naked and the Dead,* and the characters would not need to be worse than they are in the book. The fact is that you have lost the hope you had vested in us, and so you have lost your love; therefore, you see us in a much worse light than you did before, and you don't understand that the roots of our ugliness are the old ones. It is true that the evil forces in America have triumphed only after the war—with the enormous growth of corporations and the transformation of man into mass-man, the alienation of men from their own existence—but these forces were already there in Roosevelt's time. Roosevelt, you see, was a great President, but he wasn't a great thinker. Indeed, he was a very superficial one. When he took power, America stood at a crossroad; either a proletarian revolution would take place or capitalism would enter a new phase. What happened was that capitalism took a new turn, transforming itself into a subtle elaboration of state capitalism—it is not by chance that the large corporations in effect belong to the government. They belong to the right. And just as the Stalinists have murdered Marxism, so these bastards of the right are now destroying what is good in American life. They are the same people who build the expressways, who cut the trees, who pollute the air and the water, who transform all life into a huge commodity. . . .

We Europeans are also very good at this. I mean this is not done only by right-wing Americans.

Of course. It is a worldwide process. But its leader is America, and this is why we are hated. We are the leaders of the technological revolution that is taking over the twentieth century, the electronic revolution that is dehumanizing mankind. And it's depressing how Europeans contribute to it. Europeans have everything to offer America; yet it's not us who are learning from Europe, but the other way around. You also are guilty: for learning and imitating that which is worst in American life—this American need of absolute control, of a clean and sterilized environment. You believe, for instance, that we have the best hospitals in the world; it isn't true, ours are the worst ones. Our hospitals poison people instead of making them well. We have created more contagious diseases in our hospitals in the past twenty years than the rest of the world put together. Diseases that spread like weeds after each atomic explosion, and that can't be destroyed even with fire. Take antibiotics, for instance. They cure some illnesses only to produce new ones. What I mean is that our commodities are never good commodities: we have substituted synthetic fibers for silk, but the former cause discomforts that the latter never did. Our bodies are sick with the poison of commodities. It's a poison from which we won't be able to free ourselves unless we adopt a cure of great imagination. There is a kind of totalitarianism being born in America that is the essence of all the totalitarian forces of our century. It is not the same as the fascist, the nazi, or the Stalinist totalitarianism; it is a totalitarianism that resembles a sickness, a cancer. Just look how public opinion is being manipulated, how individualism, variety, dissent, the past are being destroyed, leveling everybody to a desire for superficial well-being that excludes any disagreement. . . .

Yet America was born of an act of dissent, of individuality.

Right. But let's look at its consequences. The people who came to America, who made America, were the best, and at the same time the worst, kind of people. They were unloved, they were rejected for one reason or another by their society in Europe. Because of political, economic, or religious reasons. They were rejects, in other words, who chose to come to America because they didn't want to die. Thus America was born of the seed of the most wonderful flowers and the ugliest weeds. As you know, nobody loves a weed, and it has only one desire—to live, despite the rest of nature. So what has happened to us, the descendants of those weeds? We have survived in spite of nature—with an amazing capacity to renew ourselves, to solve practical problems the like of which the world has never known. At the same time, however, we have always carried within us the insanity of the weed, an insanity that began with the origins of America. We are not a mentally healthy people. America is like a sick fat man—I say man because when I think of America, I always think of a man, never a woman—a man tied in harness who can stand his acute illness only by spreading it to others.

Why are we here then, why do you stay here instead of fleeing to Europe as other writers did: Hemingway, Fitzgerald, Henry Miller?

In the first place because I believe myself to be one of the few doctors left who are aware of the illness, and so I have to stay here rather than tend to the last glories of Europe. And then because I'm fascinated by America—by its despair, its unpredictability, its untractability. Everything can happen: it can go from bad to worse, or it can get better. If we call America sick, we must also recognize that it is not an invalid in a wheelchair, pushed around by nurses who every minute have to give it shots to dull the nerves of its resistance. Resistance in America is so intense, so brave. The young are strong; they gave me an ovation when, during a TV debate, I attacked American policy, Johnson, the Vietnam thing. Not everything in this country is ugly. Besides, you see, I feel at home here; in Europe I am lost, unsure of myself, like a fifteen-year-old boy. I like to travel to Europe, but I wouldn't want to live there. There is something in Europe I can't take all at once. Don't forget that being an American I grew up on a very thin cultural diet, and my nerves are not accustomed to being overstimulated. I am not, for instance, trained to see too many masterpieces, too many fine paintings, all in one afternoon—I get a headache in one of your museums. I used to think that this happened because I didn't like all that beauty, but then I found out what was going on. It wasn't that I didn't like it, but that I was overwhelmed by it—I couldn't digest all that chocolate in one afternoon. I used to go into a state of shock. It took me years before I could learn to derive pleasure from situations based on cultural abundance—one can tell that also from reading my books, novel after novel.

All right, let's return to America, to her decadence, the fall of the American Empire, I'm tempted to say.

Perhaps there is decay in America, but not in comparison with Europe. You'll admit that London, for example, is much more decadent than New York. No, I wouldn't use the term decadence, we are still far from it because we haven't yet reached the period that comes before decay—the Renaissance. We haven't had our Renaissance yet, and the question to ask this country, which is able to do things both wild and sublime, is whether we'll have a Renaissance to end all Renaissances, the greatest achievement mankind ever had, or whether we'll fall under the rule of a totalitarianism based on insanity that will destroy the world. Kennedy, thanks to his personality, could have been able, perhaps, to begin this Renaissance, though not because of the men who surrounded him, certainly. His advisors were intelligent and polite, of course, but they weren't great thinkers. They were pleasant, nice guys, but intellectually they were lightweights. They were people for whom deep thinking was somehow obscene. After all, Kennedy wasn't a real thinker himself. He was a little like Roosevelt: both were enchanting, had personality, and made America more fun to live in. His spell, his wit, the rich and broad life he led conquered us to the point that we would have talked about him for years. I took to him right away. Rather, to be honest, before him I had taken to his wife. A man who is married to such an eye-catching woman must be out of the ordinary, I told myself. Somebody who wants to become President of the United States should marry a pleasant wife, not an eye-catching one. A mistress can be that—nobody sees her, nobody photographs her or talks to her—but not the wife!

Yet while Kennedy was President you made a pretty strong attack on Jackie.

Because I adored her so much, I attached too much importance to her. I thought that since she was so beautiful, she ought to be wise, too, and therefore she should heed the honest voice of a man who was pleading with her not to behave so falsely. But she didn't appreciate my effort, and my social life suffered incredibly as a result of my attack on her. For years I was ostracized; you can't begin to imagine the number of parties and receptions I haven't been invited to as a punishment. But it did show that in this country anybody can criticize the President and his wife, and no harm will come of it, except that he will miss a few important receptions. European intellectuals cannot afford such luxury, not in Italy, not in France. In France, of course, they have Sartre. But he has had to pay such a high price for what he does. He has lived and still lives in constant danger—that's another reason I admire him so much. I mean, as a man. As a writer, I don't like him. When I read his stuff, I feel as if I am inside a computer lined with clean, shiny plastic; he is an odorless writer. If I were to get a life sentence and I was given a choice between the work of Sartre and Fitzgerald, I would say, "Give me Fitzgerald, for heaven's sake." But as a man he is great. I look up to him as I look up to De Gaulle, this genius who has understood that to remain in America's orbit means to destroy France. Damn, one must admire how brilliantly France has succeeded in freeing itself from America. You Italians haven't made it, though you have given up on loving us.

Perhaps because we are still hoping. Many, for instance, and I don't know whether rightly or wrongly, still have hope in Bobby Kennedy.

With Bobby Kennedy it's not a question of hope. At this time he is the most interesting political figure America has to offer, the only man who can spark some interest, the only potential candidate. After all, these Kennedys are better than they should be: they have style and individuality, and those are very important attributes for a leader of a democracy to have. It becomes easier for people to hear them out. Moreover, Bobby has profoundly changed in the last fifteen years, he is so different from the man who worked for McCarthy. And I don't think he is pretending; one cannot keep pretending for so long. No, a man who takes a stand against the war in Vietnam no longer believes in McCarthy's ideas of fighting communism to the last breath. Bobby is playing a dangerous game: he is independent enough to attract attention to himself, and at the same time he stays close enough to the central power. It's a fascinating game that makes one understand what politics is all about. What a contrast with Johnson, who in private keeps swearing up and down, but who when he appears on TV looks like a well-to-do, small-town mortician!

Many people are saying that Johnson is much more of an American President than Kennedy was.

That's exactly what's wrong with him! He has all the qualities that make Europeans hate America. Johnson is an empty

man. From a philosophical point of view he is as unpleasant
as an empty garbage can. A guy like Johnson never gives people anything, he never lets people understand what politics
is. In fact, he alienates them from political life. He's living
proof of the fact that the worst thing in American life is American politics. The only good thing about him is the way he is
shown in that play, *MacBird*. It's sad to think that he could
be a MacBird. Well, actually, if I were to meet the man face
to face, perhaps I would be able to find something good in
him. For instance, I know that he is great at telling jokes,
that he has some kind of evil charm over people. I might
even like him, if he had the guts to show himself in public
like he really is. Instead, I see only his cynicism, his preying
intelligence, his talent for manipulating politics, his lack of
ideals. I think Johnson's only ideal consists in loving his
daughters. I'm told he is a good father, to his daughters—certainly not to us. And this doesn't help us to think, to get out
of our despair. Nevertheless, I still have that hope you seem to
have lost. Because of the youth. Some of them are subhuman,
but most are so intelligent. . . .

*That is true. But they are also stuffed with drugs, violence,
LSD. Does that help your hoping?*

Theirs is an extraordinary complex generation to live in.
The best thing I can say about them is that I can't understand
them. The previous generation, the one fifteen years ago,
was so predictable, without surprises. This one is a continuing
surprise. I watch the young people of today, I listen to them,
and I realize that I'm not twenty years older than they are but
a hundred. Perhaps because in five years they went through
changes that usually take half a century to complete, their
intelligence has been speeded up so incredibly that there is no
contact between them and the generation of those around
thirty. Not to speak of those around forty or fifty. Yes, I know
that this does not happen only in America; this too is a global
process. But the psychology of American youth is more modern

than that of any other group in the world; it belongs not to 1967 but to 2027. If God could see what will happen in the future—as he perhaps does—he would see people everywhere acting and thinking in 2027 as American youth do now. It's true they take drugs. But they don't take the old drugs such as heroin and cocaine that produce only physical reactions and sensations and dull you at the same time. They take LSD, a drug that can help you explore your mind. Now let's get this straight: I can't justify the use of LSD. I know too well that you don't get something for nothing, and it may be that we'll pay a tragic price for LSD: it seems that it can break the membrane of the chromosomes in the cells and produce who knows what damage in future children. But LSD is part of a search, a desperate search, as if all these young people felt at the same time the need to explore as soon as possible their own minds so as to avoid a catastrophe. Technology has stripped our minds until we have become like pygmies driving chariots drawn by dinosaurs. Now, if we want to keep the dinosaurs in harness, our minds will have to develop at a forced pace, which will require a frightening effort. The young have felt the need to harness the dinosaurs, and if they have found the wrong means, it's still better than nothing. My fear had been that America was slowly freezing and hardening herself in a pygmy's sleep. But no, she's awake.

And what's to be done with violence? You have been and still are an apologist for violence; you must know all about it.

Yes, the best of our youth are violent. But there has always been violence in our country because from the very beginnings it has had a violent history. Let's take land, for instance. Why did we always give a mythological value to the ownership of land? Why do we call land property "real estate"? Because here land was paid for in blood: the war against the Indians, against England, the mother country. And this happened quite recently, so that we remember it well. In other words, we still have this violent attitude. And it's not enough that so many

Americans, indeed a majority, want security, quiet—no more violence, there has been enough of it in the past—it's not enough. If you keep talking to them, you'll notice that they have violence in their blood, like a hereditary disease. This of course is true for the descendants of the pioneers, the heroes who died conquering the land. Then there are the sons of the immigrants, who did not have a history of violence because they landed here when the wars were over. They are none the less violent because of it. There is in them a readiness to explode into violence, as if to free themselves of some complex, to escape their history of wretchedness. Finally there's something else in America that promotes violence: the feeling of security, the super-comfort. Those comfortable apartments in comfortable skyscrapers that can be reached only by elevators, they make people violent. I know because I have lived there. I used to live there with clenched fists; as I walked, I used to punch the walls. The house I am living in now encloses its own danger; you can't feel too safe in it, and therefore it doesn't push you to violence. Damn it, I don't like violence. But there is something I like even less, and that's a need for security. It smells of the grave and forces you to react with blood.

You dislike violence? You who have knifed a wife and can't miss a boxing match?

The knife in my wife's belly was a crime. It was a grave crime, but it had nothing to do with violence. And as for the fights, well, boxing is not violence. It's a conversation, an exchange between two men who talk to each other with their hands instead of their voices: hitting at the ear, the nose, the mouth, the belly, instead of hitting at each other's minds. Boxing is noble art. When a man fights in the ring, he is not expressing brutality. He expresses a complex, subtle nature like that of a true intellectual, a real aristocrat. A pugilist is less brutal, or not brutal at all after a fight, because with his fists he transforms violence into something beautiful, noble, and disciplined. It's a real triumph of the spirit. No, I'm not violent. To be violent means to pick fights, and I can't remember ever having started a fight. Nor can I remember ever having hit a woman—a strange woman, I mean. I may have hit a wife, but that's different. If you are married, you have two choices: either you beat your wife, or you don't. Some people live their whole life without ever beating her, others maybe beat her once and thereon are labeled "violent." I like to marry women whom I can beat once in a while, and who fight back. All my wives have been very good fighters. Perhaps I need women who are capable of violence, to offset my own. Am I not American, after all? But the act of hitting is hateful because it implies a judgment, and judgment itself is hateful. Not that I think of myself as being a good man in the Christian sense. But at certain times I have a clear consciousness of what is good and what is evil, and then my concept of the good resembles that of the Christian.

Although this may be risky, I would like to go on analyzing the sins of America through an analysis of the private sins of an American by the name of Norman Mailer. Like all Americans, you are unable to live alone. In fact, you have been married four times so far. Why are you afraid of being alone, what are you missing?

You know well what's missing: the cultural richness you have in Europe. One notices this lack as soon as one leaves New York and travels beyond the marvelous Pennsylvania countryside into the Midwest, miles and miles through towns that either are dead or were never born, in a landscape that never changes, that is not even a landscape. Here as soon as one leaves a city, one falls into the void—a void that is unlike the French, or Italian, or German countryside, a void that reminds you of Siberia. At each turn of your roads there is a masterpiece made either by man or by nature: a tree just in the right place, a church just in the right place, an old house, a store—a slice of life, in other words. Over here there is emptiness and poverty. And it is so difficult to face an empty view alone, one has to find a person to love. Or to hate. I guess you enjoy being alone, at least you are not bored, or afraid to be. You have so many things to look at, to see again, whether you are on a road or in a wood. The emotional landscape of Italian life is so rich and varied; it's a road full of curves and surprises. The emotional landscape of American life is a straight superhighway. What do we see when we drive for hours along a superhighway? If we couldn't talk to someone sitting next to us, we would go crazy. Well, perhaps you wouldn't go crazy driving alone for hours through our landscape; you have so much to remember. We don't have anything. When we are alone, we turn on a record, and we remember yesterday, the person we danced with last night, and from there we get straight back to our childhood, without fluctuating in your sea of emotions. You have been rich too long, and the great cities where man loses himself, the great expressways, are new experiences for you. Not to us. I was born and raised here, surrounded by concrete. I met nature late. I found myself at home between the skyscrapers before I could stand trees. But skyscrapers have no history, they threaten loneliness. So I need, we all need, a family: a wife, some children. If I were to live alone, I would spend every night with a different woman, partly because of the talent I have for such things. . . .

You mean to say that even your obsession with sex is due to a lack of cultural riches?

Of course. One way or another you Europeans always manage to keep your minds busy, so you can afford the luxury of abandoning yourself to sex without being obsessed by it. We can't. Without roots, having few thoughts, we use sex to fill our lives. Don't the poor and the uneducated make love more often and have more children? Sex for us is like a sport, a competition; the first thing a woman asks another about a man is: "Is he good at it?" So a man when he is with a woman thinks only about being good at it. Every time I go with a woman, I feel as if I have to defend my reputation; a pleasant but average performance would mean being disgraced in front of the whole city. We make love waving the flag, always concerned with being supermen—which is another reason, I think, for burrowing into family life. Not because of religion or morality, but because of health, a bachelor in America must be something of a sex fiend. For instance, I would be forced to throw everything into the great cauldron of sex. But isn't it ridiculous to let the best part of you drain out of your head? Actually, it's a weakness—the least forgivable weakness.

In fact, Europeans blame you for being weak. It's the most frequent objection they have after the political ones. They say that America is a country of strong women and weak men.

Certainly not weak as lovers: that's a tale manufactured by Italians to protect their national ego. America is richer financially than Italy, so, obviously, young men in Rome go around saying that Italians are better lovers than Americans, and they believe it, too. But that does not make it true. Perhaps we are weak with our women. I don't know. It's hard to say because Americans and Europeans, and especially Italians, have to deal with very different women. European women have to be in love with a man, they have to adore him, be his slave. American women believe that they must be equal with men; independence is more important to them than dedication. I don't think I can say which one is right. On the one hand, I'm inclined to say that the Europeans are right: the health, the strength, the beauty of a woman are born out of her love of a man. But if you belong to a man, you can't belong to yourself, and this in the long run affects the man, too. Slaves always end up by enslaving their masters because they become more indispensable than the masters. Look, if one is to talk about the weakness of American men, there is a much deeper and more tragic one. I once wrote that there is little honor left in American life, and that this lack breeds a tendency to destroy the masculinity of American men, to make them more feminine. What I mean by lost identity is the collective process that affects anyone who bows down to totalitarianism, anyone, that is, who loses his honor. Someone who works at a dishonorable job, for instance, someone who sells a product he doesn't believe in, or manufactures disreputable merchandise, or gives out untrue information, sooner or later loses his identity. Too many men in this country have lost or are losing their masculinity. But I will say it again: although you Europeans have lost hope, I haven't. America is still the most unpredictable nation history has ever produced. Everything can happen here. Even the miracle of becoming loved again.

New York, April, 1967

SEAN CONNERY

The Superman

If popularity can be measured by collective madness, and madness by the number of bruised, battered people, weeping women, lost children, broken ribs, upturned chairs, then what happened in Paris at the press conference and première of *Goldfinger* showed without a shadow of doubt that Sean (pronounced Shawn) Connery is today the most popular movie star in the world. Not even for Elizabeth Taylor have there been such monstrous scenes of amorous cannibalism; experts affirm that something similar once occurred over Marilyn Monroe and on another occasion over Hitler, in a Munich beer cellar, before he came into power. The difference is that at his Paris press conference there were no police, no guns, and that during the evening Sean Connery, pushed about, suffocated, crushed, ran the risk of coming to a premature, primitive end—thus proving how stupid the world can be when it falls in love with a myth, in this case the questionable hero named James Bond, agent 007, or the man who impersonates him, Sean Connery. But who is he? Who is this Sean Connery, over whom even my grandmother loses her head, even philosophers write essays? Just for a start, he is a character who says no to a queen. One day a group of actors were to be presented to Her Majesty Queen Elizabeth. Sean Connery was invited, but he replied, "Not for the world, I don't have time to waste. I don't, and anyway I don't feel like it." Friends and relations and producers had to beg and cajole until he changed his mind, grumbling, "All right, all right, I'll go, ugh, heavens!" To interview him is practically impossible: important newspapers wait months for a reply, which in ninety cases out of a hundred is, "No! Go to hell! Why should I?" Publicity agents go white in the face or curse if you ask them to arrange a meeting for you, then, telling you what martyrdom it is to work for such a brute, they furnish you with brief handouts, from which you learn that the brute was born in Edinburgh nearly forty years ago, is married to Diane Cilento, prefers to act in the theater—his best roles are in Shakespeare's *Macbeth* and Giraudoux' *Judith*. He's first rate, at all events, in Ibsen, and Pirandello too. "No! Really?" "Sure. Didn't you know? That's why it makes him angry to talk about James Bond, the ungrateful wretch," a press agent answers. "It makes him angry?" "Furious. If ever you meet him, don't try it." "And if I do try it?" "He'll hit you." "He'll hit me? Who does he think he is?" "He's the most unbearable, unapproachable blockhead you could meet. Rude, irascible," says the press agent, getting pale with anger, "and so mean that he's never stood me a beer in the two years I've known him."

There are some, you see, who don't like him. But most people do. "The first thing to say about Sean," exclaims Terence Young, the director who directed Connery in the first movie of the Bond series, *Dr. No*, then in the second, *From Russia with Love*, "is that Sean was already a damn good actor before he became a film star. In *Judith* he was so good that he acted the play itself off the stage. Good voice, splendid presence, then that special quality that we call star quality and that I've found in only one other person, Clark Gable. A lot of people say that Sean ought to be grateful to James Bond, but it's my conviction that he'd have made it perfectly well without James Bond. Maybe it would have taken him two or three years longer, but he'd have made it all the same and with better films. Bond is destructive to Sean's career, and this being confused with Bond is insulting to him." "The young man is certainly fortunate, but he deserved good fortune," says Albert Broccoli, one of the two producers of the Bond movies. "Besides, I don't know who else would have been able to carry the part. Burton, perhaps. Perhaps . . . but I'm not sure. I took to Sean straightaway, as a person as well as an actor, for the way he behaved at our first meeting. He thumped his fist on the table and knew what he wanted. When he left, Harry Saltzman, the other producer, and I watched him through the window. Together we both said, 'By God, he walks like James Bond.' " "Excellent. Exactly what was wanted for Bond: a handsome animal and a good actor," says Harry Saltzman. "He has the kind of personality you find in very few people these days. He's unexpected, explosive, unpredictable, honest. The qualities of Brando when he used to be Brando." "I've made a lot of films, and I've had a lot of partners, but I've never had a colleague as easy and generous as Sean Connery. It's impossible not to be friends with him, to admire him," says Shirley Eaton, the girl who dies painted all over with gold in *Goldfinger*. "After all, he'd be perfectly entitled to go around with his nose in the air. And he doesn't." These opinions, it is true, are not shared by everyone. Recently one magazine managed to devote I don't know how many pages to Bond without even once mentioning Sean Connery. Beneath his photographs was written, "James Bond," or, "The man himself." Idols have their enemies, it's the price of being idols.

My encounter with the idol took place in Paris, where they were shooting the Bond series movie, *Thunderball*. Terence Young and the art director, Ken Adam, brought him to have dinner with me, to break the ice, and this was he: this giant with the firm face, yet marked with lines deep as scars and large, mild, defenseless eyes, the eyes of a lamb flung down between the hyenas and the tigers of the world under pretext of doing them a favor. This was the first thing that struck you about him. And then his truly imposing size, dramatized by his excessively broad shoulders: the shoulders of a man who eats a lot, drinks a lot, and makes love a lot. And then the careless way he dressed (pants without creases, blue sweater, no tie) : the inelegance of a worker who's just left the factory, had a wash and brush up, and is ready to go out for a drink with his pals. Lastly, though you only realized it later, you were struck by his shyness: a shyness vainly overlaid by a gay, careless air, ingratiating smiles, the shyness of an adult who is discontented with himself and probably very alone, very uncertain. Truly, nobody could be less like James Bond than Sean Connery. We were having dinner in a restaurant, and a television was showing the soccer match between Inter of Milan and Glasgow Rangers. He began rooting for the Scottish team (on his right arm he has a tattoo that says "Scotland Forever"), and this enabled him to take his time, to weigh me up, decide whether or not he would do the interview. He is agonizingly diffident, as suspicious as a peasant who, finding you among his vines, scrutinizes you hard to make out whether you've stolen a grape, a leaf. I hadn't been stealing, he decided, so the next day there we were, the tape recorder alongside, to attempt the most

exhausting enterprise that could ever fall to his lot or to mine:
the interview. We chatted in fits and starts—he has a very beautiful voice, grave and halting—for three days, either in the car, or in
the hotel, or in his dressing room, and each time he amazed me
with his unexpected patience, his polite docility.

These qualities in him have in no way been affected by the
success that astounds and frightens him. His wife says so, too: "No
one can imagine how patient, docile, and good Sean is. They confuse him to such an extent with that damned Bond. You see, there's
so much tenderness in him, such need to give it and receive it.
There's one episode in his life that seems to me very significant. As
a boy, Sean used to dream of owning a motorcycle. He worked, he
saved up his money. And when the day came that he could buy it,
they told him he'd be too young to ride it. So, instead of waiting
until he was old enough, Sean bought his mother a piano, which
she didn't even know how to play. In their house in Edinburgh
they still have that piano. No one has ever played it. It's only a
piano, but it tells you all you need to know about him."

Diane Cilento came to Paris the evening of the première of
Goldfinger: small, blond, very beautiful, a woman you look at twice
in spite of her remodeled nose—the fine nose she had in *Tom Jones*
is now a charming little snub nose, goodness knows why. She's
also a very intelligent woman: as well as being an actress, she
writes books and short stories and translates. She has translated
Pirandello's *Vestire gli ignudi* from the Italian. She knows Italian
very well, her first marriage having been to the Italian scriptwriter
Andrea Volpi. Besides, the Cilento family is of Italian origin,
although they have lived in Australia for two generations. When
Diane and Sean were first married, she was more famous than he;
today the situation is reversed, and Diane has this to say about it:
"It's better this way. Bond persecutes me, admittedly, but Sean
needed success. It's good for him." We spent several hours together,
talking about herself, about the novel she was writing, about the
movie she was shortly to make in Jamaica, about her daughter
by her first marriage, about her son by her marriage to Sean, and,
above all, about Sean. At one point she exclaimed: "I don't know
how you managed to get him to talk, he's not the type that cares
much for words or can use them to express himself. But I'm sure

that anything he's told you is right and true. That's another thing I like a lot about Sean. I mean, if I weren't married to him, I'd still like him. You see, I come from a family full of men, brothers and so on, I've known men since I was a child, and there aren't many of them I'd call real men. There aren't many real men around, are there? Sean is one, without question."

He certainly is. It's my opinion too. Some time ago—we were by now good friends—Sean came to New York, where I live, and gave me a call: How do you do, let's have a drink, etc. I joined him at the small, unpretentious hotel where he was staying, and I found him eating salami and watching TV. "For heaven's sake," I exclaimed, "what the hell are you doing in New York, all alone, eating like a coal miner and watching TV like an old spinster?" "Diane and the children have not arrived yet," he replied. "All right, then go out, be with people, have fun. A big star like you doesn't miss opportunities!" "I don't like that, you know. Let's go and see a movie." Then he left the salami, and dressed as he was—he really looked like a coal miner—he pushed me out of the apartment toward the elevator. A crowd of fans was waiting for him on the sidewalk outside the hotel. He asked for the service entrance and got out through it, almost blushing. He walked all the way to the movie theater where they were showing *Darling,* and we stood in the line. There was a long line of people waiting to buy tickets. "For heaven's sake, Sean, do we have to stand in the line?" "Why shouldn't we? Others do." "O.K., Sean, I know. But since you are such a big star, let's make use of it." He didn't even answer, we stood in the line until they recognized him and let us pass without paying for the tickets—which embarrassed him to death and spoiled his fun. When the movie was over, he discovered he was hungry again: "Let's go and eat something." "O.K. What kind of restaurant would you prefer?" "No restaurant, please. They start calling you by name and being nice and asking for autographs and all that. Let's go to a supermarket and buy something there." We went into a supermarket and bought something, then we went home to eat. My maid was all excited: "He is James Bond, isn't he?" "For Christ's sake, Anne, shut up." He didn't even want Anne to set the table: "What's all the fuss? I only want something to eat." While we ate, he told us about the time he was a furniture polisher, proudly explaining how good he still was at the work, how much he still liked it. If Anne hadn't screamed with horror, he would have polished my furniture by way of demonstration. Then he got up and went away, quietly whistling with the purity of his simple soul. I mean, it is so difficult not to be corrupted by the fame, the money, the stupid adulation. And what is more a man than a man who can stand—without being corrupted—the fame and the money and the stupid adulation?

ORIANA FALLACI: *As far as I can gather, this meeting of ours is truly exceptional, Mr. Connery. I don't believe that any actor today is as difficult to approach as you are. There are certainly none who defend themselves from the curiosity of others with such ferocity, such desperation.*

SEAN CONNERY: Correct. You've said it. I hate talking about myself, it embarrasses me, it bores me. I've never understood this business. Why on earth should a man have to talk about himself, explain himself, say what he is and what he isn't? Why should a man have to open his home to journalists? They come inside, they judge how you live or don't live. Do I go into their houses to judge how they live or don't live? Do I ask them what they are or what they aren't? But you're a movie star, they say. Agreed: I'm an actor who happens to be a movie star, a money-making machine. So what? The more reason for me to refuse the degrading compromises of publicity. To take care I don't lose my head. To keep my balance. To stay a man. I mean, when what's happened to me happens to you, your balance hovers on a razor's edge. You give way just once, and you fall onto the razor and cut off your . . . in short, you're no longer a man. And I don't want to stop being a man. And then each one of us has a mask behind which he hides out of self-defense: shyness. Taking it off is like taking off your clothes: you don't always feel like taking off your clothes. It isn't always worth it. How often you like someone for the way he acts or writes, and then you see him close to, you talk to him, and you don't like him anymore, because he's not what you thought he was when he was acting or writing.

So what shall I do? Shall I go?

Silence. Stay here. Or else, suppose it is worth it. Even so, is there any point in it? Anyway, I know the image people have of me: a fellow devoid of intellectual capacity, boorish, aggressive, the image I often see in the newspapers. When I read things like that, I feel like getting hold of the heads of whoever wrote them and crushing them together like two nuts. But what can I do about it? Engage someone to go around saying, "Listen, he has a brain, too; he acts Macbeth well, too"? The moment success becomes monstrous—like the success of James Bond—and turns into an industry, it's out of your control. Someone writes something untrue, the untrue thing becomes a ball that bounces from newspaper to newspaper, from country to country, translated, copied, blown up, and you can't do a thing about it. You know, like when it's snowing and someone starts to throw snowballs. After a bit everyone's throwing them, and you can't do a thing about it.

Quite. The image they present of you is catastrophic. The least I expected on approaching you was to find myself with a black eye after the first round and a broken nose after the second. Shall we pretend that it's worth correcting the image, that there's some point in it? Shall we explain who you are?

I'm . . . I'm very much less interesting than what they say. Besides, I don't see why one necessarily has to be interesting. I'm a simple man, with few faults and few virtues. Among the latter you can count a sense of humor, a sense of the ridiculous, a sense of the value of money, a sense of morality, a sense of truth. I don't tell lies. Never. Among the defects is egotism, firstly. Then bad temper. I don't get angry easily, but if I do get angry, I get dreadfully angry. Then a little vanity perhaps, seeing I'm an actor. Then a great deal of shyness. I'm shy, but who isn't? I've yet to meet anyone who isn't. Then I'm very vulnerable. I'd have my throat slit sooner than show it, but I can be hurt by the least little thing, because at the age of thirty-four I still haven't learned to be cynical. And now I never will. And lastly I'm ambitious, but I count that as a virtue. And finally I'm Scottish, and that's the biggest virtue of all. The Scots have nothing in common with the English. The Scots are Scottish, period. So it's useless for them to compare me with James Bond. Bond is English and I'm Scottish. And I don't like the English at all because I'm Scottish, period. Or Bond . . . period.

You don't like talking about him, I know. And, as you see, I haven't yet mentioned the name. Among the thousand pieces of advice that I was given was never to mention James Bond. You'd think he was your worst enemy instead of the character who's brought you fame and fortune. But they say that at the very sound of the name James Bond you become angry and get up and go. Well then? Aren't you angry?

Angry? Why should I be?

Because I've said James Bond. 007. Bond.

O.K. O.K.! Bond. 007. Bond. They must have told you wrong. I get angry when they ask me if I'd like to be James Bond, if I'm like James Bond, if they should call me Connery or Bond, when they plague me with idiocies of that kind, not when they make me talk about Bond. Why should I? I'm not in the least ashamed of the Bond movies. They're amusing, intelligent, each one is more exacting than the last, each one is of better quality than the last. And quality isn't to be found only in the Old Vic. Old Vic or Old Smith, the hell with it! What does it matter? Above all, I certainly don't have the snobbishness or the bad taste to spit on something that gives me success and money, and anyway in my job there's room for every kind of acting. For me, playing James Bond is like playing Macbeth in the theater. I'll say more: if I hadn't acted Shakespeare, Pirandello, Euripides, in short, what is classed as serious theater, I should never have managed to play James Bond. It's not so easy, that role. It's a role for a professional. It requires movement, for example. And to know how to move well you need to have been on the stage. I'd been on the stage for four years when I made my first TV appearance, in *Anna Karenina*, playing opposite Claire Bloom. I'd been another four years in movies when they offered me Bond and . . .

And you didn't hesitate, you didn't waver, before saying

yes? Leaving aside Old Vic or Old Smith, it was a bit like taking up tap dancing after dancing Swan Lake. Eight movies about the same character are a lot. It was only to be expected that the character would eventually dog your footsteps: "Would you like to be Bond, are you like Bond . . . ?"

It was luck, my dear, and luck only knocks once. And when it knocks, you have to grab it quick and then hang on tight. Would they identify me with Bond? Would that make me angry? Too bad. For an actor, for a writer, there's always the danger of being identified with his character. Look how many people still write to Sherlock Holmes although they know quite well he doesn't exist and never has existed. Look, I didn't hesitate for an instant, particularly as the contract was so very amenable: it arranged that I would make a Bond every fourteen months, which left me time to devote to the theater, to other movies. And I've used it. In the break between *From Russia with Love* and *Goldfinger* I made *Marnie*, with Hitchcock. In the break between *Goldfinger* and *Thunderball* I made *The Hill*, with Sidney Lumet: a war film, in black and white, with an all-male cast. After *Thunderball* I'm going to make a movie in Australia, with my wife. And then the character of Bond was amusing, certain to appeal. And lastly it suited me physically. You see, I've never had a handsome face, an acceptable face. I've always had this difficult face, adult, lined; it was like this even when I was sixteen. When I was sixteen, I already looked thirty, and without a handsome face it's far from easy to break in. So, honestly, I was careful not to make too much fuss. The only thing I said to the producers was that the character had one defect, there was no humor about him; to get him accepted, they'd have to let me play him tongue-in-cheek, so people could laugh. They agreed, and there you are: today Bond is accepted to such an extent that even philosophers take the trouble to analyze him, even intellectuals enjoy defending him or attacking him. And even while they're laughing at him, people take him terribly seriously.

And how about you, Mr. Connery? Do you take him seriously or do you laugh at him?

Laugh at him? If I laughed at him, I'd be laughing at myself, at my work, and where would be the sense in that? And then being egotistical, as I said before, and ambitious, as I said before, I have to believe that what I am doing is important. Therefore, Bond is important: this invincible superman that every man would like to copy, that every woman would like to conquer, this dream we all have of survival. And then one can't help liking him. Don't you like him?

I don't know, I wouldn't like to say. As the symbol of our dreams I find him, when all's said and done, a rather sad one: this man who always wins, without morals, or ideals, or friends, rather ignorant, too, except about explosives, cards, and drinking. Forgive me, won't you? Don't be offended.

Immoral? I've never seen him steal anyone's wife, anyone else's woman, or betray his own; he doesn't have one. He likes women all right, but he never rapes them; it's they who worm their way into his bed. He kills people, he has to; if he doesn't, they'll kill him. He abides by no laws, but nor is he protected by the laws that protect others; society does nothing to defend him, he isn't known to society. He's rather ignorant, O.K., but he doesn't exactly have the time for reading Joyce. His struggle for survival obliges him to be practical, functional, to reduce everything to the verbs sniff, look, listen, taste, think. His safety depends on this and not on Joyce. He doesn't fight for old people and children, but who said he couldn't? Have you any proof? Your accusations wouldn't be valid in any court of law. Yes, sure, it would be interesting if I spoke badly of Bond. But I've got nothing at all against Mr. Bond, and I'm only too sorry he has to die.

Die? Is he ill?

I don't know, I'm not sure yet, but I'm afraid so. In my opinion we can't possibly keep him alive for more than another one or two movies. I'm convinced that *Thunderball* is the most we can do for him, the apex of his health and glory, and that after it he'll develop a worrying cough. Yet one can never tell. He's the robust type, he might last out another three or four films.

You must certainly hope so, don't you, with the money you make through him. You're a rich man now, thanks to Bond, Mr. Connery. They say you're the highest paid actor in the world, and I imagine that money matters to you as it matters to the rest of us.

I've been too short of money in the past not to appreciate it now. And at present I'm too free of illusions to reject it. I was born poor. When I was nine, I was already working seven days a week, delivering milk, and that gives you a healthy respect for money. With money you can say no when you want to say no, you can say yes when you want to say yes, you can make a good life for your father and mother when they're eighty-seven and eighty-four years old and have had to go on working until recently. With money you can make a good life for your wife and children. With money you can cultivate your dreams of independence and freedom. And I want it. I want every penny that's coming to me. I want it, and I take it. Success alone isn't enough for a man, and I've never heard that talent feeds on malnutrition. I've never believed that you have to be hungry in order to be good. No, thank you, I've already sampled the poetry of hunger, and I'm not going to try it again. Not that I'm rich, as you said, nor am I the highest paid actor in the world but . . .

I don't want to be indiscreet, but how much do you earn, Mr. Connery?

Two hundred thousand dollars a film plus 5 per cent of the takings, or four hundred thousand dollars a film if I forfeit my percentage of the takings. For *Marnie* I got two hundred thousand dollars and fifteen hundred dollars a week expenses, but I had to rent a house in Hollywood and take the whole family over. I make more on every movie, but it all goes in taxes because over and above a certain figure taxes amount to 95 per cent of one's income. Ferocious. No, I'm not really rich, but I shall be if *Goldfinger* does all right. My earnings on *Goldfinger* are mostly on percentage: it's the only way to evade the fantastic taxes. At present, all I possess of my own is the house I live in: an ex-convent with four floors, in Acton, twenty minutes from London. I don't own any land. Generally, as soon as anyone has a bit of money to play with, he buys land, but I prefer to invest in my company. Cars neither, except for a secondhand Jaguar I bought in place of my Volkswagen. The only object of value I wear is this gold watch. It's a special watch—it cost a thousand dollars—but I didn't buy it for myself, the *Marnie* team took up a collection and gave it to me. I don't like having things of value. Whenever you have any, you're always afraid somebody'll steal them, and so you live in dread. I live with very little.

They've told me that you're mean, Mr. Connery. Is it true?

I'm not mean, I'm Scottish. Because I'm Scottish, I don't like being swindled. The Scots are notorious for their meanness, and I'll tell you why. The history of Scotland is like the history of southern Italy: poverty and poverty. But if you're born poor in southern Italy, you can survive because there's the sun and you only need something light to wear. Not in Scotland. In Scotland there's no sun, there's the cold and the rain, and so as well as being hungry you're cold, too. And if you own an overcoat or an umbrella, you take care of it, you keep a grip on it, and you don't want anyone to take it from you. I'm not mean. I'm a simple person, I was born and grew up in a place where you're content with very little: that's a very different thing. For example, I don't care much for clothes, clothes like Bond's, I mean. It doesn't agree with me to go around in ties and well-pressed suits as Bond and the English do. Ugh, the English! . . . If you see me wearing a tie and a well-pressed suit, it's because I have to go somewhere: to the theater, to a restaurant, to a business appointment or something. There's nothing I can do about it. I'm miserable wearing a tie; I am, miserable. And all those buttons, hats, shoelaces, shoes. Dreadful. Ugh! Dreadful. And then you won't often see me going places, in London. I like staying at home, barefoot, with my wife, the children, friends coming to dinner. On Sundays we always have friends in; I have fun doing the cooking. Yes, I can cook and pretty well, too. I can make an excellent casserole. I cut up the onions very fine, fry them gently in butter. . . . I learned to cook in the Navy, and then during all the years I was a bachelor; Diane and I were only married two years ago. I have few vices, none really: a cigar after a meal, a few glasses of beer. Beer's the drink I like best. I like whiskey too, so long as it's Scotch. But I prefer beer. What are you laughing at, eh?

Nothing. I was thinking of all the women who think of you as being one thing and . . .

Oh! It's not me they like, it's James Bond. I know perfectly well it's James Bond they're thinking of when they look at me like that. I'd just like to pick out one of them, at random, and say, "Come on, let's go," carry on with her like Bond does, and see what she'd do. At the very least, she'd send for the police. So as I was saying, I'm fond of beer, what else? By way of staff I only have my secretary and a nurse for the children. I don't have a chauffeur, and I never shall have. I hate being waited upon, it makes me ashamed. I've never understood why a burly man with two legs, two arms, and two hands should let himself be waited upon by someone else who's maybe smaller than he is. But this must also be an inheritance from my past; in my home we never had the money to have ourselves waited on. My father was a truck driver. My young brother—he's eight years younger than I am—is still a house painter in Edinburgh. You see, meanness has nothing to do with it, it's just a matter of simplicity. You see, even my likes are simple: soccer. What I really wanted to be was a soccer player. I was, what's more: center forward for Manchester United.

Now that's something I'd like you to tell me about, Mr. Connery.

Sean.

Sean. That's something I'd like you to tell me about, Sean: how it came about that from being a soccer player you became an actor. Everyone knows that you went on the stage very late, when you were already a grown man. And it certainly wasn't the sacred flame of art that drove you into the theater; it was chance.

Naturally. I've always lived like that, I've always taken up whatever came my way, at random. I've never had precise plans, precise hopes, I've never been driven on by any precise dream—apart from soccer. I left school, grade school, when I was twelve, and since then God knows the jobs I've done. Whenever I got fed up with a job, I changed it. I can't stand discipline; it can't be helped, my mind is willing but my body refuses, that's all there is to it. I entered the Navy when I was sixteen, and when I came out, at eighteen, I became a coffin polisher. The government had given me a study grant so I could choose a career, I chose polishing, goodness knows why, and I finished up in a funeral home in Glasgow. When this acting business came my way, I was working for an Edinburgh daily paper—just a worker, of course. I used to put the rolls of paper in the rotary presses. One Sunday they sent me to London, where I heard that they were looking for people for the musical *South Pacific.* I went for an audition, there was nothing to lose, and they took me. So then I quit printing, and for two years I sang and gamboled as a chorus boy in *South Pacific.* I was twenty-three when I faced the choice of soccer or acting. I chose acting, thinking that it wouldn't prevent me from playing soccer. Bullshit. Firstly, every time you start playing, they yell: "Be careful, you'll break a leg; if you break a leg, the movie will be held up; if the movie's held up, you'll be liable." Then for soccer you need twenty-two players, and I can never find the other twenty-one. I've had to fall back on golf, which is less dangerous and you only need two to play it. But soccer is something else altogether. Oh, soccer's great. How's Inter doing?

Fine, thank you. And having left soccer for the stage, you began to study acting?

Nothing of the kind. I studied . . . I'm not saying that Inter is a bad team; far from it, it's very good. But it's full of foreign players. How can you call it an Italian team?

Quite right. So what did you study, Sean?

Of course Glasgow Rangers is a real Scottish team. All Scots from the tops of their heads to the soles of their feet. They didn't deserve to lose against Inter yesterday. Did you think that penalty kick was fair? Let me tell you, the Glasgow Rangers full backs are . . .

Yes, yes. So what did you study, Sean?

I didn't study, for heaven's sake! You never find a woman who can talk about soccer. They know all about everything else, but they don't know the first thing about soccer! The hell with it! I didn't study. I studied a bit of movement and action with a Swedish teacher in London who had been a dancer with the New York City Ballet. And then I took up reading. I made myself a list of books, and I read them. Joyce's *Ulysses:* God, what an effort. Proust's *Remembrance of Things Past:* my, but that was a sweat. In fact, I never finished it. And then *My Life and Art* by Stanislavsky. And then *An Actor Prepared.* And then the whole of Ibsen, everything. And then Pirandello. And Shakespeare and all of them. I used to read in the library, I used to spend whole days there. At the same time I used to go to the theater to watch how others acted and . . . that's all. That's all: if you do that, and you do it well, and you're not a fool—you'll see—you'll become an actor. And when you are, you like it so much that you don't care about anything else—except soccer. You see, people sometimes ask me why I'm an actor, being the kind of fellow I am. Well, it isn't for the money. You can make money in soccer, too. It's for the fantasy, the way you have to get inside someone else's skin, imagine him, understand him, recreate him with tragedy or humor: translate him. I mean, it's great to put across fantasy. It's a constant surprise how reality is harder to put across than fantasy. I never forget that Stephen Crane wrote a very fine book about war, *The Red Badge of Courage*, although he'd never been in a war. And then he wrote a very bad book called *Shipwreck*, although he had been in a shipwreck. And this explains a lot of things. It explains, for example, why a person might take refuge in idealisms and might not want to have his . . . cut off by publicity. It explains why one gets angry when one hears oneself asked: "Would you like to be Bond, to be like Bond?" It explains why, for all one's healthy respect for money, at a certain point instead of being satisfied with the money one goes to Oxford to act Pirandello and earn only seventy-five dollars a week, paying one's own hotel bill. I turned down a good part and a heap of money in the film *El Cid* in order to go to Oxford and act in Pirandello's *Vestire gli ignudi*. For seventy-five dollars a week, paying my own hotel bill. Well, I'd die if I didn't do these things, I'd die. When I was under contract to Twentieth Century Fox and couldn't act what I wanted, I nearly died. In fact, I broke it, the contract.

You'll have been asked this before, Sean, but I'll ask you all the same: Did you expect this success?

Of course I expected it; anyway I hoped for it. When you love your work, and you're sure you do it well, you always hope that others will notice, don't you? Besides, you see, success is a point of view, there are so many degrees of success. What does it mean, saying that now I'm successful? International success? Agreed. But I was successful before Bond, too. In England I was considered a successful actor. A strange phenomenon is taking place, today in England: an artistic renaissance, I'd call it, comparable to the one that exploded in Italy after the war with the harvest of Magnanis, De Sicas, and, why not, Lollobrigidas. They're making movies like the Bond movies, *Tom Jones*, turning out actors like Peter O'Toole, Albert Finney, Tom Courtenay, and me. A rather wild generation, maybe, excessively rebellious, but good, full of talent. So the merit isn't all mine, personally. And one has to be careful not to get a swollen head, one has to remember that success is relative, temporary, it depends on others and has its ups and downs. Phew! What a lot of talk. Couldn't we give over and go and have a beer?

In a minute, in a minute. Just two more questions. This one, for example, which I was asking myself a little while back, listening to you, Sean: I was wondering what else, besides soccer and your career, might interest a character like you—such as, I don't know, politics, for example.

Not in the least. I've never voted since I was born. What's the point? Things go on just the same, and politics is all a question of money: the more money you have, the more successful you are in politics. I'm not a monarchist, but I'm not a republican, either. I mean, I've nothing against the Queen, but I honestly don't lose any sleep over her and her relations. I'm not a reactionary, and I'm not a socialist, either, although I see the world from an essentially economic point of view. It's all a question of money, my dear, money! I feel sympathy for the workers of course; I was one of them. But I've never deluded myself that they're Jesus Christs. God! I lived too long among them not to know they're no Jesus Christs. Ideologies leave me cold. I've never liked people who talk, I like people who get on with things and do them well and do them thoroughly, without speeches. I'm a practical man. Do you see what I mean? I admire something done, accomplished, successfully finished, not something theorized and philosophized about. Between conquered and conquerors I choose the conquerors, always. Nothing appeals to me more than strength, energy, enthusiasm. . . .

So then, Sean, let's finish with a little test: the names of three men and three women whom you admire, for whom you feel respect and envy.

Uhm! Eh! Uhm! Let's see. . . . The first is Khrushchev. I've always watched him carefully, and I've always felt infinite respect for him. That sense of humor of his, that appetite for living, that nonconformism. Great man. I don't know what I wouldn't give to meet him and tell him so. The second is Stanley Matthews, the soccer player. He's fifty-one, and he still plays soccer. I'd like to be him. The third is Picasso: to me he has the same virtues as Khrushchev. As for women . . . let's see . . . women . . . let's see . . . odd: you know, I can't think of a single one? Yet I like them, I like them a lot, I respect them, I esteem them, I often find them even superior to men. . . . Do you see what I mean? I'm one of those who still find women devilish attractive, irreplaceable . . . well, that must be why. I mean that, whenever I think of women, I can never get away from the sex element. The liking and even the admiration, even the respect, I feel for a woman always have sexual origins. I can't help it. A character like me, who loves life and appetite and strength, can't get away from sexual desires. And so, when he stops to assess a woman, he can never make out where that thing finishes and pure admiration begins. Do you see what I mean? Khrushchev doesn't provoke any sexual desires in me, nor does Matthews, nor does Picasso. With them there isn't that alarming little complication. Alarming, isn't it?

Eh, yes. Alarming.

In fact, I find women very alarming, very worrying. Always. And picking out one whom I just admire and nothing else . . . let's see . . . yes: Greta Garbo. For her talent, her dignity, her silence. And yet, no, even in her case I can't get away from the fact that if I'd ever been close to her . . . well . . . in short . . . I'd have been very attracted to her, apart from her talent, her dignity, her silence. So, after all, the choice doesn't stand. Phew! Tell you what we'll do: we'll forget about women for a

moment and take the names of two more men. One is Hitchcock and the other is Noel Coward. For the above reasons. And
now let's go and have a beer.

Paris, March, 1965

H. RAP BROWN

I'm All Ready to Kill

One of the heroes of the Negro revolt in America is a young man, twenty-three years old, with a markedly African nose, light-tea colored skin, and hair so curly that many believe he wears a woolen wig. He also wears whiskers, with downturned tips. He was born in the South, his father was a factory worker and his mother a domestic servant—both very religious and quiet. He was studying sociology, but without too much success, when he dropped out. Now his profession is that of a full-time revolutionary. In May, 1967, he became the leader of a powerful youth movement with a quite inappropriate name: Student Non-violent Coordinating Committee, or SNCC. The outgoing president of SNCC, Stokely Carmichael, introduced him to the press with the words, "You will be very sorry that I left after you see him in action. He is really mean." And he is. By his own admission, he has been arrested so often he has lost count of the number of times. He answers a request to list his various crimes and indictments with "Illegal possession of weapons, attempted burglary, threatening, incitement to riot, bootlegging, breaking the peace, sexual offenses, assault and battery, and so on." His name is Hubert Brown, but he prefers to use the name Rap Brown even on official documents. He became Rap by popular acclaim, as a result of his habit of crying "Rap them, baby!" to the crowds he was haranguing. Another sentence he likes to use in ghetto meetings is: "We have built America, and we will destroy it." A slogan he has often repeated goes as follows: "If you give me a gun, I'll shoot Lady Bird," wife of "that crazy wild dog, that Texan outlaw who sends white murderers to kill black people"—an expression he uses to define Lyndon Johnson from the safety afforded by the indisputable freedom of speech that prevails in the United States.

Congress and the FBI hold him largely responsible for the uprisings of 1967, and an inquest has been opened to ascertain to what extent such responsibility involves conspiracy. His ties with China and Cuba are said to be strong. He was indicted in Richmond, and a week later in Alexandria, for incitement to riot and for arson. These indictments could cost him twenty years in jail. The charges stem from events that happened in Cambridge, Maryland, during the summer riots. Everything appeared to be quiet in Cambridge till Rap came into town and climbed on the roof of a car. "Detroit has blown up, Newark has blown up, Harlem has blown up," he screamed, "it's time for Cambridge to blow up, too!" An hour later hell broke loose, people died, others were wounded. A shot grazed Rap, too, on the left side of his forehead. Clutching his wound, Rap disappeared in the direction of a part of the town that forthwith exploded in flames and was soon completely destroyed. Next day he was arrested at Washington airport. He was freed on ten thousand dollars bond. Undaunted, he took off for Alexandria, where he began to instigate violence again. They arrested him again—another ten thousand dollar bond. This is why Negro revolutionaries love him, hold him to be a martyr. In their frustration they have selected him to replace Cassius Clay as the new Spartacus.

The interview that follows, a very unusual concession on Rap Brown's part, since he hates and despises every white person, took place in the headquarters of SNCC, in New York, on August 4, 1967. Some young gum-chewing Negro girls looked at me insolently and made me wait for a long time, as if reluctant to let Brown know that "the white cat" had come. Eventually I was shown in to him. He was sitting at a desk, with his fingers in his nose, exploring its cavities with scrupulous concern and finally extracting from it things he deposited here and there with obvious satisfaction. On his brow a band-aid, a tiny one, hid the bullet scratch. The interview was painful and took a long time—it cannot be said that he overwhelms one with his intelligence. To ask him for a coherent answer is like asking a hemophiliac for blood. It took a lot of effort to make sense of his replies. Nevertheless, the interview amounts to a precise document of the tragedy that is tearing the United States asunder—a tragedy that not even the most pessimistic onlooker could have foreseen, and a tragedy that appears to have no resolution. H. Rap Brown is not alone in his racism, his hate, his desperate thirst for vengeance. America is full of Rap Browns, full of people who think, talk, act the way he does, while whites who are the Negroes' friends, who fought for years on their side, look on hopelessly.

ORIANA FALLACI: *Mr. Brown, it has been said that the blacks are organizing trained guerrilla outfits in various American cities, and that your movement has something to do with this. Is it true?*

H. RAP BROWN: Of course it's true. We blacks are fighting America. And since we can't wage a real war—we have no big guns, and if we had them, we couldn't use them; besides, we are numerically inferior—obviously we have chosen guerrilla warfare. It's the best tactics for us, and it's easy. We work in the most strategic points of the whole country, in the white man's factories, his fields, his homes. We can sabotage and destroy without any trouble—often without even having to shoot. We can, for instance, destroy the telephone lines, the railroads, the airports, the electrical and electronic installations. Every city in the United States works on the basis of an electronic system, and its destruction would paralyze the city itself. So from city to city, we'll make America kneel down, we'll ruin her economically. At the same time we will apply ourself to violence. That's why we are studying modern guerrilla techniques, like the ones used by the Viet Cong. Our black brothers who are fighting in Vietnam for white Americans are learning indispensable lessons about modern guerrilla warfare. They are trained in it every day. When they return here, they will be useful to us not only as soldiers who are not afraid to kill or to die but also as masters in guerrilla warfare. Of course the main problem with using violence is weapons. But every American Negro has a rifle or a gun, and Molotov cocktails are easy to make. Moreover, we'll have access to weapons. I can't say more, but we'll have access to weapons.

And when is this struggle supposed to begin, Mr. Brown?
Tomorrow, even today. It depends on them. It depends on

Johnson, the administration, the whites. If they, fail to eliminate the conditions that have caused the past riots, we'll take the offensive—we are ready. The revolution hasn't started yet, these past riots have only been a rehearsal for the revolution that will involve all American Negroes. But every riot is more sophisticated, better organized, than the one before. We have no time to lose—Johnson, Congress, the Senate, the FBI are getting ready an anti-Negro conspiracy. There is an anti-riot law being passed in Congress that's aimed against us. For us violence is necessary. It was the whites who taught us to be violent, violence is a part of American history and culture, like apple pie and the Fourth of July. You turn on TV and see cowboys shooting, people fighting and killing each other— violence here is a symbol of maleness, it's the only attitude the white man respects. Nonviolence has been a failure; besides, it was a method discovered for us by white brains—first by Kennedy, then by Johnson. Johnson blames me for having lit the fuse. He's the one who did it.

This is why you would like to kill Lady Bird?

It should read "Johnson" instead of "Lady Bird." That's an old story. When they wanted to draft me and send me to Vietnam, I told them, "I won't use this gun to kill the Viet Cong. The Viet Cong are not my enemies. It wasn't they who bombed the Birmingham church in which four black girls died, and no Viet Cong has called me 'nigger.' If the Army gives me a gun and tells me to kill the enemy, I'll follow instructions and shoot Lady Bird. She is my enemy." Of course, I meant Johnson, but if I had said that, they would have thrown me in jail. Instead, they refused to draft me because I was defined as being dangerous and undesirable. "Why Johnson?" you'll ask. It's simple: Johnson is a symbol of the white power that is our enemy, just as, before him, Kennedy was the symbol of that power. None of us has been fooled by the chatter of the late President Kennedy and Civil Rights and all that. When

Kennedy spoke of Civil Rights, he was a businessman pushing his line: Civil Rights were a fraud that benefited him economically.

It seems to me that while it was Johnson who passed legislation helpful to the Negro, it was Kennedy who proposed those laws. Tell me, Mr. Brown, is there any President in American history for whom you could feel some sympathy or gratitude?

Not one. Kennedy was an enemy of the blacks—besides, he was capitalist, and capitalism in the United States means oppression of the black people. And if you mention Lincoln, who freed the slaves, etc., you'll make me laugh. Lincoln was concerned with the nation, not with the slaves. He couldn't care less about the slaves, he wanted to save America, and that's it. He was white, like George Washington, who owned slaves. Washington is not my hero, Lincoln is not my hero. My heroes are patriots like Malcolm X, Mohammed Ali, whom you whites call Cassius Clay because you don't even want to recognize his name, or Robert Williams, who left the United States and went into exile in Peking, where he now works for us. We get the paper he prints in Peking every month, in English. It is distributed in every Negro community, from the Atlantic to the Pacific. It's called *Crusade*. And then Stokely Carmichael is one of my heroes, because he's gone to Cuba and is liable to get arrested when he returns.

Mr. Brown, to what extent is Fidel Castro helping you?

I don't know what Carmichael has arranged in his talks with Castro. I know Castro has made some offers, but at this point there is nothing definite. We'll decide, when Carmichael returns, whether to accept those offers. It all depends on whether Castro agrees to our conditions. And our conditions include the demand that it is we who will decide what the Cubans can do for us, and what we can do for them. Right now we don't need them too much, but in the future their help may become essential. So far, there is between Cuba and ourselves only a positive non-alliance—just like that between all other groups whose goal is to liberate a country. This is so because we are not a Civil Rights movement any longer. That's dead, thank God. We are a movement for Human Rights; that is, we are leading a revolt built on an international basis and not tied down to the geographic structure of the United States. Cuba is our friend, likewise all the countries where the United States is present with its colonialist oppression—Latin America, Vietnam, South Africa, Puerto Rico.

And how about China? To what extent is she helping you, Mr. Brown?

I don't know if Robert Williams, that true black patriot, is preparing direct help from Peking. Nor would I be authorized to reveal it if I knew. Of course, we blacks feel that we have much more in common with the yellow Chinese than with the white American. Chinese are colored people, too. And the United States has treated China as badly as it has treated us; for instance, it still fails to recognize that country, so superior to the United States in intelligence, technological development, social assistance, and justice. There are seven hundred million Chinese, and the United States pretends that they don't exist; just as there are twenty million blacks, and the United States pretends that they don't exist.

Mr. Brown, are you or are you not Communists?

The blacks are just as communist as the Pope is. We are not interested in political ideologies—these are tales circulated by that cowpoke, Johnson. I bet his grandmother was a Communist. Not me. If the blacks stand with the socialist countries, it is because all the countries that have achieved independence for themselves through revolutions later became socialist—and not by chance: it's obvious that once a people frees itself, it will reject capitalism. That system is symbolic of America and its tool of oppression, the dollar. And then we blacks like revolutions. The will of the people has to be kept in use, and there is no better way to do so than through revolutions. This explains also why we have declared war on the United States. We are fed up with little political concessions that don't change anything. We are fed up with being given aspirin and hearing it called progress. We want what's owed us, and we'll get it.

Mr. Brown, you are talking about waging war against the United States. But aren't the Negroes in the United States Americans? Isn't America their country, their home?

We are black. Therefore we are not American; at most, we are Afro-American. We don't feel American. We live inside the United States as one of its colonies. No Negro can afford the luxury of feeling American because every Negro is against all that is meant by "American"—imperialism, colonialism. Every Negro is a victim of this nation, the most decadent, immoral, degenerate country in the world. Like that white man, G. B. Shaw, said, "This is the only country that progressed from barbarism to decadence without passing through a civilized stage." Feel American? When America is practicing genocide against us? Blacks are only 10 per cent of the population, but 21 per cent of the soldiers fighting in Vietnam are black, and 30 per cent of the soldiers who die in Vietnam are black. Why? It's simple: because more blacks than whites are drafted, because more blacks than whites are sent out in front. And when they don't kill us in Vietnam, they kill us here—with hunger. In Alabama five hundred children die of malnutrition every year; the conditions under which they have to live are still those of three centuries ago. Then there is legal genocide: when a black has to stand trial, you can be sure he'll get the maximum penalty—as happened to Mohammed Ali. Then there is scientific genocide, or birth control. They pushed it only in the black communities, because they don't want to increase the black population.

Mr. Brown, in Alabama things aren't at all like they were three centuries ago, and birth control is being preached everywhere, though more among the poor than the rich—as it should be. But not all Negroes are poor—there are forty-seven Negro millionaires in America.

A black millionaire is treated just like a poor black. In America there are only two colors, white and black, and not even money can have a neutral color. Someone who talks like you do is attempting to break black solidarity and claim that rich blacks bear the same guilt as the whites do. You are wrong: rich blacks are my brothers even though they have millions stashed away in the banks, because in the concentration camps they want to net the rich as well as the poor. In the last two years they have set up thirteen concentration camps for blacks: in New Jersey, in the Midwest. They are just like the ones that during World War II were used to house the Japanese, and they are waiting for us to fill them.

Concentration camps? I've never heard of them. In the United States it's difficult to keep a secret. . . . How come your congressmen have never mentioned it?

We have no representatives. We had one, Adam Clayton Powell, but they took him away under the pretext that he was a thief. The others are slaves in the white man's service, like that filthy Edward Brooke who was elected by whites. He doesn't represent any blacks, he represents the state of Massachusetts and its white families. American blacks have never taken part in government decisions, American blacks have never been allowed to act politically. Black Americans have always been only a physical presence and nothing else, beasts of burden and nothing more. And every time that they tried to get their rights, they were told, "If you don't like it, go back to Africa." We have no intention of going back to Africa. We feel close to Africa because Africa is our past and a man without a past has no future, but we want to stay here. America belongs to us as much as it belongs to the whites, and they have a debt that's still to be paid, because it's us who built this country. We carried every brick, we raised every skyscraper, every bridge. . . .

Let's be fair, Mr. Brown. You've got to admit that some of those bricks were carried by the Italians, the Irish, the Poles, the Jews, the Englishmen who were the first to build.

We have made America, we made it! And we will destroy it! If one day we decide to leave for Africa, we will destroy everything before we board ship. Level everything! The only thing left behind us will be a pile of smoldering ruins!

Mr. Brown, it would be hard to find a racist who is more racist than you are, a man more filled with hate.

Of course I'm a racist, just like Lyndon Johnson, like Kennedy, like Lincoln, like Washington, like all Negroes— because all Negroes are racists. Everybody who lives in America either is a racist or will become one. One cannot stay neutral: one must stand on one side or the other, without mixing colors or ideas—white with white, black with black. Integration is impossible. We are not interested in it and don't want it. Neither do we want part of the United States for ourselves, otherwise they'd come to bomb us dead. The only reason they haven't bombed us so far is that we live in their cities. What we want is to rule our fate by ourselves, which means to have control when we are in the majority, to own America like they own it, to be free financially and politically—and never to marry them, in no ways. Hate has its use. I'm full of it, like all blacks are. Hate, like violence, is necessary for our revolution. There's never been a revolution without blood and hate. And why should this hate be repressed, when the white man's hate for us has been out in the open for so long? Hate is a tool, a tactical weapon. A black man cannot allow himself to love a white, to treat him like a brother—otherwise he could not love himself. A black man who loves himself must hate whites.

Any white man or only American whites?

All white men who are against blacks. All whites who have control over blacks. That means all whites. I know there are whites who claim to be on the side of the blacks. We don't give a damn—that was a line that worked two years ago but doesn't work any longer. So a white man says to me, "I'm with you." Is it true? And even if it is, so what? He stays white, part of a society that has always been my enemy. And when progressive whites ask us, "Why do you refuse our help?" We answer, "All the help we need is guns, or money to buy some." No, the whites cannot help me to be free because I'm already acting in freedom. Their assistance is superfluous. If they really want to fight with me, I'll tell them what we tell Castro, "Be my guest, but on our conditions. It's we who decide when to shoot, whom to shoot at, or how to shoot."

Mr. Brown, is there anything in the Christian faith you can accept? Is there anything in it that speaks to you when you speak to crowds asking them to burn and to kill?

No. My people is my religion: the blacks. I'm certainly not a Christian. Although Christ was black, a detail the whites have always concealed from us, Christianity is Western, and to adopt it would be like adopting America. If we respond to Christianity, after each slaughter we get a preacher with a cross. We don't need preachers and crosses. We need to answer slaughter with slaughter. For four hundred years the church has been used among the blacks as an instrument of tolerance—that is, oppression—and it's still used to keep them quiet and blind. Now it's over. Nothing makes me laugh as much as that speech of the Texan cowpoke asking blacks and whites to forget in prayer the Newark and Detroit riots. Who among us could fall for such miserable gimmicks? We are not the fools our fathers were when they said "thank you" for an aspirin. We see clearly now, and we're determined. Many among us believed in God, but two years ago they told us that God is dead, so we began to believe in ourselves. It is by believing in ourselves—not in God, not in Christianity—that we have learned to kill.

Mr. Brown, it's one thing to talk, and another to act. Are you quite ready to kill?

I'm all ready for it. And I will kill.

New York, August, 1967

INGRID BERGMAN

The Lady in Gray

I really cannot picture Ingrid Bergman in Sweden: on the stony island where she spends the summer with her third husband, Lars Schmidt, or in cold, monotonous Stockholm, where she was born at the end of World War I. The white nights that for six months of the year grip you in a longing for darkness and the long nights that for the other six months grip you in a longing for light do not suit her restless spirit. The methodical character of her compatriots, who never park their cars where parking is prohibited, who never forget to stand in line to buy a postage stamp, and who are so meticulous that they even nationalized their young hoods, using them during specified hours for public services (letting them hang around for the rest of the day in a special enclosure that belongs to the city), does not suit her need for adventure.

When I was in Stockholm, I stayed in a small hotel facing the Royal Academy of Dramatic Art, where she herself once studied and where Max von Sydow, Ingrid Thulin, Gunnar Bjornstrand, and Ingmar Bergman are still studying today. From the window of my room I used to watch in amusement as they entered at eight in the morning or came out at six in the evening: punctual as factory workers, attracting no more notice than schoolteachers, anonymous, dressed in gray. And I used to reflect that Ingrid Bergman could never have been one of them. Ingrid Bergman is at most about as Swedish as Peer Gynt, who fled on the eve of his wedding to Solveig and went wandering all over the world, returning to his village only when he was on the brink of death. In fact, like Peer Gynt, she fled from Sweden when very young. She has known many loves and many lands, she has been an American in America and an Italian in Italy, and in France she is a French-woman, with a husband who also has something of Peer Gynt in him. Of all these lands and loves the one that has left the strongest impression on her is the strongest country: the United States. And

51

in the United States, land of adventure, with its skyscrapers, gangsters, Broadway, popcorn, I can picture her very well indeed.

The place is a swimming pool in Beverly Hills, California. The time is a Sunday afternoon. The characters are two women who have known each other for years—one a journalist, the other an actress named Ingrid Bergman. They talk—smoking, drinking vodka—now in English and now in Italian, a language that Ingrid knows very well. Roberto Rossellini taught it to her, and their three children are Italian citizens. They talk like friends. It is a conversation during which memories grow in an attempt to explain a life that has been so widely discussed: the life of a woman and an actress. Twenty-eight years have passed since she came to America, eighteen years since she left America, looking for new shores and new hopes in that Europe she belongs to. For some, it was the love story of the century; for others, it was the scandal of the century. It did not last forever. Now she is the wife of Lars Schmidt, the Swedish producer. She is changed. Her face is no longer the face that was so much loved and then hated. The velvet smoothness is gone. Here and there you can see small wrinkles, though her beauty is untouched and her body still perfect. In Eugene O'Neill's *More Stately Mansions,* she is the irresistible mother of a twenty-six- and later a thirty-six-year-old man, and also a grandmother. This could be true in her life. Pia, the daughter born of her marriage to Dr. Peter Lindstrom, is now thirty. Robby, the first son of the marriage to Rossellini, is now nineteen. Isabella and Ingrid, the twins, are now sixteen. She tells me with pride. She is a very proud woman.

She also is a very misunderstood one, especially in the country where this conversation takes place. This country saw her as a Joan of Arc, immune from sins or terrestrial desires, and grew angry when she revealed herself instead as a Peer Gynt. Peer Gynt is the most popular hero of Scandinavian literature. The village where he lives is a prison to him. He escapes in his youth but comes back to his sweet Solveig when he is very old and about to die. He is a dreamer and a fighter and a scoundrel and an adventurer—very human, very alive, therefore great. Ingrid is, too. Listen to her while she talks, just before sunset begins, in a glory of red and gold, on a Sunday afternoon.

ORIANA FALLACI: *Should a movie be done on your life, Ingrid, it could begin from this Sunday afternoon in America, almost thirty years after your arrival in Hollywood: the right time, the right place, to make up accounts of a life.*

INGRID BERGMAN: Thirty years, my God. When I think that almost thirty years have passed since the day I came here from Stockholm, I say, "It isn't possible." I realize that it's true only when I look around and don't recognize what I used to see in 1939. At that time Hollywood was so small, a village. There were fields where now there are roads. And the old streets are so changed. They're wider and bordered by enormous buildings, skyscrapers, banks. Weeks ago, Pia and I went on a pilgrimage to the places that were familiar to us: the school where she studied, the house where we lived. We almost couldn't find them.

And the people . . . many of my friends, my colleagues, are now dead. Gary Cooper is dead, and Humphrey Bogart, and Spencer Tracy, and Clark Gable, and Tyrone Power, and Claude Rains, and David Selznick, and Cecil B. De Mille—so many, so many. When the others come and see me, I feel as though they also bring along the ghosts of those who are gone. And the others, the live ones, are changed like the streets. Cary Grant came, and Gregory Peck, and Joseph Cotten, and Jennifer Jones, and Billy Wilder, and William Wyler, and George Cukor, and Lewis Milestone, and God knows how many others, and each of them was a shock for me. Because I saw my wrinkles in their wrinkles. You know, one looks at herself in the mirror every morning, and she doesn't see the difference, she doesn't realize that she is aging. But then she finds a friend who was young with her, and the friend isn't young anymore, and all of a sudden, like a slap on her eyes, she remembers that she, too, isn't young anymore.

Let's go back to that time, Ingrid, for a moment. It is now 1939, and Ingrid Bergman is twenty-two years old. She is here to play in her first American movie, Intermezzo. *She is . . . how is she?*

She is a girl, always happy, enthusiastic, and she is the mother of a twelve-month-old child. She has come with her child and a suitcase containing a few dresses. Her husband has remained in Stockholm because there is a war in Europe, and should it spread to Sweden, he wants to be at home to be useful. He is a doctor. She feels rather alone, and she speaks practically no English. She only says, "How do you do?" But she says it with a big smile, so everybody loves her, even the producers who lose sleep over her ice cream. She likes ice cream too much, banana splits in particular, and she eats so many of them that she puts on weight, and they cry—nicely, though. You know, until I fell in love with Roberto and left them, I had a very special place in the heart of the Americans. And I didn't know why at that time. I understood later that my success was a woman's success more than an actress' success. They were so used to the European prima donnas, those who break mirrors to get things, wear jewels even in bed, and walk holding a tiger on a leash. They were intrigued, then conquered, by the Swedish girl who had arrived with a child and a suitcase. Women, I think, liked me before men. And men identified me with their wives, their mothers, their sisters. Not accidentally, all the publicity went out about my simplicity, the fact that I didn't use any lipstick. Times were ripe for such a novelty, and you know that talent is not enough without timing. The combination created the love.

Yet ten years later, that love turned into hate—as strong and vast.

Even stronger. Their hate submerged me like a tempest, furiously, and I remained so surprised and so hurt. I did not comprehend it. Only now I do. Well, you called me Peer Gynt because Peer Gynt must go around the world always seeking new dangers and new adventures. There is much truth in your interpretation. But that never was the American interpretation of me. Because of my face, which was washed with soap and nothing else, Americans never saw me as a Peer Gynt. They always saw me as a sister, a mother, even a nun. A nun does not fall in love with an Italian. My falling in love with Roberto was too much of a betrayal for them. Don't forget that it happened in 1948; now it would be different. The new generation that knows me through the movies seen on TV doesn't think as in 1948. The young people react with astonishment when they hear the story of the hate that burst around me. They ask: "Why?" And when they are told, they smile, saying, "Is that all? So what?" But nobody smiled in those years. I didn't either. I can smile today, when a journalist comes with the question: "Have you forgiven the Americans?" Of course I have. After eighteen years! It is over, enough! If a drop of sorrow remained, it vanished the night I first appeared on the Los Angeles stage, and all Hollywood was there, and the applause went on endlessly, and I didn't know what to do. I walked up and down feeling embarrassed and grateful. And when it finally ended . . . I opened my mouth, and I had a blackout. I knew the words, but I couldn't pronounce them.

Yes, they applaud you again. However, there is still a sort of unconfessed uneasiness when they speak of you. I have found it in many.

It is because they still don't understand why I fled. They don't know, for instance, that I didn't flee just because I had fallen in love with Roberto. It was something else, something more. In a certain way, Roberto was the instrument of my flight, the consequence of a deeply matured tiredness. For years I had dreamed of escape. I only waited to find how to escape and where to. Some people around me had felt it; a few knew it. Sam Wood, one of my directors, once said in an interview: "Ingrid? I often watch her while she swims in the ocean, far from the shore and without fear for the sharks. One day, you'll see, she will swim and swim and swim, always farther, and she will never come back." In Hollywood, I felt locked in a prison. The ice creams were not enough, nor was the success. Pia's father had joined us, but I was so alone. The only talk I heard was talk about money and career. I had left the provinces for other provinces. For heaven's sake, I don't want to be unfair to Hollywood—Hollywood gave me so much—but I love either big cities or the country, and Hollywood wasn't a big city or the country. I moved between my house and the studios. There was not a museum to go to, not a concert hall, not a theater. And I only knew actors, directors, producers. I heard much later that many writers lived in Hollywood; nobody ever introduced me to them. And God knows, I needed it. I had seen so little in Sweden, I was looking for life; I wanted to see, to learn. I lost my mind while thinking that beyond the mountains, the ocean, there was a large, unknown world.

And you never felt any tie, any affection, for the village and its golden gates. Is that so?

Never. I was there for ten years, and still today I consider those ten years as a parenthesis in my life. In America I had only one bond: New York. My heart yearned for New York. New York was the freedom and the big city and the theater. I don't know how to explain my joy when I went to New York to play *Joan of Lorraine*. I dived into Broadway as one dives into the sea on a hot summer's day. The pleasure to walk along Fifth Avenue, finally, to enter the museums, finally, the art galleries, finally, the concert hall, finally! And those beautiful shops full of things, and lights, and crowds. And those amusing restaurants, Chinese, Italian, French, Hungarian. And those people from all over the world. New York offered the entire encyclopedia of life to the Swedish girl who had come to America with only a suitcase. I have always loved New York. After all, my destiny took shape in New York. It was here that a Swedish elevator boy had said to a lady working for

Selznick :"I have seen a marvelous Swedish movie, *Intermezzo*.
You should see it too." And she had seen it, then Selznick had
seen it, then he bought the rights to remake it in Hollywood
and called me there.

But you didn't escape to New York, you escaped to Rome.

I saw that movie by Roberto. It was done with nothing, and
it was so unbelievably beautiful that I fell in love with Roberto
before knowing him in person. When I met him, I only had
the confirmation of being in love with him. And I knew I had
found my road. A rough road, if you wish, but I have never
been very wise. Do you see what I mean? Things came to me
asking to be done, and I did them—spontaneously, without
asking whether it was wise or not. And the day after, I could
say, "Maybe I shouldn't have done it." But years later, I always
realized I was right in doing them. Yes, Roberto *was* my road.

*Your road or another road? Peer Gynt didn't stop in Italy,
either. You had never become an American, and you never
became an Italian.*

I did, much more than you believe. I was more Italian than
I had been American. If I never became completely Italian, it
was because it was too late to transform me at that point.
Roberto tried, very hard, but he didn't succeed. Somehow, I
was still a product of Hollywood, and this prevented me from
becoming as Roberto wished and hoped. All my Italian friends
understood it, and that is why, for the Italians, I will always be
a stranger, though I speak Italian and three of my children are
Italian. Consider their love for me: it isn't possessive, it never
was. When my marriage with Roberto was over, they let me
go without screaming. Deep in their hearts they always knew
that I wouldn't remain, that Peer Gynt's destiny is to keep
going, maybe to come back and to leave again. When I stop
somewhere, I cannot stop forever. I might hope for it, but a
foreboding pinches my mind and says: "You'll not stay, you'll
leave."

Peer Gynt does stop in the end. When he's old and is going to die, he goes back home. Ingrid, will you ever go back home to Sweden?

No. I like to go back for a sentimental journey, but never to stay. I do not feel Swedish. I am happy I was born Swedish because this means having a tough education—at least it did in my time. But I couldn't live there. Neither could I when I was eighteen or nineteen, when I went to Germany to make movies. Sweden is too far from the rest of the world, farther than Hollywood. Even psychologically, you feel there as if you are confined on an island. Besides, I have nobody in Sweden but friends. Would you believe me if I tell you that I am more at home in Italy than in Sweden? Yes, I never became completely Italian, but Italy is my second country. What a strange thing to say, even for me. When I left Roberto, I did not believe that such a feeling could last. But it does, and it will. I had been happy with Roberto in Italy.

Once, on French television, you said you preferred Italians. I happened to be in Paris. I remember that the interviewer asked you who were the best people in the world, and you said the Italians were. The interviewer was very put out. Was that just to be provoking?

I never mean to be provoking. I always say only what I think. I said the Italians were the best, and I'm sure of it. There's a human warmth in the Italians that you don't find in the French. If I ask a Frenchman where such-and-such a street is, he doesn't even answer, he can't be bothered to help me. If I ask an Italian, he not only answers me but takes me there, and as he walks along with me, he tells me half his life story: when he was born, and where, and of whom, and about his aunts, his cousins, his in-laws. For me this is a quality that not even the Americans possess. Americans help you, too, but with money. I don't know who it was that said, "Maybe the Americans won't be the first to go to the moon, but they'll be the first to give money to the moon's inhabitants."

Do you feel you have anything in common with Italians?
Anything in common? . . . No-o-o! Ah! You noticed the silence? I hesitated a long time before answering. I've hunted around, but I can't find anything. I am too different, too Nordic . . . You know what I mean?

I think so. Years ago you told me: "The difference between you Latins and we Nordic people is basically and simply this: you get angry over trifles, and you show it; you forgive easily, and you show it. We get angry only when something serious happens, and we don't show it; we forgive only with difficulty, and we don't show it. And so it looks as if you are the only ones to suffer or feel joy, and you don't realize that we suffer just as violently, we love just as violently." Anyway, something to that effect. On that same occasion we talked about America and Europe. You told me that at first . . .

At first I didn't care much either way about America or Europe. What I cared about was success. You know, when we're young, we don't think of much. Or we only think about success. For me, at first, the most important thing was success. Now . . . now I don't know. You see, when you say success and you're referring to your career, people wrinkle their noses because they think an actress wants success in order to get fame and money. I've never sought success in order to get fame and money; it's the talent and the passion that count in success. Do you see what I mean? Heavens, this is a difficult thing to explain. What I mean is that everyone is born with a talent: a talent for writing, for sewing, for acting. . . . And this talent is love, passion. And so, when you do your work gladly, as an actor, for example, you don't do it only to become successful. You do it, without success, at the cost of sacrificing very important things.

Are you referring to family? In other words, do you mean that career is more important than family?

Oh, Lord! How can one say that career counts more than family? Put like that it sounds terrible, because career is inevitably bound up with money and fame. What I mean is that, especially when we're young, passion for work counts more than family. And, indeed, very few actresses have given up their careers at the height of success; those who have probably have done so because their careers were going badly. Grace Kelly is the only one who gave up her career at the height of success, with the result that now she'd like to take it up again. And if the public hadn't cried out against it, she would have done so. But why, I'd like to know, should a woman have to choose just the one thing and give up the other? Why? Being an actress doesn't make you a bad wife or a bad mother. I am neither a bad wife nor a bad mother, yet I cannot bear the idea of leaving my work forever. I might abandon it for a week, a month, a year, but not forever.

Does this mean that for you being an actress is a means of existence, a necessity, your very life? That giving it up would be like giving up life?

That's right. That's what I mean. Nothing else.

Ingrid, where is your home now?

I have three homes: one in Paris, one in Rome, one on the island off the west coast of Sweden that Lars bought for our marriage. We spend the summer there. I go to Rome in the winter, when the children go to school. My real house is in Paris, with Lars. Paris is the place that fits me better. Lars knows this because Lars is the man who has understood me best. I should say he is the only person who has ever understood me—as a woman, as an actress. And he accepts me as I am, without fighting, without trying to change me. Unfortunately, we met too late. Or perhaps we met at the right time, when we both were mature enough to love each other. Patience comes with aging, and aging makes you forget jealousy. Lars had me when I was an adult whose curiosities had been fulfilled, whose tolerance had begun to exist. The others had me when I was a girl kidnapped by dreams or a woman tormented by uncertainties. I was so restless when Roberto arrived. I was so young when Pia's father met me. Sometimes I wonder if my un-happiness with Hollywood contributed to breaking up my first marriage. No, it didn't. The break would have come anyhow, when two people get married too young and reach maturity along different roads. . . . You look thoughtful, what do you think?

I was thinking that you have a beautiful life, Ingrid, a full one.

A very beautiful life. A very interesting life. A very lucky life. I realize it especially when I consider others' lives—so boring and gray and motionless. They can't even cry because they have nothing to cry about, and how can they survive without crying? I've had ugly moments filled with tears. But they were never stupid moments, stupid tears. Even sorrows sometimes are fortunate. The only sorrows that I am not grate-ful for are the sorrows that I had as a child. My mother died when I was two years old, my father died when I was thirteen years old, the aunt I lived with and loved as a mother died in my arms six months after my father. Perhaps it was because of my training in big sorrows that I could stand the minor ones. The fights with Pia's father, the insults that for years followed Roberto and me. My whole happiness with Roberto was poi-soned by those insults. It was hard to see a man as talented as he badly treated because of me. All the movies we did together were rejected, remember? I never stopped thinking that if he had not done those movies with me, for me, his success would have continued gloriously. Our love, my love, broke that suc-cess. And yet I have no regret. I will always repeat that, should I live my life again, I would live it exactly as I have lived it, without any hesitation. Because I am capable of gratitude, I can see the good I have had. I am not like those people who take everything for granted and never say thanks.

And youth, Ingrid? Don't you regret the loss of your youth?

No. . . . O'Neill says that getting old is a natural thing, and we must not be afraid of the natural. The trees age, and the animals, and everything that is alive. We must die. And since we must die, we must age. Isn't it fortunate that we can age? If I am aging, it means that I did not die young. No, I am not even afraid to look old. I will never get really old because I don't know indifference and I ignore bitterness. If something unpleasant happens to me, I put it behind me, and I keep thinking that there is always another day—which is good for the wrinkles, too. My only fear is of becoming ill and ending my life in a bed. But I can still get by with little sleep, and never before three in the morning. And I tell you how old I am: I am fifty-two. Write it down. And also write down that I am proud to be fifty-two. Because at fifty-two, I am a happy woman.

Los Angeles, August, 1967

NGUYEN CAO KY

Man of Destiny

He is the most famous man in South Vietnam and also the most hated. Reactionaries hate him because he is the most hostile enemy of the reactionaries; liberals hate him because he is the most hostile enemy of the liberals; Americans hate him because he is the most hostile enemy of the Americans. And there are many who think he will not die of old age, that someone will try to eliminate him very soon. He knows it. Not by chance, he likes to define himself as uncomfortable, dangerous, without friends.

At first glance you wouldn't know it. He is a Vietnamese like many others, neither tall nor short, neither too strong nor too fragile. Physically he distinguishes himself from the others only by his moustache (Vietnamese don't usually wear them) and by a certain air with which he seems to oblige you to remember that he is Nguyen Cao Ky, Commander of the Air Force, Vice-President of the Republic. He is not cordial. He smiles very rarely, and he is always wrinkled up in a bad mood, filled with preoccupation, exuding a detachment that skims the arrogance. When he shakes your hand (he has very beautiful hands, rather feminine), he looks at you so distractedly that you would say he is not even looking at you. Yet, when you go looking for news about him, you learn with surprise that beyond that severe, scowling, discouraging appearance there is a very colorful personality, one of those that popular magazines emphasize—women's magazines in particular.

They would tell you, for instance, that he is a real ladies' man. Before he married his second wife, no one in Saigon could compete with him in certain adventures, and until three years ago this was his principal claim to fame: he did not deny it. On the contrary, he supported his reputation with pride, explaining that every woman loves the pilots: "Perhaps because flying represents to her eyes something new, a daring way of life." They would tell you that, besides this, he was a playboy, a heavy drinker always frequenting nightclubs. You can tell it, they say, from the way he combs his hair, the way he wears that mauve satin scarf around his neck, from his unstudied, casual look and his uniform always so ironed, too ironed, which he wears at all times, the same suit he used when he jumped at night into North Vietnam on secret missions: all black and close-fitting. With such a suit he seems a bat with a giant rose at his neck—but what an elegant bat.

Others will tell you that no, inside he's a sentimentalist, that he abandons himself to these harmless characteristics because of an old despair, the disappointment inflicted by his first wife, who was French and took advantage of him. When married to her, he was a good boy; he became a playboy when she left him with five children and he went to live with that show girl. Think of it: a prime minister who goes to live with a show girl, committing to her his children. If you understand such a drama, they say, then you realize how tender he is, how kind, how thirsty for a normal family. Then you will believe that it was for this very reason that he married his second wife, as good and as beautiful, eleven years younger yet wise, whom he met on an Air Vietnam flight to Bangkok. Then you will believe that in Bangkok he invited this air hostess who studied math at the University of Natrang to dinner, along with the entire crew, that seven days later he introduced her to his children to make it clear that he wanted not only a wife for himself but also a mother for them. Besides, his wife will confirm the story, she'll even add that he is a good father, a good husband, that since the day they got married, he has never given her a reason to doubt his fidelity, that it is not true what people tell about the day he flew to Hue for a sentimental journey and she followed him on a military plane. He did order the control tower to forbid her landing, but the order was given "because the weather was bad, the landing dangerous." She was joining him because he wished to spend the weekend with the family. "People are so nasty."

Finally, others will tell you that he's superstitious, that he believes in horoscopes to a hysterical degree, questions the astrologers before serious decisions, that he was very happy when his second wife gave birth to a girl because he already had four sons. (In Vietnam four sons mean good luck, five mean misfortune.) The

astrologer, they say, had announced to him that a daughter would
bring him a future full of good promise, a son would bring him
disasters. That is why, they add, he called his daughter Duyen,
which means "strange magic." He denies it with indignation. But
he does not deny that his fondest amusement, his real relaxation,
is watching cock fights. In his house at Tan Son Nhut he keeps one
hundred cocks, and every Sunday afternoon he organizes a show
that ends in a hecatomb of blood: feathers strewn all over, breasts
and necks and legs torn to pieces. Not satisfied, he goes looking for
cock fights wherever they take place; he crosses half Vietnam by
plane and jeep and enters Viet Cong zones without escort just for
that. He admits it, explaining that cocks are a pretext, in reality
those trips are useful, they allow him to make contact with the
peasants. He likes peasants. With them he doesn't have a distant
relationship, with them he smiles jovially and shows all his teeth,
which are white and strong and as frightening as the teeth of a
wolf. With them he shakes hands in a very friendly way. He believes in them as much as Ho Chi Minh and Mao Tse-tung do. He
claims that Vietnam's renaissance depends on the peasants, not on
the intellectuals. Intellectuals are not able to fight because they
are not able to suffer, and they are not able to suffer because they
have never been hungry.

Before becoming a pilot, his dream was to be a farmer. But he
comes from Hanoi, of a family of Mandarins. In other words, he is
of aristocratic descent. From his tastes, you wouldn't guess it. He
has little interest in "good" music, he listens to Brahms or Beethoven when he wants to get sleepy. When he's awake, he prefers
the Twist and Rock and the Beatles. He doesn't go to the movies—
such an easy place to get killed—but he often projects motion pictures in his house, and they certainly are not very "deep"—Westerns and James Bond movies. With books it's the same. He reads
detective stories; his wife says that he possesses an entire library
of them. Once a French journalist, François Pelou, went to visit
him at the Independence Palace and saw, over his Vice-President's
desk, two detective stories and a Bible. "Congratulations, I see
you are dedicating yourself to serious literature," Pelou said, pointing to the Bible. "Someone just gave it to me," he answered with
irritation, then he took the Bible and threw it away. He is not

religious; he's a confessed atheist. He recalls that when he was a
soldier and his mother prayed to Buddha for him, he made fun of
her. He declares he has never faced the problem of the existence of
God and adds that he couldn't care less about whether God exists
or not.

In the light of these anecdotes, therefore, nobody would dare to
judge him as a representative character, a man whose destiny was
and is to enter into history of this war, the only possible leader in
a country painfully poor in leaders. Yet he is. And you realize it,
with astonishment, when you listen to him for more than ten
minutes. The man is not stupid. He has something to say, and he
says it without fear. To begin with, he is a socialist, but not a pink
socialist, undecided between reforms and compromises. He is a
Marxist-socialist, exactly like his enemy Ho Chi Minh. Like Ho
Chi Minh, he does not believe in democracy as we accept it, in
freedom as we interpretate it. In his eyes the rich are indisputably
corrupt, the poor are indubitably innocent; social revolution is
the only answer to the problems of Vietnam. And not a pacific
revolution, not a constitutional revolution, it must be a violent
revolution—a bloody one if necessary.

The most extraordinary thing is that he expresses this belief
without pronouncing the formulas "capitalism," "class struggle,"
"dialectic." He has never read Marx, and he hasn't the slightest
idea of what "Marxism" means. He has arrived at his ideological
conclusions all alone, by instinct, confusedly, between a detective
story and a cock fight. And it would be difficult to explain to him
that such ideas are not new, that someone wrote them down a hundred years ago. Even more difficult is it to tell him that the war in
Vietnam is substantially due to the conflict that surrounds these
ideas, that consequently he's on the wrong side of this war, that
if destiny had put Marx's *Das Kapital* in his hands, he would now
be with Ho Chi Minh, firing mortars into Saigon. In other words,
he is ignorant, with no desire to read anything other than a detective story.

Things being like that, it's a mystery how he could become first
Prime Minister and then Vice-President of the government most
hated by any Marxist. And if "mystery" is not the right word, then
we must admit to have understood nothing about Vietnam and

what boils in there. It is not unusual, when you tell a responsible Vietnamese that Nguyen Cao Ky speaks like a Viet Cong, to get this answer: "But most of the Ky generation speak like Viet Cong." And perhaps the most dangerous enemy that the Americans have in Vietnam is not the ascetic old man who studied in Moscow and whom the North Vietnamese tenderly call Uncle Ho, it is this young man with a mauve silk scarf, this pilot whom they hosted for eight months at the airbase in Maxwell, Alabama, and whom Henry Cabot Lodge referred to as "my second son."

The interview that follows took place in a house on Rue Cong Ly, where the Vice-President lives during the daytime with his family. At night the family transfers to the Independence Palace, where they sleep in a room adjacent to his office, on mattresses placed against the floor. Armed guards guard the palace; the atmosphere around them is tense, suspicious; the children have learned how to keep their heads down and get covered as soon as they hear a gunshot. When Madame Ky says, "We live like soldiers," her porcelain face becomes a portrait of sadness. Ky's face stays imperturbable. For him the risk is normality, the death's threat is routine. And a blind faith holds him: the faith that he can walk through that death's threat like an invulnerable god. Maybe he's a visionary; maybe he knows very well what he's doing. Maybe he will end as a Lumumba; maybe he will win as a little Napoleon. Others, as ignorant as he is and as controversial, were able to succeed. This reporter made no judgments, she limited herself to telling you what he said. Ky spoke to her for hours, with a steady voice and hard eyes. It was a Sunday afternoon in March, 1968, and the artillery thundered around Saigon.

ORIANA FALLACI: *General Ky, many disconcerting things are said about you, but the most disconcerting I have heard is what you said about yourself a few days ago: "I know that someone is trying to kill me. But this someone will not be a Communist."*

NGUYEN CAO KY: Exactly so. If someone kills me, it will not be a Communist. It will be someone on the other side, someone for whom I am much more dangerous than I am for the Communists. Not all the evil is on the communist side. The corruption is among us, among our leaders. Nine out of ten are corrupt. And as I am the only one to recognize it, to admit it, many people hate me, and it is in their interest to eliminate me. Politicians don't like me because I am not a politician, because I am not a diplomat, because I denounce this regime as an inefficient one, an incapable one, and because I say that democracy exists in it only in name. Americans don't like me because I tell them what I think, and I accuse them of lying. Americans say that they are here in the name of their principles of democracy and freedom. I do not believe them; at best I believe them 50 per cent of the time. Americans are not here for democracy or freedom, they are here to defend their interests. And their interests do not always coincide with the interests of Vietnam. Americans are here because they want to stay in Asia, to fight communism in Asia, not because they care for us. They do not understand what we need, they do not understand our tragedy. Look at that Robert Kennedy who always talks about corruption in Vietnam as if it were here only. He's a very rich fellow, this Kennedy, and I would like to know if his father was ever involved in corruption. And I would like him to come here, not to send that kid brother of his, but he is too afraid to face reality. He says: "Democracy, freedom." Words. His concept of democracy and freedom is simply ridiculous to me, because it is always these big powerful countries that talk about democracy and freedom that are the colonialists. They begin by saying: "We are here to help you." And then they become bosses, and then they become colonialists. Enough of that.

General Ky, are you speaking about revolution?

Of course I am. What Americans do not understand is that South Vietnam needs a revolution to counter the ideal of revolution from North Vietnam, to demonstrate that not only in North Vietnam is there a need for justice. Americans want to institute in South Vietnam a certain kind of democratic regime involving respect for the laws, freedom of speech, and so on. Elections. But what do elections mean to someone who is dying of starvation? What do legislative power and executive power mean when all you need is a bowl of rice for your children? When you go to the villages and you speak to the peasants about voting, they answer that they are hungry. They don't care about democracy; they care about social justice. So for me democracy means social justice, that is, distribution of the land, building of houses and schools, no more starvation. It does not mean what it means to the Americans, to Mr. Kennedy. I am not interested in the elections that Americans recommend; they don't mean a thing in this country because here people vote out of ignorance and indifference and fear. In most cases, the men who have been elected in South Vietnam are not those the people want; they do not represent the people. The people voted for them because someone told them to vote for them. Our last elections were a loss of time and money, a mockery. They were useful only as a means of electing a regime that is wrong and corrupt and weak, that would fall immediately with a revolution. It is hard for me to say so because I share the responsibility for those elections, I stood as a candidate and was elected, and I now serve as Vice-President of the regime so endorsed. But at least I recognize the evil where the evil is. And I say that laws must be changed, because what we now have are laws that defend the rich. We need new laws to defend the poor.

General Ky, this is what Ho Chi Minh says, what the Viet Cong say. This is socialism, Marxism.

Who denies it? I am not afraid of the word "socialism." It is the Americans who pronounce the word socialism as if it were a dirty word. When I spoke with Cabot Lodge, I used the word socialism, the word "revolution." I said: "Freedom? Freedom of what? Of expression? The freedom we need in Vietnam is the freedom from want, freedom to get that bowl of rice. Let us first build a country in which nobody starves, then we will talk about freedom of expression, of legislative power and executive power." You say I am a Marxist. It is not the first time that a European has said that to me. So maybe I am a Marxist. Who cares? I don't know Marx, or Engels, or any of these white people who were born in Europe. They set down theories, and I have no time to lose with theories. Frankly, I don't read. I am not even ashamed to admit that my education is rather poor. I did not go beyond high school, and I stopped studying when I was eighteen years old, when the French closed the schools to send us to war. I am a pilot. I have spent my life with airplanes, not reading the books of this Marx and this Engels. It doesn't interest me in the least to know that this Marx discovered that the poor must not be poor. I don't need his discovery to know such an elementary thing. I am yellow-skinned, I am an Asiatic, and I know what my country needs much better than all those white people who write books.

The fact remains, General Ky, that if you read those books you would realize that you are saying the same things as those you are fighting. Could you tell me why you fight the Communists?

Well, as I told you, I only know what I see here in my country. And what I see about the Communists in my country . . . well, I don't like it. I mean, I don't like to see a son condemn his mother in the name of a party; I don't like a party that destroys the family and the family sentiments in the name of an ideology; I don't like a society in which a man becomes a member of a party. Thus, although it is true that I am against the freedom that causes disorders and prevents social justice, it is also true that I am against dictatorship. I don't know how to explain it. Maybe I can explain it this way: I don't like the Catholics, and the Communists resemble the Catholics very much. They belong to the Party exactly as the Catholics belong to the Church—fanatically. This is why I fight the Communists. But certainly I don't reproach them for their program of distributing riches, and I agree perfectly with them when they take the land of the rich and give it to the poor. I agree perfectly with them when they give a rifle to a peasant and say to him: "Fight for a better life." I agree perfectly with them when they abolish the privileged classes, and when they say that the system of division of classes is wrong. As Confucius says, we must raise the poor and lower the rich until they meet at a level at which everybody can live harmoniously, totally integrated.

General Ky, did it never occur to you to think that you may be on the wrong side of the barricades? Did it ever occur to you to think that you could well get on with Ho Chi Minh?

Well . . . if my destiny had been different, I could have been on his side. But what would I be today? I would be a little functionary lost in the cadres of the Party, like thousands of others, completely silenced by them, and I wouldn't be able to do a thing. Staying on this side of the barricade instead, I am Nguyen Cao Ky, and I can do something; for if it is true that one swallow does not make a summer, it is also true that one swallow announces the summer. Of course, everything would have been easier for me on the other side of the barricades. Probably I would be less unhappy there, too. But I also would be impotent, and I could not dream of my revolution. Let's take Ho Chi Minh. Sometimes people ask: "Would you like to know him?" Honestly, I am not interested, and do you know why? Because he belongs to another generation. Certainly he is a good leader, but he is old. He is over seventy, and I am thirty-seven. What could we say to each other? It is not that I despise the old, I belong to a country in which venerability is much respected. But when we speak of revolution, of social justice, of building the future of a country, the old people have nothing to teach us. People like Ho Chi Minh do not belong to this century, their systems are obsolete. If we listen to them, we will repeat their same mistakes.

However, General Ky, should you one day realize that you are unable to carry out your revolution, that you have chosen the wrong side of the barricades, would you be ready to go to the other side?

No. When a man chooses an ideal, or a way to realize an ideal, he must follow it until the end—without changing his system. Should I realize, sooner or later, that I have chosen the wrong way and the wrong side of the barricades, I would prefer to die. I know very well that my choice is not easy, that it will be very painful. I know very well that the Communists and I have many dreams in common, common targets, common aims. I know very well that the system on this side of the barricades is wrong, but there would be no sense in abandoning a wrong system for another wrong system. No, I will never go with them. I'd rather die than admit to have chosen the wrong way. The only thing that I could admit then would be that my choice was not very practical.

Do you really believe you'll succeed, or do you only dream of succeeding?

I believe in my destiny, so I believe I will succeed—unless they kill me. If they don't kill me, I will win because I am not with the minority. The mass of the people—the poor, the peasants—are with me. And it is on the poor, on the peasants, that one must count for a revolution, not on the intellectuals, on the middle-class people. He who is not hungry does not shoot well, if at all. My revolution must be done with the peasants and by the peasants and for the peasants.

This is what Mao Tse-tung says.

Mao Tse-tung is Chinese, and the Chinese have been our enemies for four thousand years. Our history demonstrates that the Chinese only want to absorb us, destroy us, and what a Chinese says can never agree with what a Vietnamese says. We hate them, the Chinese, in the South as well as in the North. And when some Americans say that Ho Chi Minh will ask the Chinese to intervene in this war with their troops, I answer, "You are crazy." Ho Chi Minh is a Vietnamese, and he hates the Chinese as I hate them, and he knows that calling in the Chinese would be the mistake of his life. Should the Chinese come to Vietnam, we all would reunite, South and North, Communists and Nationalists, and we would fight them together, and all our problems would finally be resolved, and our country would not be divided anymore.

General Ky, what do you think of the Viet Cong? What do you think of this fight between brothers? Can you consider the Viet Cong as brothers?

A brother is a man who is with me when I am sad and when I am happy. A brother is a man who thinks like me, and the Viet Cong don't think like me. They speak my language, they have the same blood and country, but they are not my brothers. The most I can do is to feel pity for them when I see them dead. This may scandalize you, but should you have put the same question to the Americans during their Civil War, they would have answered the same thing. Now the Americans are united. A day will come when my country will be united, too, like America, and I will not shoot what you call my brothers anymore, they will not shoot me anymore: this is our destiny, and the destiny I am fighting for. Until that day don't ask me to like them, I leave this privilege to you Europeans. You Europeans have fallen in love with the Viet Cong. Everything they do seems good to you; everything we do seems bad to you.

We are the villains, and they are the heroes: it's just like a Western. You admire them, you have taken sides. Should we attack the North, the whole world would arise against us. But they infiltrated into the South, and the whole world accepts it. I have not yet understood if yours is romanticism or idiocy.

Maybe it's only respect, General Ky, for instance, respect for their courage, their faith. You must admit that it takes a lot of courage, of faith, to go barefoot against tanks.

Who denies that they are brave, that they have faith? Sure they have it—a lot. They are Vietnamese. But also our soldiers have guts. It is you Europeans who accuse them of cowardice, I don't know on what basis: when you watch a battle, you always watch the Americans, never the Vietnamese, as if the war could be fought only by the Americans. All right, Americans fight, and I thank them for this. But they are not alone, and if the North Vietnamese were not infiltrating into the South, we would not need the Americans. We would be able finally to settle our own damn businesses without the Americans. We have no less guts than the Viet Cong. I personally am not less courageous than a Viet Cong. Oh, you're full of admiration for the Viet Cong for their Tet offensive. Well, it certainly was a brave offensive and an intelligent one. I would call it a rather respectable offensive. But we were not less than they. They only have more discipline than we have, more training, because they have organized themselves since 1954, and we started only three years ago.

General Ky, in your judgment, why was the Tet offensive a failure?

It was a failure because the Viet Cong believed the statements that the American press and the Vietnamese press have been making for years: that we were the cowards, that they were the lions. They lost because they thought that our soldiers would not react and that the population would immediately pass over to their side. They lost because they had wrong information, and because they had not understood that the mass of the population does not want Ho Chi Minh or me, it wants only its bowls of rice. They lost because they did not have me to guide them. If I had planned the Tet offensive, I would have won because I know what is required to shake the indifference of my people. You have to wake up their consciences. And to wake up their consciences you have to recognize their right to bowls of rice. You have to make them fight for those bowls of rice, and then no army, no atomic bombs, can stop them. They lost because their leaders are old and foment revolutions in an old-fashioned way, using the books that were written a hundred years ago by white people. Their leaders reason as Americans do, interrogating computers, not common sense. And then, militarily speaking, they lost because of a few stupid mistakes. First of all, they had not enough troops. Second, their troops were not sufficiently armed or sufficiently trained. They did not occupy the right places at the right times. They wasted time on the American Embassy, for instance. Who cares about the American Embassy? How can you waste energies and lives on the American Embassy? They should have taken the Tan Son Nhut airport, they should have taken the radio stations, they should have spoken to the people, to raise them up: "Here we are, in Saigon. No more Ky, no more Thieu, no more Americans. We are the government now, we are your friends." I would have done that.

Maybe they will next time? General Ky, do you think they will attack again?

Sure they will. As soon as they recover from their terrible losses—they have lost about fifty thousand men all around the country—they will attack again. And this will happen very soon in my judgment, let's say in May or June. They will attack Saigon because the decisive battle will take place in Saigon, nowhere else. It is the Americans who publicize Khe Sanh and the places like Khe Sanh. The North Vietnamese are not stupid, they know very well that Khe Sanh has no importance, not militarily, not strategically, not politically. They have no intention of wasting themselves in transforming Khe Sanh into a Dien Bien Phu. They want Saigon, the capital, the population. The war will be decided in Saigon. But I don't think they will win. If they win, it will mean that they are right and I am wrong, that their revolution is just and that there is no need for my revolution. And they won't win, because to win you need a general uprising of the populace.

General Ky, are you not tired of this war?

No, it is you Europeans, you Americans, you white people who think that the Vietnamese—both in the South and in the North—are tired of this war. It is not true. And the reason is that we have never known peace or happiness; we are habituated to death; we are not afraid of it. Take my case. I don't even remember the first time I saw war, I was born in it. I was a child when the Japanese were here. And then the Japanese went away, and the so-called Allies—the Chinese—came. And when the Chinese went away, the war with the French began. And when the French went away, this war began. Every day for us could be the day of our death. We are ready for it, we are Asiatic, that is, fatalistic. We believe in destiny, and we are used to the sufferings. You white people don't understand. You white people give too much importance to life, to the length of life, to the comforts of life. You are not really able to sacrifice yourselves for a dream. If you had been in a war as long as this one, you would have given up a long time since.

You don't love the white people, General Ky, do you?

I don't. I am too proud to love you. I am too proud of being a Vietnamese, Asiatic, yellow. I've never thought that the white race is a superior race, on the contrary. If I were religious, which I am not, I would say, "I am the son of Buddha, I am the son of God, I am God. I am the man that God sent to save this country and unify it and give it one day the role it has to have in Asia." You have to realize that the future is here among us, not among you whites. Europe is old, tired, dusty, and

America should not be called "The New World" anymore, it should be called "The Old World." Its time, your time, is over —which is why I couldn't care less for your criticisms about us and about me. Take all that noise about the General Loan episode—I mean when he shot the Viet Cong. Of course I blame him, but I understand him: his gesture was the gesture of a man who loses control when he has seen many of his men killed. But I want to have the right to judge a Vietnamese who kills another Vietnamese. And I don't transfer that right to anybody else. I don't recognize that anyone else has that right.

You don't, but we take it, General Ky. And the results are not always very beneficial for you. Are you aware of how hated you are?

Yes. People always seem to expect the worst from me, people abroad especially. I remember when I was sent to Australia, and the posters called me "Butcher, Murderer, Dictator." When they realized that I was not that bad, they reacted in total amazement: "We waited for a butcher and we find a small, nice gentleman," one newspaper wrote. I know I am still accused of being an admirer of Hitler: ridiculous, simply ridiculous. It all started because, one day, when I was Prime Minister and we had a coup every day, I exclaimed in exasperation: "What this country needs is a Hitler." I meant a strong man. I chose Hitler out of paradox and rage. But then the English Parliament raises the problem and sends me its ambassador to ask for an explanation. With what right? With the right of the white race? I answered him, "If you come as a friend, I can explain it all to you. But if you come as an ambassador, get out of here; because if you assume the right to accuse me of admiring Hitler, if you forbid me the right to choose to admire Hitler, soon you'll be assuming the right to oblige me to admire your queen. And I don't, for the simple reason that she is a queen and I think that queens and kings and princes and princesses are grotesque in a modern society looking for revolution."

General Ky, is there anybody in the world whom you ad-
mire, apart from yourself?

I don't admire anybody except the poor who fight for their
bowls of rice. So let's use the word respect instead of the word
admire. Well, I respect De Gaulle, for the way he fought in the
Resistance and for the way he brought back prestige to France.
I respect Churchill, for the way he fought during World War
II. Then Stalin, for the same reason. But maybe, instead of
Stalin, I should say the Russian people, for their patriotism,
their courage. Ho Chi Minh, I don't know, it's difficult for me
to judge Ho Chi Minh objectively. And then I respect my
cocks when they fight. As you know, I am not a rich man. I
possess nothing except one hundred fighting cocks. And the
reason I keep them is that I respect them. And the reason I
respect them is that they have courage. They fight until death
even when the adversary is bigger and stronger and blinds at
the first clash. To have courage is the most important thing
in life, important as having an ideal. And I have an ideal.
And if they don't kill us, I will win because I have courage and
an ideal, which are more important and useful than culture.

You are a man in trouble, General Ky. You could also lose
your life.

Well, for a man like me there are only two solutions: to win
or to be eliminated. So maybe you are right when you say
that I am a man in trouble. But perhaps it is even more right
to say that I am a tragic man. The fact is that it is always tragic
to be a Vietnamese. To be a Vietnamese means to be in the
middle of the struggle between two giants, three giants, who
don't give a damn for you and use you as a gun to shoot at each
other: America and Russia, America and China, Russia and
China. We are the pretext for their vanity, which looks only
at the achievement of power, of supremacy. And in such a
struggle we risk being squashed without pity. Even Ho Chi
Minh knows this plain truth. Even you Europeans. Everybody
knows. Everybody but the Americans. But trying to explain

this to the Americans would be as hard as trying to explain to them that socialism is not a dirty word, and that there is no other answer to the civilization that they propose to us. Theirs is a civilization of robots. It is impossible to talk with the Americans, not because they don't want to talk, but because they don't understand. Once I tried, with a specialist in foreign aid. He wanted to know why Americans are hated so much in the world today, in spite of all the help they give. I said, "Because it is not what you give, it is how you give it." And he asked, "How should we give it?" So I said, "I could teach it to you. But it would take tens and tens of years. Better, generations and generations. Better, a civilization of thousands of years." He did not understand. He could not. He was too much a product of a world dominated by computers, by technology, by the three giants who use us Vietnamese and the small countries like Vietnam as instruments in their struggle. If I am unable to win, it will be only because one man alone can no longer win in a world dominated by those giants, those computers, that technology. That will be the only reason.

Thank you, General Ky.

Thank you, for having listened to me. You see, I am a very lonely man. Very lonely. Really lonely. It happens so rarely that I can talk with someone—I mean someone who really listens to me. And when it happens I feel happy, because I feel less alone.

Saigon, March, 1968

GERALDINE CHAPLIN

In the Shadow of Father

On that beautiful face of hers, which "from forehead to nose is mother's face, from nose to chin is father's," Geraldine Chaplin has three beauty spots, forming a triangle: one is above her mouth, one below her right eye, and one below her left eye. The one above her mouth she manages to conceal, more or less, with make-up, but not the ones beneath her eyes. And as they actually adjoin her lashes, they look like two black tears: the motionless, continual, heartrending tears of a little clown. She smiles, and the black tears are still there. She eats, she smokes, she sleeps, and the black tears are still there, to remind her of an unadmitted sadness, the heavy responsibility that nobody envies her: being the daughter of Charlie Chaplin. During our conversation I never took my eyes off those two beauty spots, the two black tears, and even if she hadn't been so touching, so sincere, they would have been enough to cancel out the scant indulgence with which I had approached her, this twenty-year-old who has everything: charm, beauty, illustrious name, success, easy career. Without so much as raising her little finger, let's admit it, she has got where other people fail to get after years and years of effort; it was enough for her to appear doing two or three steps in a ballet, barely a role at all, for the world to fall in love with her, international society to fling wide its doors, and the cinema to beg her to accept star parts.

But is this really such good fortune? The answer to the question lies in the following interview, which took place in Madrid, where Geraldine Chaplin was making her first movie, *Un beau matin d'été*. Naturally the film has nothing to do with father's films; indeed, goodness knows what father thinks about it, father doesn't say anything, father's waiting for her at the finishing tape. As for mother, she says and thinks what father says and thinks, and as father . . . father. Father. That incredible, exacting, terrifying father, who has as much glory as progeny. My interview with

81

Geraldine Chaplin lasted several hours. Geraldine, who is shy, spoke hesitatingly, bashfully, and whenever she said anything especially serious, her voice would become a whisper, trail off into silence, fade away. I had great difficulty picking it up on the tape recorder, even with the volume turned up to maximum. Only when I asked her if she feared that father of hers did her answer come loud and sure. And because of what she told me, I forgot to ask her the very thing I most wanted to know: whether she loved him, that father of hers.

ORIANA FALLACI: *No doubt you realize, Geraldine, that this interview is due to a name, to a relationship, to the fact that you are Charlie Chaplin's daughter. This might sound discourteous, perhaps it is. But the curiosity and the interest you arouse everywhere are also due to the same thing, let's admit it. Leading newspapers spread news about you, famous film directors fight over you, proud countesses court you, and yet it can't be said that you have so far distinguished yourself by any particular achievement. Yours is a typical case of a person who becomes someone before they've even done anything and . . .*

GERALDINE CHAPLIN: Done anything?!? Damn all, you mean. Look, I'm twenty. And twenty years might not be many, but they aren't few, either. There are people who by the time they're twenty have done masses of things, but I've done a fat nothing, except be Charlie Chaplin's daughter. Publicity, when you get it, is always for some reason, either good or bad. But I get it for nothing: for being Charlie Chaplin's daughter. It's unfair, I know, it's plain ridiculous. In fact, my father is angry, very angry, and he's right. For example, take what happened when I first appeared in that ballet, *Cinderella.* I only had two little parts, each of which lasted a minute, or less, yet there wasn't a seat to be had in the theater, and the papers were full of photographs, everyone wanted to interview me, and it was all so disproportionate, so embarrassing. Goodness knows what people thought. You understand? Every time a ballerina did a solo, they took her for me, and down would come the applause. When I finally came forward to do my two or three pirouettes, and it became clear that the little Chaplin girl was only going to do two or three pirouettes, their disappointment hit me like a gust of wind. I felt I could hear them saying, "Well, is that all?" I felt mortified, humiliated. I thought they'd picked me because I was good, and now I discovered that they'd only picked me for the sake of the publicity that goes with my name.

Such are the problems of inheritance, Geraldine. You yourself admitted it in your rather original remark: "A lot of people inherit wealth or a title. I have inherited a surname." And when you inherit something you always have to pay duties; the greater the inheritance, the heavier the duties. But still, as well as the duties, there are the advantages.

Agreed. And the advantages are remarkable. If you want to start a career, any career, and your name is Chaplin, you don't have the slightest difficulty getting started. Everyone wants you, everyone's after you, everyone reveres you. Nevertheless, the disadvantages are equally remarkable, believe me. If your name is Chaplin, people expect a lot of you. They expect too much. And you must be good, you have to be. If you're not good, they take umbrage, they make fun of you, their respect turns to scorn. But if you are good, they take it for granted. And whatever happens, you never know whether it's to your own credit or due to your name. Oh, it's hateful to think that if you do make a go of something, it's just due to your name. It's hateful to think that if you fail, you'll be crushed with shame, because of your name. There are times when I think it would be a lot better to have an unknown name.

Then why don't you change your name, Geraldine? A lot of people, in your situation, have changed, do change, their names. So why do you use the name?

Because I'm proud of it, obviously, very proud. Because I'm glad to be Charlie Chaplin's daughter. And also because it would be pointless to change it, it's too late. By now everyone knows who I am. Everyone recognizes me, apart from the fact that I take so very much after my father and mother: from forehead to nose is mother's face, from nose to chin is father's. Not only that: ever since I was a child, I've been photographed with them, and if I called myself Geraldine Smith, you know what people would say? They'd say: "Geraldine Smith, Charlie

Chaplin's daughter." The definition "Charlie Chaplin's daughter" will follow me all my life, even if I change my name a dozen times. And so I might just as well go on keeping the name, as Jane Fonda does, for example, Henry Fonda's daughter, or Susan Strasberg, Lee Strasberg's daughter. And I might succeed, too. They've both succeeded, haven't they? The only trouble, apart from this positive obligation to succeed, is that you never know whether people give you a contract because they think you'll succeed or because you're Chaplin's daughter.

And you aren't cynical enough not to care about it, not to be excessively hurt by it?

I get so hurt that when they asked me to go for my first screen test, I said no, I didn't want to. Or rather, I tried not to want to. And then I knew that father would be angry; after all, he'd already been angry about the ballet, hadn't he? But the offers kept on coming in, pouring in, and the moment came when I couldn't hold out anymore. And now I have at least five movies lined up: this one with Jean-Paul Belmondo that I'm doing in Madrid; the next one to be made in Italy, directed by Da Risi and written by Zavattini; a third one also to be made in Italy, directed by De Sica and written by Zavattini; a fourth, which will be *Doctor Zhivago,* playing opposite Omar Sharif, I don't even know which part it'll be; and a fifth to be made with Paramount, which will be *Anne Boleyn*—the part of Anne Boleyn, my God!

Heavens, Geraldine! To the best of my knowledge, no movie star has so many films lined up.

I know. But it's hard to say no when you're in demand, even harder when your father happens to be Charlie Chaplin and he keeps saying, "Do something, do something!" For the sake of doing something I enrolled at the Royal School of Ballet in London. I wanted to be a ballerina, I can't imagine a finer career, and above all my father was happy I should be a ballerina. But I realized that I'd never be a great ballerina, and so I might as well give it up straightaway and try something else.

Because, you see, it's not enough to be a good ballerina; you have to be a great ballerina, and this wasn't the case with me. Firstly, I'd started too late, when I was already fifteen, so my technique wasn't grade one. Then, to be honest, I didn't have the necessary dedication to dance eight hours a day, not to drink, not to smoke, not to eat, to be half nun, half robot. And what would have been the outcome? The outcome would have been that I'd have been a disappointment to myself and to father too. I'd have spent my whole life being middling, a member of the corps de ballet, the ones who earn sixty dollars a week, and, after all, I have to keep myself, don't I?

One question, perhaps indiscreet, Geraldine: Didn't your father help you, isn't he helping? Would you really have had to live on the sixty dollars a week and nothing else?

My father paid for my keep when I lived with a family in London, and now he pays, or rather he was paying, the rent of the apartment I've been living in since I moved to Paris. But my father thinks that a girl of twenty should support herself, and I think so too. Obviously I could always telephone home and say, "I'm in a mess. Send me a check. Thank you." But I've never done it, and I never intend to. A while back, for example, I was broke—but really broke. But I didn't ask them for a thing. Luck came to my rescue. I happened to meet a photographer friend, Willy Rizzo, and Willy said, "How's it going, Geraldine?" Fine thanks, I told him, but I've got money problems. So then Willy said, "Why don't you pose for some fashion photographs, Geraldine?" Immediately, thanks, I replied. And so I posed for fashion photographs for four days, for a feature that *Marie Claire* had commissioned Willy to do, and in those four days I earned no less than two hundred thousand francs, a fantastic amount, and so I didn't ask my father for anything. The money has kept me going up to now. And it goes without saying that I can live on very little. The apartment in Paris isn't even a proper apartment, it's a basement with one room, a kitchen, and a bath. The only convenient things about it are the telephone and the separate entrance. As for clothes . . . look, this suede jacket was given to me by my sister-in-law, Noelle Adam, Sidney's wife. And all that's more than enough for me. Look, three years ago I came to Spain with some friends. Our money was stolen as soon as we got there, so you know what we did to keep ourselves? We started singing and playing the guitar in the bars. We'd get a few pesetas together and buy ourselves a plate of fried fish. Of course it would have been more comfortable to stay in Vevey, living the life of the daughter of the king, but it didn't suit me. And I did right, didn't I?

The more so as you no longer have to sing in bars, Geraldine. They're offering you crazy sums of money to act in these movies. Crazy for a beginner, anyway.

My God! For this film I've already been given 10 per cent, and I'd never seen so much money all at once. It's even disgusting, the amount they pay. When you think that a wretched ballerina works and sweats and breaks her feet for years and years and years to earn in a month what I'm earning in a day! Crazy. I talked about it to father, too. Heavens, the money they spend on making a film! Father says, "True, but more people go to the movies than to the ballet." Well, it's still crazy. But that isn't really the point. The point is: Do I deserve it? This isn't just rhetoric, believe me; it's pride. Like the business of succeeding. Will I succeed? Will I succeed in not making a fool of myself and of my father? My part in this movie isn't difficult, the Da Risi film might have been written for me, but the others . . . Anne Boleyn . . . my God . . . and if I don't succeed . . . my father. I'd never seen a film camera before I did my screen test, and so I'm going around asking for advice, and some people tell me to study diction, some tell me to study singing, some tell me to study diction and singing, some tell me not to study anything. . . .

And what does your father tell you, Geraldine? It seems to me that no one could help you resolve these kinds of doubts better than he.

He tells me . . . nothing. That is . . . not much. It's true
I don't ask him anything. Not because we aren't on good terms,
the way they say, eh? On the contrary, I go home whenever I
can, in the holidays, for example. We telephone each other
from time to time, but . . . we never talk about my career. He
doesn't want to interfere, so much so that I don't even know
what he thinks about my becoming an actress. . . . I think he's
waiting for me at the finishing tape, to judge me. . . . For the
moment all I can say is that he's angry, very angry, about all
the publicity. . . . My father, you see, is a difficult man . . . very
difficult. He expects a lot, perhaps he expects too much, and
you can't argue, in view of the fact that he's done so much,
in view of the fact that he's been so good, so . . . and if I don't
succeed . . .

The future frightens you, doesn't it, Geraldine? Yes, it
frightens you. In fact, one would say it frightens you more on
your father's account than on your own. This onerous name . . .
this continual comparison . . .

The comparison. You've understood. The comparison. For
myself, if I failed, I could go and work as a shop assistant. But
everyone would know that Geraldine Chaplin, Charlie Chaplin's daughter, a failure, is working as a shop assistant. Michael,
my brother, left home and for some time worked as a delivery
boy in a greengrocer's shop, and everyone knew that Michael
Chaplin, Charlie Chaplin's son, was working as a delivery boy
in a greengrocer's shop. Then Michael took some coins out of
the fountain at Marble Arch, not that there's any harm in
taking coins out of the fountain at Marble Arch, even the
judge said I don't see why anyone shouldn't take the coins out
of the fountain at Marble Arch. But everyone knew that
Michael Chaplin, Charlie Chaplin's son, had taken coins out
of the fountain at Marble Arch. Of course, if I do fail, I shall
face my father and tell him calmly, "I've failed, Father." But
if it really happens . . .

It won't happen, Geraldine. You are very beautiful, very photogenic, and you have what it takes to be someone. You have that certain something that spells success. I'm right, you'll see. But still, I do understand: it certainly can't be said that the Chaplin name is always lucky. It wasn't lucky for Charlie, Jr., the oldest son, or for Sidney, the second. . . . And so one can't help wondering: Why do you all wind up in show business? Why don't you try something different that will spare you the risk of cutting a poor figure?

Because it's in our blood, obviously. It wasn't only father who was an artist; mother also wanted to be an actress. And our grandparents on father's side were actors and singers in music hall. And our grandfather on mother's side was a playwright. There's nobody in our family who hasn't, in one way or another, had something to do with the stage. I didn't believe in these things, but now I have to. I can't find any other explanation, seeing it can't have been the environment I grew up in that influenced me. The atmosphere at Vevey is simple, bourgeois. Movie people never come to our house, and nobody, nobody at all, ever put it into my head or Michael's or Sidney's or the others' to go into show business. My parents wanted me to go to university, but ever since I was a child I've felt an unreasonable love of music, of the stage. Meeting actors, I have always been lost in admiration. Every time I meet an actor or an actress, I look at them as if they were goodness knows who. Seeing, or rather re-seeing, my father's films gives me real joy. And then, look, it's useless, comparisons will always follow us. For example, I like writing, too. From time to time I write short stories, but then I hide them, in shame; my grandfather on mother's side was called Eugene O'Neill, and who has the courage to write when his grandfather is called Eugene O'Neill? I don't want you to think that I feel hard done by, that I consider myself unlucky. I consider myself, and I am, a very lucky girl, a girl who's had everything and a thousand

times more than other girls—a father who's a genius, a marvelous mother, a comfortable life, an intellectual background,
affection, but . . .

Geraldine, how long is it since you saw your father?

A long time. I should have seen him in London for the
publication of his book, but I couldn't go because Boris, my
dog, was sick. I thought he was going to die, my Boris, and so
I had to choose between Boris and my father's book. And I
chose Boris. So I don't even know if father is pleased about this
first movie of mine. No, father doesn't come here to Spain.
Father never sets foot in Spain. And then it isn't as if I find it
very easy to talk to father, to talk about myself, I mean. Not
because he's seventy-five and I'm twenty; I get on well with
people of any age, and very young people often irritate me. No,
it isn't a matter of generation; it's that father is so strict, difficult. . . . But, yes, perhaps age does have something to do with it.

*I'd say so. But how about your mother, Geraldine? Apart
from the fact that your mother is only thirty-nine, it must be
easier to have a heart-to-heart talk with your mother, isn't it?*

My mother is a saint—truly, a saint. But I find it very difficult to talk even to her. My mother, you see, is nearer my
father's seventy-five than my twenty. Because, you see, people
don't understand. They don't know. People say: "What about
your mother, Geraldine?" Well, my mother tries to keep everything running smoothly, to keep everyone on good terms, but
she's so much in love with my father. People don't understand,
they don't believe it. They'll never understand, they'll never
believe how, why, such a young, beautiful woman, who could
have become a star in her own right, married anyone she
wanted, could have fallen in love with a man nearly thirty-
seven years older than herself. But that's how it is. The two of
them live in a world of their own, a fairy-tale world, a world
from which anyone else is excluded and . . . people should
just see them. He still courts her as he did in the first days, she
still blushes as she did in the first days. It's even very touching,

but one feels shut out. And one thinks . . . well, one thinks that perhaps it isn't even worth asking advice. And then I'm shy, terribly shy, like my mother, in fact like my father too—nobody knows that my father is shy. We're all shy in our family. We love adventure, but we blush for nothing and people frighten us. You know that up until a few years ago I used to cry when I had to go into a room full of people? Well, I don't cry nowadays. But I'm still shy just the same, because I've discovered, you see, that the world is wicked. I've always been disappointed in people, and the more important the people, the more I've been disappointed. Not that I take too much to heart though, you know. On the contrary, I've learned one important thing about people: that you musn't expect to find yourself, a reflection of yourself, in other people; you have to take people for what they are, that is, different from yourself, always. And then you can accept them, people.

Who helped you to understand this, Geraldine?

Nobody. I found it out for myself. I've always found everything out for myself. By thinking. For myself. By seeing. For myself.

You were a very lonely child, weren't you, Geraldine?

Oh, no! You can't be lonely when you have seven brothers and sisters. And children have a happy life in the Chaplin household. They play and laugh and sing and make a lot of noise all the time, and there's always something going on, an argument, a quarrel. . . . And then mother gives them a lot of her attention, father loves them very much; children are never unhappy, never lonely in the Chaplin house. Everything's simple in the Chaplin household, while you're children. It's later that things become a bit less simple. It's later that you begin to think for yourself, see for yourself, decide to leave the nest. And so I've left the nest, Michael's left the nest. . . . I was, naturally, the first to leave it. After me it was Michael's turn, and at present he's studying speech and drama in London. After Michael it'll be Josie's turn; she's the beauty of the family, fantastically beautiful, even more beautiful than my mother. After Josie it'll be Vicky; she's very gifted, and she'll certainly wind up as an actress, too, and . . .

And your parents will be left more and more lonely?

Lonely! My father and mother will never be lonely as long as they both live, and for every child who leaves, another arrives. The last one was born eighteen months ago, but will it be the last? And then they're used to seeing us go. As soon as the girls are ten years old, my parents send them to a convent. I went to a convent, too. I only left it to go to London, to the ballet school.

To a convent, Geraldine?!? Odd that Charlie Chaplin sends his daughters to a convent. It certainly can't be said that he has any sympathy with the Church. And why on earth does he send you to a convent?

For the discipline. My father's fanatical about discipline. And I am too; in that respect I'm very much like him. Besides, I was so wild, when I was ten, that I don't know what would have happened if the nuns hadn't brought me up. They were strict, the nuns, as strict as my father, but they were so gentle too. And gentleness is so lovely, and I'm very happy I spent those years with the nuns. And then the nuns gave me something I didn't have, they gave me religion and . . . you see, we Chaplin kids were never baptized into any religion. That's the way father wanted and wants it. We'd never heard any talk of God, we'd never heard a prayer and . . . well, now I'll tell you a very silly, very odd thing. The first day I went into class, all the girls were standing up, praying. I didn't know about praying, you see, and so I thought they were reciting a lesson. But the second day they stood up again and recited the same lesson again, so I thought, that's odd, didn't they say the same lesson yesterday? I turned to one of the girls and asked her: "What *are* you doing?" "We're praying," she said. "Praying?" I said. "Yes, praying," she said. "Praying to whom?" I said. "Praying to God," she said. "God who?" I said. And . . . silly, eh? Odd.

No. Go on, Geraldine.

Well, the girl looked at me in amazement and didn't say any more. So then, when the lesson was over, I went to the nuns and asked the nuns who God was: Was He the head of the school? The nuns said yes, God was also the head of the school. So then I asked the nuns if I could meet this head of the school, and the nuns replied that this head of the school was very good and was taking care of me. If I spoke to Him, He would listen and . . . well, it was like a fairy tale, only more beautiful, much more beautiful, and I believed it. Then, suddenly, I didn't believe it anymore. Suddenly I decided that the tale was like the story of Father Christmas who gives presents to children. For years I'd believed in Father Christmas, but one day they'd told me that he didn't exist, that it had been father and mother all the time, and I felt they'd just been putting me on. So I thought that God was like Father Christmas, and I said to myself, "What nonsense. Fairies, Father Christmas, God, none of them exists, and they're putting me on." And I said as much, angrily, to the nuns. And the nuns, gently, explained to me that it wasn't like that, that God was different, He was something more than fairies and Father Christmas, even if I couldn't see Him. And I was happy again, and I loved the nuns, and I loved God too. Silly, eh? Odd, eh?

No, Geraldine. On the contrary, beautiful. The only odd thing, the only silly thing, is how we are always fated to disobey. Some are born Catholics and become atheists. But you were born an atheist and have become a Catholic. But is it really true, Geraldine, that until you were ten you'd never heard God spoken of?

No. Never. Maybe the word had been mentioned by someone, sometime, but I'd never taken any notice. Certainly I don't remember it. My father says he'd have liked to be religious, that it would have been a great help to him, but he just can't be. If he could, he says, he'd put more trust in people. My father is a man with no illusions, and we all grew up without any illusions—except for the early years, when we thought it was Father Christmas who brought us cookies. It was horrible finding out that instead it was mother and father who used to bring them. By now even the youngest children know that the cookies come from mother and father, that there's no such person as Father Christmas.

Listen, Geraldine. When you realized that you believed in God, when the nuns spoke to you about God, that is, did you ask your father and mother for any explanation?

Oh, no! I really couldn't have asked my father, apart from the fact that it's such a personal thing. My mother . . . you see, mother isn't religious, either. Mother believes everything father believes and doesn't believe anything father doesn't believe. And so I kept it to myself, just cheering myself up with what I'd discovered, and I didn't even mention it to Michael. And then I didn't think about it all that much, you know? I don't think about it all that much even now. It's just that I still like the idea, and one thing is certain: if I had to choose a religion, I'd choose Catholicism. In fact, sooner or later I will choose it. Sooner or later I shall be baptized—when I've overcome all my doubts. I've already overcome a great many, you know? Oh! You *are* looking at me in a funny way!

I'm looking at you with sympathy, Geraldine. And with surprise. I'd been told you were spoiled and willful, superficial, and proud, even somewhat silly. Let's go on with our talk. Tell me about these doubts you have overcome.

Firstly, snobbery. There's nothing in the world I hate as much as snobbery. I absolutely cannot understand why people take such an interest in countesses, princesses, movie stars, millionaires, and so on. I absolutely cannot understand why countesses, princesses, movie stars, millionaires, and so on give themselves such airs. Men like my father, like Picasso, are entitled to give themselves airs, but those idiots who haven't done a thing apart from possess a title or millions of dollars! Bah! Oh, I know what you're thinking now. You're thinking: then why, Geraldine, do you go to their cocktail parties? Look, I hardly ever go and then only to take with me someone they don't like, to be rude and noisy, and to annoy them and show them that I despise them. All right, you say, but you've let yourself be adopted by these people, Geraldine. Why did you let them adopt you? For fun, of course. I had no end of fun at the debutantes' ball they gave in Seville. They had me there for much the same reason as you'd hang up an advertising sign and . . . my God! I've never laughed so much in my life. I couldn't even bear to look at myself in the mirror, I looked so grotesque. Dressed all in white, in a magnificent gown by Castillo, and my hair done by what's-his-name, Alexandre . . . I looked like a high-class French poodle. You know, the per- fumed sort that belong to silly rich women, who because they don't do a thing and can't do a thing, spend their time in dogs' beauty parlors. And when the poor dogs emerge, they don't look like dogs at all, they look like powder puffs, idiotic little monsters. . . . Well, that was me at the debutantes' ball in Seville. And the others . . . poor girls, the others. I looked at them and thought: if you could only see yourselves! If you had the eyes and the brain to see yourselves! No, I've no doubts about it: I'll never be one of them. I want to be free, free to dress badly, to jump on a train and go to Greece if I happen to want to go to Greece, to jump on a plane and go to America if I happen to want to go to America. I don't want to be a powder puff for countesses and snobs.

America. . . . You left America when you were eight, Ger- aldine, when your father and mother left for good. Do you bear a grudge against America, too, Geraldine?

No, I don't. I've been back there two or three times, and I like it a lot. Having grown up in Europe, having been brought up in Europe, by now I'm completely European, I'm in no way at all American. But I like America a lot, and I'm glad to be going there because of that contract with Paramount. I've made adorable friends, in America, I've had terrific fun there. I've found nothing horrible about Hollywood, and, well, I know America didn't treat my father well, but one can't bear grudges forever. It was so many years ago, don't you see? So if I have to go to America to further my career, well, I'll go to America.

Clear. And one last question, Geraldine.

Oh, I know what the last question is. It's about my fiancés. Well, look, I've had seven fiancés. Two of them I've never even seen. The other five I scarcely know. I'm the most engaged girl in the world, I am, and the extraordinary thing about it is that I'm always the last to know I'm engaged—the newspapers or the snobs always hear about it before I do. It happened over El Cordobés, the bullfighter. It happened over Govilov, the leading male dancer at the Opera. It happened over Antonio Peralta, who's a brotherly friend. I don't even take it to heart anymore. When I happen to meet them, these fiancés, I just say, "Good morning. Did you know I'm your fiancée?" Naturally I have a few flirtations. If you don't have flirtations at my age! But fiancés, no, look, I swear it. Nor am I in love. And if you ask me if I've ever been in love, I'd say I don't know. And if I say I don't know, it probably means I never have been. That was your question, wasn't it?

No, Geraldine, that wasn't it. My question has nothing to do with fiancés. It was . . .

Then, I get it, it was about marriage. And what can I say about marriage? I shall get married, certainly. Everyone in the Chaplin household gets married. But I don't know when, I don't know whom to. To get married you need to have the wifely calling, like my mother, and will I ever have it? You see . . . for anyone like me who has witnessed a love as great and incredible as the love that has bound, binds, my father and mother . . . well, you feel crushed by the fear of never finding one like it. You search for it, a love as great as the love of your father and mother, and you know very well that you'll never find it, because miracles like that only happen once in a hundred, two hundred, years. And so you feel a bit jealous, unhappy. You think: I'll never have what my father and mother have had, such a miracle, such luck. My father's had such luck in his life! He's also had griefs, troubles, humiliations, but in the end everything turned out all right for him, everything! And he's had fame, respect, riches, love, everything! Even love! Everything! And a child, once he's grown up, compares himself with him . . . and thinks that things will never turn out as well for him, he'll never be as good . . . as lucky . . . he'll never have so much love . . . and . . . that was it, wasn't it, the question?

Well, Geraldine, it was, and yet it wasn't exactly that. It was also something else. I'm going to ask, and I beg you to answer me sincerely because, I believe, it's a very important question, a question that, obviously, concerns your father. This, Geraldine: Are you afraid of him?

Of my father?

Yes, of your father.

Certainly I'm afraid of my father. . . . Certainly. Very, very afraid. And not only because he's so unbending, so difficult, so strict. Not only because he always turns out to be right in the end, whatever he says or does. But because . . . because . . . how can I put it . . . I feel this constant reproof, this constant comparison, because I feel I'm in his shadow all the time, all the time, like all of us. And I feel . . . yes, I feel that only when I'm no longer in his shadow, when I'm no longer afraid of him, that only then will I finally be able to do something myself.

Madrid, November, 1964

ANNA MAGNANI

Tragic Mother

Of all the actresses I know Anna Magnani is the only one to send a telegram to thank the writer of an article when it appears. So I can't understand why they call her ill-mannered or proud, or why they paint her as a common woman who lives on foul language and beans. For me she's a lady, one with whom I have always got on well. Besides, you can tell she's a lady by her home, which is on the top floor of the palazzo Altieri. Her apartment is full of antiques, books, original paintings, and so enclosed in an aquarium-like silence that even her dogs and cats move around in it as weightlessly and softly as fish. A common woman or an ill-mannered or proud woman would live in a villa with a swimming pool and a jukebox. She would answer publicity with raspberries.

Adjoining her own apartment is one belonging to her son, a handsome young man and the biggest thorn in her heart: as is now common knowledge, he was struck down by poliomyelitis and can only walk with orthopedic aids. I have been to Magnani's home many times, and I have never seen her son, who they tell me is touchy and rarely smiles. But on each occasion his presence has been as real and as acute as if he had come in and sat down on the sofa with us. Whatever she might be saying, la Magnani always ends up talking abut her son; whatever she's doing, she ends up remembering her son. He is the measuring rod of her life, the condition of her life, the aim and object of her life. La Magnani is making a film? It means she needs the money for her son. She isn't? It means she's staying with her son. And I believe that it's on account of her son that she fears illness so much, that she hates death so much. She hates death as she would hate a person who must be killed: grimly, desperately. She is quite unable to accept it as the logical and inevitable conclusion of the journey that begins when we are born. "It's so unfair that we should die just because we are born," she said to me.

Along with death, la Magnani hates her neighbors. I think her friends could be counted on the fingers of one hand, and the men she has loved are few—certainly not as many as they say. La Magnani believes in no love other than maternal love; she believes in no ties that are not blood ties, those that tie you to the creature who is separated from you when the umbilical cord is cut but on whose stomach is left, like a scar, a tidy hole. On the subject of this kind of love she expresses herself with scorching tenderness; on the other kind of love she expresses herself with bursts of scornful laughter that show her strong teeth, like a wild animal's, and fling wide her mouth as far back as her tonsils. Love for children is eternal; love for men who take you to bed comes to an end: "And when it ends, you cry a bit, but you get over it." Cynicism, together with contempt, is her great strength. Even when she's being kind, she is so with cynicism; even when she's generous, she is so with cynicism. Always she feels that it isn't worth it, that there will be no reward for kindness and generosity either in heaven or on earth. Nobody is less loved than the lady bountiful or people who indulge in forgiveness. And Christianity for her is a philosophy to be treated warily: "God is conscience"—no more than conscience.

My interview with la Magnani took place one afternoon when she was having trouble with a tooth. The tooth had developed an infection. The infection had swollen her cheek, and it would be inaccurate to claim she was beautiful. She never has been, with her fragile, short body, her thin, starved-looking legs, her lined face, like a man's. Moreover, even her movements were brusque, like a man's, and her clothes, too: pants and a dreadful sweater, which had been darned in two places. As she talked, she covered her cheek with her hand and engulfed me in those tremendous eyes of hers. She would sit, or rather crouch, in an armchair like an animal that is cold, then, suddenly, stand up and start walking up and down, and then stop, equally suddenly, and kneel on the floor. Her words came helter-skelter, her thoughts came from the pit of her stomach. It was dark in the drawing room, nobody at all came to disturb us. When there was no longer anything more to be said, she wanted to listen to herself. Competently she ran back the tape, pressed the button, and, as her voice filled the room, burst into scornful laughter. She laughed scornfully for as long as her voice could be heard.

ORIANA FALLACI: *An odd thing happens to me every time I meet you, Signora Magnani: I am always most curious to speak to you as long as I'm making ready to see you, and yet I find I have nothing to ask you as soon as I have you before me. Those dark, brooding eyes, those fierce teeth, that look of a wounded bird that doesn't know where to beat its wings . . . they're the wings and the teeth and the eyes of the most mysterious and transparent woman that the mythology of the cinema has ever invented, with your knick-knacks, your cats, your dogs, your immutable sadness masked by vivacity. . . . I felt the same thing the first time I interviewed you in this room. You are like a book that is already written: the more incomprehensible it is, the more you reread it—but it is written.*

ANNA MAGNANI: God! Don't tell me you've come to make something sad and depressing of me? Today, too, when I'm happy; I've had a tax rebate, I'm full of amazement at their humanity and my own skill. . . . Yes . . . a three million seven hundred thousand lire rebate. . . . They were killing me, slaughtering me, but I spent two months studying the problem: why they make you pay this, why they take away that, the demands, the appeals, the tax year. Then I went to tackle them by myself, like Daniel in the lions' den, without even a lawyer. . . . Ha! What a sight: those pallid faces, those weeping eyes, like animals at bay! It looked like a chapter out of Kafka's *Trial.* At one window there was a little old woman fighting over five thousand lire, trying to convince the clerk that she just couldn't pay, I shouted, "Can't we help her, eh?"

And this painful irony of yours, the constant bitterness with which you regard the world, your capacity for transforming even income tax returns into metaphysical tragedy . . .

What are you driving at? What do you mean? And me feeling like a lizard in the sun! Why this determination at all costs to show me as some withdrawn, solitary, disillusioned

Electra? What must I do to convince you that I'm cheerful, that I'm jumping for joy, that I laugh, that being la Magnani tickles me to death, that I get a great kick out of it when people recognize me in the street, when the policeman directing the traffic calls, *"Ciao, Nannarè"?* Now you're even bringing out the Roman dialect in me, you are. What I mean is, it's the same old story. It's like when people are amazed because my home is full of good taste and books. How many times do I have to explain that I wasn't a waif or a stray, that I went through high school, that I learned the piano for eight years, that I went to the conservatory of Santa Cecilia? . . . Or like when they insist that I was born in Egypt of an Egyptian father. Rubbish. I was born in Rome, my mother was from Romagna and my father from Calabria. If you don't believe it, I'll show you my birth certificate. My mother went to Egypt after I was born. She was eighteen and unmarried, which in those days was a scandal. So she went to Egypt, and I stayed with my grandmother, here in Rome. Because—get this straight—I'm not the least ashamed to repeat that I don't have my father's name. I have my mother's, I never knew my father, all I know about him is that he came from Calabria. So why do they want at all costs to make me Egyptian?

All right, Signora, all right. I'll write that you're Roman. Don't upset yourself. Let's talk about something else. Don't upset yourself. I hear that you are going to Paris, to make a movie with Autant-Lara. And that you're no longer going to do S'agapo, *with Rossellini. . . .*

We aren't going to do it, and I'm very glad. What can I say? I've worked better with Rossellini than with any other director. Whenever he was setting up a sequence, it was always the sequence I'd have shot if I'd been in his shoes. And yet, whenever something keeps me apart from Rossellini, everything starts going fine for me and I get on miraculously well. No, it's not because of what you're thinking, my dear: Rossellini hasn't left any marks on me, I don't allow any man to mark me. And, seeing the name has come up, let's speak plainly. For years you journalists have gone on talking about my great passion for Rossellini, but shall we tell the truth? It was Rossellini who wouldn't leave me alone, who wouldn't let me move a step, not I who ran after him. If I had shared that great passion, I would have been able to keep it alive, be sure of that. I wouldn't have let it escape. Let Rossellini say what he likes. He says so many things, Rossellini. Not long ago he even said he'd not seen *Open City* and *Paisà* since he made them, while in fact he'd seen them with me a month before in a film club. God! We aren't going to talk about love, are we?

Who would dare, Signora Magnani? I prize my skin, and when I'm with you, I never feel it's very safe. I know very well that few actresses habitually defend their personal feelings with such ferocity as you do. Besides, wasn't it you who some time ago said: "Love is a thing I find very troubling. Love is staying at a standstill, and at the end of it you're left empty-handed."

I might have said it in a moment of depression: love in itself, as long as it lasts, doesn't trouble me at all. It gives you courage, security, helps you to ignore other trifling things. I believe in this. It's in great passion that I have never believed. Give me one example of a great passion, a true one, with Christian names, surnames, and addresses, not some legendary one, and I'll believe it. You see? You're silent. Great passions, my dear, don't exist: they're liars' fantasies. What do exist are little loves that may last for a short or a longer while. That's why, every time I've loved a man, I've never let it overwhelm me. I have loved him, I've even been jealous of flies touching him, but I've known all along that it had to end. And when it ends . . . you cry a bit, but then you get over it. Two, three months later, you meet him in the street, and it seems impossible you could ever have lost any sleep or shed any tears over him. Pouf!

It's odd, Signora Magnani, you have such a masculine character, you always say you hold men in greater esteem than women, "for me to accept a woman she has to have an almost masculine dignity and character," and yet you talk as if you attach very little value to men.

Look, none at all. The fact is that women like me can only become attached to men with stronger personalities than their own, and I have never found a man with a personality that would overshadow mine. Women like me can submit only to men capable of dominating them, and I have never found anyone capable of dominating me. The men I've found have always been—how shall I say?—darlings. God! You cry over the darlings, too, of course, but they're one cent tears. Incredible though it sounds, the only man over whom I didn't cry one cent tears was my husband: Goffredo Alessandrini, the only man, of all I've known, for whom I have ungrudging respect and of whom I am really fond. Whenever I see him I feel a great tenderness.

I know that you have a role in Alessandrini's next movie, taking no payment for it, solely to make it easier for him to come back to Italy and make his movie. This is very handsome, very generous of you.

It's only a tiny role: seven days' work, at most. It's so tiny it didn't even exist originally; it emerged when they wrote the script. But it was a role that suited me, and as he didn't dare ask me to do it, I told him: for you I'll do it for nothing. Alessandrini is an excellent director and a man who has been very unfairly treated. He's been out of Italy for at least four years now, since he emigrated to Argentina, and now that he's coming back, he's going to find himself up against a wall of hostility. I must help him. There's nothing between us anymore. Even if we didn't manage to get a divorce, I live my own life and he's started a new family. But I must help him all the same because he deserves it. Of course, it wasn't all a bed of roses, even with him. When I married him, I was only a young girl. And as long as I was his wife, his infidelities gave me more horns than a basketful of snails. I did nothing but weep and moan—I'd like to meet the woman who puts up with infidelities like a stoic—but, in spite of this, there was always such true honesty in him, such true humanity, such true elegance. My dear Oriana, I might use foul language, but I do hate bad breeding. Quite apart from the fact that foul language is a privilege of the few and doesn't necessarily signify bad breeding, in Alessandrini there has always been a complete and utter absence of bad breeding: the bad breeding shown by being calculating, having no understanding, not being able to forgive. And . . . God! Isn't this more than love? Apart from the fact that this much vaunted love is no longer indispensable to me, I can live without it now. Oria, what's that little smile about?

Nothing, nothing at all. I was only thinking, Signora Magnani, that you don't seem particularly fond of people in general. When you aren't talking about them with immense scorn, you're talking about them with immense pity. I wonder whether you manage to have any friends.

Few. In one way or another they always manage to hurt me or betray me. Being betrayed in friendship is always much worse than being betrayed in love. People in general . . . I lose a lot of time over people; I always try to do good even if it isn't on a monumental scale. But when all's said and done, we have very little understanding of each other. It's so rarely that you meet a human person among people. Animals are more human than men, and every time I'm struck by this thought, I really get the urge to get away from it all, to retire into the country, where there's no one to see me, among the horses and the hens. Truly, for six months I've been looking for a little place in the country. Help me find a little place in the country. Oh, how marvelous not to use a car anymore, not to smell the stink anymore, not to have to put up with people anymore. This morning in Via del Tritone I nearly fainted, there was a traffic jam, and the din of the horns, the stink of gas, the lack of air. . . .

Do you mean to say, Signora, that you wouldn't consider it a

calamity to be no longer an actress, no longer la Magnani: one
of the best known women in the world? I don't believe it.

If you don't believe it, why are you here? Stop this contrap-
tion going around and around and take a walk with some nice
young man. If you don't believe it, I'm offended; I don't tell
lies. Oriana, my girl, I can't wait for the day when I can stop
being an actress and stop being hounded by the world I live in!
I like popularity, I've said. So what? Who'll take it away from
me if I go and live in the country? I'm proud of the career I've
had. So what? Who'll take it away from me if I let everything
drop? I don't like movies anymore, my dear. The day has gone
when I deluded myself that making movies was art; I'm not
dreaming anymore. Movies, today, are made up of festivals,
cannibalism, the idiocy they call lack of communication,
intellectuals who always make out that they're teaching something and undervalue the public, forgetting that the public
is composed—all right—of insecure individuals, but, put
together, these insecure individuals become a miracle of
intelligence. And intelligence won't put up with being led by
the nose by imbeciles who preach from the pulpit. Listen:
what I think about the cinema is what my son wrote when he
was twelve years old in the school magazine of his Swiss boarding school: "When I go to see a film, I want to be amused. If
it also teaches me something without my realizing it, so much
the better."

Agreed, agreed. I remember very well when you told me:
"I can't abide fools, better a rotter than a fool. Nor can I abide
intellectuals. Intellectuals are so seldom intelligent. Very often,
an intellectual person is one thing, an intelligent person
another." But then, why do you always mix with intellectuals?
And your great friend Tennessee Williams, how do we fit him
in?

Tennessee is a child with a child's purity and a superhuman
goodness of heart: a man of intelligence rather than an intellectual. When I'm with him, I never talk about intellectual

things: I talk about everyday things, about personal affairs. But with intellectuals you always talk about the same things; they're a lot of bores, and they're never generous, never ready to forgive, to understand, to learn from other people. I have mixed with them, I do mix with them, it's true. But it's part, or rather it was a part, of my mistaken policy not to live in too much isolation, not to play the holy cow, not to be as difficult as they say I am. Oria, for my whole life they've plagued me with stories about how proud I am, how arrogant, ill-mannered and foul-mouthed, in short, about my bad character, with, "Anna, you can't talk like that," and, "Anna, you can't act like that." They kept it up so long that I finished up believing them, and I attempted that stupid betrayal of one's real self that is called self-improvement. You tell me: Am I such a bad character, then?

I'd say that you are a character. Anyone who's a character is said to be a bad character. People always mistake self-respect and love of justice for bad character. Let them trample you underfoot, let them humiliate you, let them shout their viva il duce, *and they'll say what a nice character you are.*

Then I'm not. For instance, take my alleged hostility toward Marlon Brando when we made *Pelle di Serpente*. Marlon's a fine fellow, his only fault is that he plays the star too much. He knows he has that stupendous magnetic face, and he never forgets it. I'm terribly fond of him, I admire him, but one day when I was feeling on edge, he comes up to me and starts provoking me. "I know why you're in the dumps, I know." "Be quiet, Marlon. You don't know a thing." "I know, I know." "Be quiet." "I know." "What do you know?" "I know you want your name to come before mine in the credits." Jesus. I wanted it, but that wasn't why I was in the dumps, and if he hadn't provoked me, I'd never have admitted it, I have too much pride. But he fanned my pride, and I told him, "Yes, I want my name to come first in Italy." "Why?" says he. "Because it's my due." "Because you're an ambitious woman," says he.

"And what do you call yourself?" I say, after which I repair to my dressing room. Well, he had the bad taste and imprudence to follow me there and continue the argument. My bad character, pardon, my good character exploded. "I," I told him, "would never have asked you such a thing. I would have waited for you to offer it to me like a bouquet. But as you haven't offered it to me like a bouquet, I'll tell you that you're a low common fellow with no breeding." He went white and got out, and I got what I wanted. Ah, if they think they can make a pathetic figure of me, they're wrong. I'm not a weak woman, I'm a woman who knows what she wants, who's always known. Nothing has ever come my way by chance, nothing—except for the success of *Open City* and the reputation it gave me. I was so convinced that to become somebody in films you needed blue eyes and a sweet little face. . . . Anyway, I became "la Magnani" by chance, but now that I am, I want them to say, "La Magnani is a bad character."

They say it, they say it. Even though at times I've seen you act the gracious lady like the most insufferable of gracious ladies, they say it.

I used to act like that for my own amusement, to prove to myself that I could act the gracious lady, but where did it get me? Bad films, films that were mistakes. I started acting the gracious lady with Castellani, and the result was *Nella città l'inferno.* I went on acting the gracious lady with Monicelli, and the result was *Risate di gioia.* And I even acted the gracious lady with Pasolini, and the result was *Mamma Roma,* a movie that was a box-office mistake too. And whose fault are mistakes like these? My own. Nobody ever blamed Marlon Brando because his movie *Desirée* was a disaster. But everyone blames la Magnani for the failure of her movies. In Italy there's a strange custom: when a movie fails, the actress gets the blame. Everyone forgets I'm not a drama-school type actress, that my work comes off only when I'm free to do what I want, like a writer when he writes or a painter when he paints, that I can't knuckle down to technique, that I have to be creative. And then I'm bored stiff with these everlasting parts as a hysterical, loud, working-class woman.

You could turn them down. You could go on the stage. I've always thought you'd be a splendid Lady Macbeth or an extraordinary Marguerite Gautier. But every time you go back to the theater, you draw in your horns like a snail. One might think you were afraid.

Afraid yourself. Snail yourself. My dear girl, if I don't work in the theater, it's because the theater takes up your whole life, and my life for me is my son, and I care more for my son than for the theater. I've already left him too much for me to leave him again. Remember that for the last eighteen years I've been the man of the family, and if I go away, who will look after the family? Those ladies with husbands—and I don't envy them, believe me. Ugh! A husband! What a drag, what a bore —are free to devote themselves to art. But me! You and your lady-macbething! Take *Mother Courage*, which I should have done on Broadway. They'd been asking me for eighteen months, and you know what Broadway means. Well, could I go off for eighteen months and leave my son who is studying and needs me? Could I take my son to New York with me and worry day and night, thinking, "Where is he, what's he doing?" I don't know, I don't know. There are women who can reconcile the two things, family and career, but I can't. Have a child yourself, and then see if you can go gallivanting around the world whenever you fancy. Children are like puppies: you have to keep them near you and look after them if you want to have their affection. And if you succeed . . . listen, my son has a good-looking mug, he's sensitive, he's good, he's intelligent. . . . He's worth all the careers in the world. . . . But watch out. If you make me out to be all sugar and honey, the big-hearted mom, I'll strangle you.

You won't strangle me. There's no sugar and honey about you, and I'm far from convinced that you're even big-hearted.

There's room for so few people in your world, apart from la Magnani and her son.

Oh, yeah? Listen to the little squirt! What do you think I am, then? A robot with a plastic heart?

Not at all. You're . . . you're Anna Magnani. And Anna Magnani is what you told me yourself you are, in Venice, six months ago. You were huddled on your bed, I remember, your hair as wild as Benvenuto Cellini's "Medusa," stroking one of your jewels and muttering: "La Magnani is a person I can't stand, I don't like. But she's simpatica, I have a soft spot for her." Then you said: "Me, when I pray . . ."

Yes, I adore jewels, but more to hold in my hand than to wear. Ah, the feeling you get holding a diamond in your hand! It seems to bore into your skin, to burn, to breathe. It's like holding a bit of the moon in your hand.

. . . then you said: "Me, when I pray, I feel I'm to be pitied." Do you really pray, Signora Magnani? Listen, Signora Magnani, I'm going to put you a question I often ask in these interviews: Are you a religious person?

Let's take things a step at a time. I never feel pity for myself; I hate pity, particularly self-pity. That sentence came from someone else, or you made it up. As for praying, I do pray—and how. Religious . . . yes, I think so. Definitely, yes. God, there must be something bigger than me: a kind God who's helping me. And then, you know, God is conscience, and I'm so much at peace with my conscience. I've made plenty of mistakes, but I've never done anything bad. I don't forget the wrongs that are done to me, often I can't forgive them, but I don't take my revenge: revenge is as cheap as bearing grudges. Being like this makes me strong as a lion, gives me a strength that makes me afraid of nothing.

Even you must be afraid of something, Signora Magnani— of growing old, for instance. Aren't you afraid of growing old?

No, providing it isn't my brain that grows old. Wrinkles on the face, you know, are bearable. Especially if you had a good enough time before they came. But wrinkles on your brain, what a horrible thought!

Of dying then. Aren't you afraid of dying?

Yes, I am, very afraid. I'm always thinking about it, about death. It's so unfair that we should die just because we are born. Death is an end. Why should we end? A man should end when he wants to end, when he's tired, sated with it all, not before. God, there's such disparity between the sweetness that comes with birth and the exhaustion that comes with death. Birth is a healthy, joyful crying; death is a tragedy. We should at least die with the blissful unawareness with which we are born. And you know what I think? It might be fairer if we were to be born old and die as babes. Jesus, what a conversation. Now you'll make me out to be tragic and depressing. But I'm not a tragic and depressing woman. I'm . . . Oria, what am I?

I already told you at the start: a book that is already written. The more incomprehensible the more you reread it. But it is written.

Uhm! Boh! Mah! All this intellectual stuff! Oria, don't come over all intellectual; be intelligent, tell me what do you think of me?

I think . . . I think you're a great man, Signora Magnani.

Rome, April, 1963

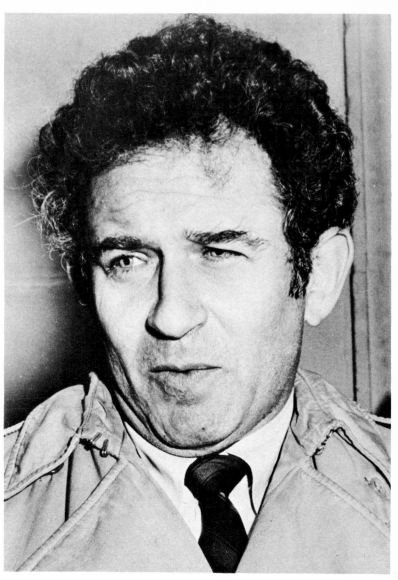

Norman Mailer

Sean Connery, with Diane Cilento

Sean Connery, with director Terence Young and the author

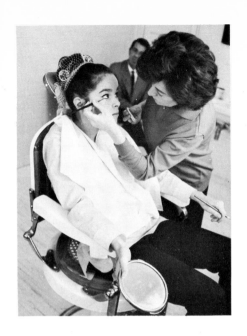

Geraldine Chaplin

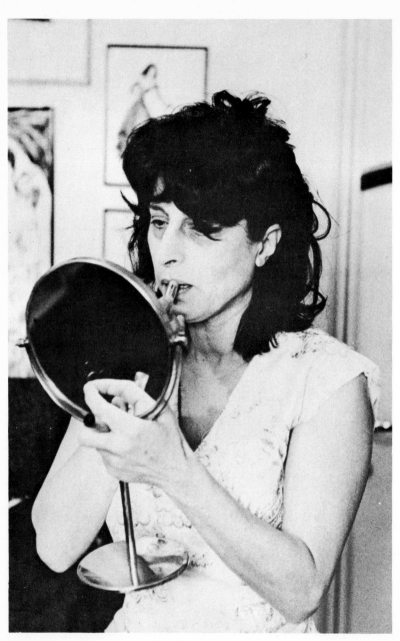

Anna Magnani

The Duchess of Alba, with some of her own paintings

The Duchess of Alba, with Goya's "La Cayetana"

Federico Fellini

El Cordobés, on his farm outside Cordova

El Cordobés

HUGH HEFNER

I Am in the Center of the World

First of all, the House. He stays in it as a Pharaoh in his grave, and
so he doesn't notice that the night has ended, the day has begun, a
winter passed, and a spring, and a summer—it's autumn now. Last
time he emerged from the grave was last winter, they say, but he
did not like what he saw and returned with great relief three days
later. The sky was again extinguished beyond the electronic gate,
and he sat down again in his grave: 1340 North State Parkway,
Chicago. But what a grave, boys! Ask those who live in the building next to it, with their windows opening onto the terrace on
which the Bunnies sunbathe, in monokinis or notkinis. (The
monokini consists of panties only, the notkini consists of nothing.)
Tom Wolfe has called the House the final rebellion against old
Europe and its custom of wearing shoes and hats, its need of
going to the restaurants or swimming pools. Others have called it
a Disneyland for adults. Forty-eight rooms, thirty-six servants always at your call. Are you hungry? The kitchen offers any exotic
food at any hour. Do you want to rest? Try the Gold Room, with a
secret door that you open by touching the petal of a flower, in
which the naked girls are being photographed. Do you want to
swim? The heated swimming pool is downstairs. Bathing suits of
any size or color are here, but you can swim without, if you prefer.
And if you go into the Underwater Bar, you will see the Bunnies
swimming as naked as little fishes. The House hosts thirty Bunnies,
who may go everywhere, like members of the family. The pool also
has a cascade. Going under the cascade, you arrive at the grotto,
rather comfortable if you like to flirt: tropical plants, stereophonic
music, drinks, erotic opportunities, and discreet people. Recently,
a guest was imprisoned in the steam room. He screamed, but nobody came to help him. Finally he was able to free himself by

breaking down the door, and when he asked, in anger, why nobody came to help—hadn't they heard his screams?—they answered, "Obviously. But we thought you were not alone."

At the center of the grave, as at the center of a pyramid, is the monarch's sarcophagus: his bed. It's a large, round bed, and here he sleeps, he thinks, he makes love, he controls the little cosmos that he has created, using all the wonders that are offered by electronic technology. You press a button, and the bed turns through half a circle, the room becomes many rooms, the statue near the fireplace becomes many statues. The statue portrays a woman, obviously. Naked, obviously. And on the wall, there are the TV sets on which he can see the programs he missed while he slept or thought or made love. In the room next to the bedroom there is the laboratory with the Ampex video-tape machine that catches the sounds and images of all the channels; the technician who takes care of it was sent to study at the Ampex center in San Francisco. And then? Then there is another bedroom that is his office, because he does not feel at ease far from a bed. Here the bed is rectangular and covered with papers and photos and documentation on Prostitution, Heterosexuality, Sodomy. Other papers are on the floor, the chairs, the tables, along with tape recorders, typewriters, dictaphones. When he works, he always uses the electric light, never opening a window, never noticing that the night has ended, the day begun. He wears pajamas only. In his pajamas, he works thirty-six hours, forty-eight hours nonstop, until he falls exhausted on the round bed, and the House whispers the news: He sleeps. Keep silent in the kitchen, in the swimming pool, in the lounge, everywhere: He sleeps.

He is Hugh Hefner, emperor of an empire of sex, absolute king of seven hundred Bunnies, founder and editor of *Playboy:* forty million dollars in 1966, bosoms, navels, behinds as mammy made them, seen from afar, close up, white, suntanned, large, small, mixed with exquisite cartoons, excellent articles, much humor, some culture, and, finally, his philosophy. This philosophy's name is "Playboyism," and, synthesized, it says that "we must not be afraid or ashamed of sex, sex is not necessarily limited to marriage, sex is oxygen, mental health. Enough of virginity, hypocrisy, censorship, restrictions. Pleasure is to be preferred to sorrow." It is now discussed even by theologians. Without being ironic, a magazine published a story entitled " . . . The Gospel According to Hugh Hefner." Without causing a scandal, a teacher at the School of Theology at Claremont, California, writes that Playboyism is, in some ways, a religious movement: "That which the church has been too timid to try, Hugh Hefner . . . is attempting."

We Europeans laugh. We learned to discuss sex some thousands of years ago, before even the Indians had landed in America. The mammoths and the dinosaurs still pastured around New York, San Francisco, Chicago, when we built on sex the idea of beauty, the understanding of tragedy, that is our culture. We were born among the naked statues. And we never covered the source of life with panties. At the most, we put on it a few mischievous fig leaves. We learned in high school about a certain Epicurus, a certain Petronius, a certain Ovid. We studied at the university about a certain Aretino. What Hugh Hefner says does not make us hot or cold. And now we have Sweden. We are all going to become Swedish, and we do not understand these Americans who, like adolescents, always speak of sex, and who, like adolescents, all of a sudden have discovered that sex is good not only for procreating children. But then why are half a million of the four million copies of the monthly *Playboy* sold in Europe? In Italy, *Playboy* can be received through the mail if the mail is not censored. And we must also consider all the good Italian husbands who drive to the Swiss border just to buy *Playboy*. And why are the Playboy Clubs so famous in Europe, why are the Bunnies so internationally desired? The first question you hear when you get back home is: "Tell me, did you see the Bunnies? How are they? Do they . . . I mean . . . do they?!?" And the most severe satirical magazine in the U.S.S.R., *Krokodil*, shows much indulgence toward Hugh Hefner: "[His] imagination is indeed inexhaustible. . . . The old problem of sex is treated freshly and originally. . . ."

Then let us listen with amusement to this sex lawmaker of the Space Age. He's now in his early forties. Just short of six feet, he weighs one hundred and fifty pounds. He eats once a day. He gets his nourishment essentially from soft drinks. He does not drink coffee. He is not married. He was briefly, and he has a daughter and a son, both teen-agers. He also has a father, a mother, a brother.

He is a tender relative, a nepotist: his father works for him, his brother too. Both are serious people, I am informed.

And then I am informed that the Pharaoh has awakened, the Pharaoh is getting dressed, is going to arrive, has arrived: Hallelujah! Where is he? He is there: that young man, so slim, so pale, so consumed by the lack of light and the excess of love, with eyes so bright, smart, vaguely demoniac. In his right hand he holds a pipe; in his left hand he holds a girl, Mary, the special one. After him comes his brother, who resembles Hefner. He also holds a girl, who resembles Mary. I do not know if the pipe he owns resembles Hugh's pipe because he is not holding one right now. It's a Sunday afternoon, and, as on every Sunday afternoon, there is a movie in the grave. The Pharaoh lies down on a sofa with Mary, the light goes down, the movie starts. The Bunnies go to sleep, and the four lovers kiss absentminded kisses. God knows what Hugh Hefner thinks about women, men, love, morals—will he be sincere in his nonconformity? What fun, boys, if I discover that he is a good, proper, moral father of Family whose destiny is paradise. Keep silent, Bunnies. He speaks. The movie is over, and he speaks, with a soft voice that breaks. And, I am sure, without lying.

ORIANA FALLACI: *A year without leaving the House, without seeing the sun, the snow, the rain, the trees, the sea, without breathing the air, do you not go crazy? Don't you die with unhappiness?*

HUGH HEFNER: Here I have all the air I need. I never liked to travel; the landscape never stimulated me. I am more interested in people and ideas. I find more ideas here than outside. I'm happy, totally happy. I go to bed when I like, I get up when I like: in the afternoon, at dawn, in the middle of the night. I am in the center of the world, and I don't need to go out looking for the world. The rational use that I make of progress and technology brings me the world at home. What distinguishes men from other animals? Is it not perhaps their capacity to control the environment and to change it according to their necessities and tastes? Many people will soon live as I do. Soon, the house will be a little planet that does not prohibit but helps our relationships with the others. Is it not more logical to live as I do instead of going out of a little house to enter into another little house, the car, then into another little house, the office, then another little house, the restaurant or the theater? Living as I do, I enjoy at the same time company and solitude, isolation from society and immediate access to society. Naturally, in order to afford such luxury, one must have money. But I have it. And it's delightful.

Seventy delightful millions of delightful dollars. Who could imagine, Mr. Hefner, that naked women have such a value?

I did not, for sure. I did not even hope it. I created the magazine only thirteen years ago, with fourteen hundred dollars. *Playboy* came at the right time, when the United States was experiencing a sexual revolution. My naked girls became a symbol of disobedience, of the triumph of sexuality, of the end of Puritanism. The first issue of *Playboy*, with the calendar of Marilyn, came in 1953, just when the American began to discover the hypocrisy surrounding sex—a social hypocrisy, a legal hypocrisy. Publicity is based entirely on sex, but for every advertisement showing a girl in a bikini, you find one hundred young men who get married as virgins.

In Europe the cult of virginity has been always directed to women only; in America it has attacked both men and women. Puritanism is more violent here than Catholicism is in Europe; it put down roots here better than in England, which is now fifty years ahead of us. In America, sex has always been justified and made legal by marriage. This is the reason for our ferocious anti-sexuality, our dark anti-eroticism. Do you know that, theoretically, two adults who make love in total agreement but are not married can be arrested and put in jail? And so we live in fear, in terror of being blackmailed. We live in mental dirtiness. Until a few years ago, movies that portrayed a man and his wife in the same bed were forbidden. To publish *Playboy* was like waving a flag of freedom, like screaming "rebellion" under a dictatorship.

A flag with a bunny: not too solemn for such a solemn crusade, Mr. Hefner. I have often tried to find some explanation of the excitement caused by that rabbit.

The rabbit, the bunny, in America has a sexual meaning, and I chose it because it's a fresh animal, shy, vivacious, jumping—sexy. First it smells you, then it escapes, then it comes back, and you feel like caressing it, playing with it. A girl resembles a bunny, joyful, joking. Consider the kind of girl that we made popular: the Playmate of the Month. She is never sophisticated, a girl you cannot really have. She is a young, healthy, simple girl—the girl next door. The sex that we fight for is innocent sex. Anybody can join. We are not interested in the mysterious, difficult woman, the *femme fatale,* who wears elegant underwear, with lace: she is sad and somehow mentally filthy. The *Playboy* girl has no lace, no underwear; she is naked, well-washed with soap and water. And she is happy. She does not suggest fetishism or masochism. She suggests laughter, simplicity, and her nudity is spontaneous. In other times, nudity implied a sense of guilt. They photographed a naked girl, against a white wall, for instance, and hid her head and did not mention her name. *Playboy* girls have a first name, a last name, an address, a family. They belong to good respectable families from every point of view, financial, social. No, madam, we never choose poor girls. Poverty brings sadness with it, a sort of dirtiness that becomes evident even on a naked body. And the *Playboy* girls have a very high morality. After all, if the Bunnies accept a date, they lose their job. Private detectives find out if they accept a date. The Bunnies are . . . are . . .

. . . inaccessible and familiar, like the Statue of Liberty. O.K. But are they not ashamed to pose naked in front of a photographer? Do they consider that moral?

Morality has nothing to do with nudity. The glorification of sex does not prohibit being moral. Those good girls are very happy to pose without dresses, and their parents are happy, too. The sexual revolution, the fight against Puritanism, is changing the old generation also. And do not forget that being Playmate of the Month means a passport to TV and the movies, generally. And then we pay them well: twenty-five hundred dollars for posing and twenty-five hundred dollars for promotion. So girls write continuously, offering to be photographed. And many wait years before the Great Day comes. The new generation is not anti-sexual. Fifty per cent of the population of the colleges read *Playboy*, and many girls who pose naked for *Playboy* come from the colleges.

What about actresses? It must be terribly difficult to get them to pose with nothing on.

On the contrary: we never have problems with the actresses, *Playboy* is such a vehicle of publicity. First they pose naked and use that publicity, then they express their indignation and use this new publicity. But they never reach the point of taking legal action. The quarrel with Carroll Baker, for instance, was not caused by the fact that she was naked in those photos. She knew that she was naked, didn't she? Actresses . . . you know . . . I would lie if I said that they are my favorite girls. Actresses never have any sexual effect on me, the *femmes fatales*, the old ones, or the intelligent ones. I mean, I don't feel uncomfortable with an intelligent woman. Simply, I do not know what to do with her. Now let us consider the *femmes fatales* and the aged ones. Very often the *femmes fatales* are the aged ones, and vice versa. Jeanne Moreau, for instance: a good actress, but, as a woman, she tells me zero. No, no, I do not really like this Moreau. The same thing with the Greek one—what is her name?—Melina Mercouri. I don't know, certain women make me think of the Parisian striptease, and the striptease never appealed to me. Zero. And zero to Greta Garbo. Zero to Marlene Dietrich. I mean the Mata Hari type. Do I make myself clear? It is difficult to judge at a distance. Can you judge Rudolph Valentino? But I find nothing sexy in Greta Garbo or Marlene Dietrich. One would say, looking at them, the myth discourages sex. The most beautiful women, the most attractive ones, are always the unknown ones.

What does the American expert in sex, Hugh Hefner, think about Bardot, Loren, Liz Taylor, Ursula Andress?

Among all the international beauties, Ursula Andress is without doubt the sexiest, she is absolutely sexy. Ursula is completely attractive—completely. Her health is attractive, and her bosom. Her sportive look is attractive. Elizabeth Taylor . . . oh! Absolutely no. She was sexy enough some years ago, when she did *A Place in the Sun.* But now! Really. Virna Lisi . . . no. She tells me nothing, I don't get the message. Carroll Baker: zero plus zero, the last one in the world to send me messages. Jayne Mansfield . . . for heaven's sake! Don't even speak about her. Brigitte Bardot . . . well . . . yes . . . sexy, very. Especially when she was young, at the beginning of her career. Marilyn Monroe, oh, yes! I got the message. Not as much as from Brigitte, but I did. Sophia Loren . . . you see, I like Sophia more as a human being than as a woman. I think she is *simpatica*, yes, I like her, though I do not know her personally. And I think that when she was twenty years old, she had a fantastic body. But that is all.

Do you know what I am wondering, Mr. Hefner? I am wondering if you like women, beyond the sex, I mean.

Well, socially, mentally, I enjoy more being with men, I admit. When I want to speak, to think, I stay with men, not with women. This doesn't mean that I do not consider women important. On the contrary, I am the first one to recognize that women have been relegated to an inhuman role, that sexual emancipation cannot be achieved without the sexual emancipation of women, that the highest price of anti-sexuality has been paid by women. . . . But men have been too much and too often slandered, in America especially. Weak, they say, frightened. Obviously, they are frightened. Men gave women something that women had the right to have, no doubt, but now this turns against them. It's a reciprocal fear that puts women against men and men against women. Women want to compete with men, want to take the male role, and so the problems of men become the problems of women, and the two sexes get confused. What does it mean today, being a man or woman?

But what place has love in all this? Or does love have a place in all this?

I have always said that sex without love is better than nothing, that sex is still a very beautiful thing, even when it is only sex. But sex with love is better. The pleasure is doubled when it involves a feeling. I am romantic, I believe in love. At times, I have fallen in love; I imagine it will happen again. Obviously, it would be easier for me, with all the women I might have, to put myself in the situation of not falling in love, not to be wounded. But I would pay too high a price. If you cut off the possibility of being wounded, you cut off the most fascinating side of a relationship. As you see, I am not cynical.

What a surprise. And I bet that you believe in marriage. And I bet that you are a faithful man. And I bet . . .

I believe so much in marriage that I, myself, do not marry to avoid making a mistake. I do not discourage people from getting married. Those who get married after the age of thirty probably will have a happy marriage that includes physical faithfulness. If a man desires another woman, he is not totally happy with the one he has already. I am in favor of marriage because I think that marriage is the only way to procreate children and raise them. I do not agree with women who have children without a husband. Why should they, if technology today permits us to make love without having children? Unless a woman is very strong, she is not ready for such an experiment. Yet marriage is not for me because I have no time for the husband's role. I have no time to give up variety, adventure, my work. I am married to my work, to my philosophy, and this is a marriage that does not permit any divorce. I was married once, when I was twenty-three years old, to a girl I met in school. I am not sorry to have been married. It permitted me to have two children and to have no curiosity about it. But I do not think it will happen again. In fact, I always keep what I call my special girl—the one that I care for more than the others, the one that I stay with most of the time. The problem of being faithful does not even exist in such a situation. I do not ignore other girls. Let me see if I can explain this. Right now, my special girl is Mary. It has lasted three and a half years. But in the meantime I have had many less important relationships. Before Mary, there was Cynthia. During that time, too, I had various relationships. Before Cynthia, there was Betty, and another girl whose name was Joyce. This covers thirteen years. Anyhow, I would like to make it clear that those never were pseudo-marriages, they were cohabitations, which, unfortunately, provoke jealousy in some women.

And you? Are you jealous, Mr. Hefner?

Sure I am. I wouldn't like Mary to be sexually involved with someone else. When this happened with some of my special girls, I was rather hurt. In my relationships, I do not look for equality between man and woman. I like innocent, affectionate, faithful girls who . . .

Do you mean you would never love a woman who has had as many men as you have had women, Mr. Hefner? A woman who accepted and applied your philosophy?

Not in the least. I never looked for a woman like me. I wouldn't know what to do with a Hugh Hefner in skirts.

Mr. Hefner, you have a daughter fourteen years old. What would you think if she would pose in four years, let's say, for Playboy?

Well . . . let us see . . . personally I would be pleased, I think. I would consider it a compliment to me and to my work, I think. But I wouldn't like my daughter to have a promiscuous life. I would not like my daughter to be immoral. . . . O.K.! I understand your criticism. Then let us look each other in the eye and confess the truth. Intellectually, I may think in a certain way; practically, I may act in another way. I am the son of two devoted Methodists, I am heir to a violent anti-sexuality, and my head tries to separate the emotional prejudices, but this does not mean that I succeed in the effort. This does not mean that I can divorce myself from my education, which is a puritanical education, the typical education of a typical American man, the education of a society that never absorbed the European sophistication. I am disillusioning you, I know. Somehow, I am scandalizing you, I know, as I know that I might look old-fashioned in your eyes. But there is nothing that can be done about that. I am and I remain a combination of incoherences that I uselessly try to reject. I wouldn't be honest toward you, toward myself, toward those who will read about us if I do not confess such a simple truth.

This is noble, Mr. Hefner, this is correct. But here the donkey falls.

What did you say?

Nothing. It's an Italian way of speaking.

What does it mean?

It means that while I'll go to hell, you'll go to paradise, Mr. Hefner. There among the saints and martyrs, together with your Bunnies, you'll go to discuss the sex of the angels.

Do they have sex?

They don't.

Chicago, February, 1966

JEANNE MOREAU

"Femme Fatale"

I met Jeanne Moreau in the studio belonging to Mademoiselle Rozan, her press agent and friend, with whom she stays when she is in Paris; her own house is at Versailles. Our appointment was for three o'clock in the afternoon, and promptly at three o'clock in the afternoon Mademoiselle Moreau appeared, with her pinched little face, her fragile little body, her aura of perfume and illness. She was wearing a dress by her friend Cardin, she had short chestnut hair, and she wore no makeup. This, it seemed to me, made her look far from sexy, although everyone says she is sexy, the sexiest woman in the world. As soon as Mademoiselle Moreau came in, she began paying me compliments, saying she had read one of my books and would like to read another, she had liked that one so much. In some trepidation I thanked her, unsure whether to believe her. Then I decided not to believe her and went on to explain to her how the interview would go. She listened, nodding almost as if she were learning an interesting lesson, then replied, "I'm ready." She was as punctual in her replies as she was for our appointment and made no errors of syntax or grammar, which is extremely rare for a movie star. She enunciated her words with perfect diction, phrasing her sentences as if she were dictating to a shorthand typist, with periods, commas, semicolons, and quotes all in their right places. And, most remarkable of all, she never said anything silly. Our conversation was quick and cost me no effort: not only because Mademoiselle Moreau is intelligent and very clever, but also because, unlike most intelligent and very clever women, she enjoys female company, feels at ease in it. We were consequently able to talk about absolutely anything, even about the relationship with Pierre Cardin and about the reputation she enjoys as a *femme fatale*. The reputation is hers and hers in abundance, but you wouldn't think it to look at her and even less to listen to her. Mademoiselle Moreau sets great store by morality and is sorry to think that today love is practiced like a sport, a pleasure, and no more. Our interview was lengthy. When it was finished, Mademoiselle Moreau said it had been very brief. She rose, bowed, and left.

ORIANA FALLACI: *The first time I saw you, Mademoiselle Moreau, was six or seven years ago, while you were working on a movie here in Paris. You were sitting on a bench, smoking, still, silent, ignored by everyone, and I stopped to watch you because, I remember, I was struck by your face. "Who's that?" I asked the press agent who was taking me around. "An actress from the theater," he told me. "Her name's Moreau." The name meant nothing to me at the time, and I moved on. Afterward, however, I more than once found myself reflecting on your face. Not that it was a particularly beautiful face, as faces go I had actually found it a little on the ugly side, with that bitter mouth, those sunken cheeks, those dark ringed eyes. But it was an unusual face, a face unlike any other, and it bespoke an obdurate patience, a waiting quality I had never seen before. It was almost as if, I don't know, as if you were sure of obtaining sooner or later the success that you have today. Almost as if this success were your God-given due.*

JEANNE MOREAU: In fact, I was expecting it, I was expecting it, I was expecting it, as you expect a seedling after planting a seed or a child after conceiving. More than that: I wanted it. And not because of the money, the envy of others, or the outward signs of what is called popularity, but because of a kind of bet with myself and other people. I have always liked things that are difficult, I have always had the urge to open forbidden doors, with a curiosity and an obstinacy that verge on masochism. Everyone said that a theater actress couldn't act in films, and I came from the theater; acting for me was the gospel, the love of the spoken word. Everyone said that to succeed in movies you needed a big bust and a photogenic face, to look like Martine Carol. I was on the skinny side, and you can see the kind of face I have. And so I accepted every movie that was offered to me, without asking who would be directing it, without asking who my partner would be, without asking whether they were paying me or not. I was determined to have success. I had been waiting for it, this success, since 1948, and then it came with *Lift to the Scaffold*. If you work it out, you'll see that my celebrity dates back barely five years. For this reason it hasn't given me much of a thrill. Apart from the fact that it doesn't depend only on me—it's team work—I've accepted it as something that was my due.

And something that doesn't much matter to you now, I'd say. Your face hasn't changed much, as usually happens to someone who has success. The waiting look has vanished, but there remains the obdurate patience, the tranquillity of one who doesn't believe in miracles.

It does matter to me, it does matter to me. Success is like a liberation or the first phase of a love story. Feeling oneself looked at, admired, encouraged, affects one like the love of a man one loves: your hands gesture more freely, your step becomes surer, your face more beautiful. A face, you know, is a matter of what you're used to. When you're used to it, in the end you find it beautiful. No, I don't think success is harmful, as so many people say. Rather, I believe it indispensable to talent, if for nothing else than to increase the talent. The more I talk about what I am, the more I realize that it was absolutely indispensable to me. Or do you think I'm wrong?

I don't think anything, Mademoiselle Moreau. With all the articles that have been written about you, I still don't know who you are. If I had to describe you now I couldn't find anything more to say than this: a woman who is educated, elegant, probably very intelligent, who is wearing a dress by Cardin and talks like the printed page.

Firstly, I'm the daughter of a peasant who was the son of a peasant, and of an Englishwoman from Lancashire, a dancer at the Folies Bergère. One can't get away from that. My father is now living in the country with his peasant relations and his cows, and my mother is living in London with my sister: my parents are separated. Neither of them ever had the blessing of any exceptional culture, although my mother has always been more refined than my father. Neither of them has ever been rich. Indeed, after the 1936 crisis they were left very poor, and I grew up in this poverty: not actual beggary but indisputable poverty. Being an actress has also meant this to me: shaking off the memory of the fifth floor in Montmartre, stairways that stank of cooking, the promiscuity unavoidable when many poor people live on the same landing. Like my father, I love the country and view the big city like a provincial, but like my mother, who became a dancer to get out of Lancashire, I've always wanted to be somebody.

That's strange, Mademoiselle Moreau. Seeing you today, one would think you were a woman who has always lived in comfort, or at least had a nursemaid, or at least went to a middle-class boarding school.

Oh, no! I feel very nostalgic about my childhood, but it wasn't a privileged childhood. I went to state grade schools and high schools on scholarships, nothing else. But I began to read very early: at thirteen I had already read Zola, and I had an obsession for literature. I was a sickly child, condemned to very long periods of convalescence, and during convalescence I would read until I wore out my brain and my eyes. My vocation for acting goes back to that: the pleasure in words and the desire to repeat them aloud to somebody else. I would learn by heart Racine and Anouilh, give the text to my mother so that she could correct me, and recite it. Naturally when I told my father that I wanted to be an actress, he went raving mad. To a simple person like him such a job was like prostitution, a scandal, and then there was another way he wanted to get me out of that fifth floor in Montmartre and the stink of cooking. At that time, in France, it was fashionable to become a civil servant, a post office employee, a teacher. He wanted me to be a post office employee. The sophistication people see in me is a recent acquisition, like my confidence and poise. The truth of the matter is that there are still a lot of things I can't grow out of: my fear of people, for example, my embarrassment at being stared at. If I have an appointment in a café, quite often I can't make myself go in. At the movie theater, I always go in and out while it's dark. And then I was taught good manners, very good manners, although I realize that good manners can in fact lead to grave misunderstandings. My father was very strict; he taught me not to show off. My mother was very correct; she taught me self-control. Does that surprise you?

A little. They always draw two pictures of you: either the intellectual who reads herself to sleep with Voltaire and Rousseau, Giraudoux, and Diderot, or the emancipated modern woman who takes no notice of what other people say, who considers nothing taboo, and who's free of any sexual or social inhibitions.

Doubtless I am, but not as the myth would have me. I think the public see me too much as they see me in movies, and I'm always playing unorthodox characters. In *Lift to the Scaffold* I was a woman who together with her lover arranges the murder of her husband. In *The Lovers* I was a wife with a lover who suddenly falls in love with another man, makes love with him all night, and at dawn goes off with him. In *Jules and Jim* I was the woman of two men united in eternal friendship. In *Les liaisons dangereuses* I was a faithless and amoral woman. My private life is rather different. My private life . . . no, I never talk about my private life. Not that I like to cloak myself in mystery—there's very little mystery about me—but I do wish other people wouldn't poke their noses into it: that's all. Not from modesty, from good sense. It's already so very difficult to sort out one's own problems when there's nobody knowing and watching; imagine what it would be like with the world knowing and watching. You see, I know very well that success is helped by publicity, but I can't help detesting it: I know too many actors who've ruined their whole existence because of it. Think of those poor wretches who get married to avoid a scandal. Ah, yes, in a world where a man and a woman can perfectly well live together without getting married, actors are the people who get married most because, if they go to bed without getting married, people sit in judgment on them. We shouldn't let ourselves be influenced by other people, and it makes me laugh when actors say, "It's impossible, you can't get away from the press, from people's curiosity." I was divorced from my husband, I went to divorce court, before a judge, in broad daylight, and there wasn't a single columnist, not a single photographer. Why? Because I hadn't let them know. And so everyone thinks I'm still married.

Thank you for your information. However, I didn't mean to sound indiscreet and ask you things I personally couldn't care less about, Mademoiselle Moreau. I only wanted to talk with you about a character, your own, that is not renowned for conformity.

Feeling uncomfortable when one reads something about oneself in a newspaper isn't conformity. Certainly, I'm not a conformist. I've always led my own life tranquilly and at the same time without the anguish of wondering what other people will say about me. Not courageously, because one doesn't after all need so much courage, but not fearfully, either. I have lived, let us say, in freedom, or, better, in illegality, considering that after five years of marriage I was separated. And people always confuse illegality with emancipation and modernism. "Heavens, she isn't married, she isn't divorced. They saw her with such-and-such, they saw her with so-and-so, this time she's going too far. . . ." A woman who's boss of her own life always goes too far in the eyes of the righteous, and I'd be lying if I said that I like having this reputation for going too far. A woman is a woman, and she can't do what a man can do. A woman is slave of her woman's condition even if she enjoys a social status identical to that of men. It's so-called freedom. . . . You know, even freedom is a form of slavery.

Are you condemning the freedom everyone believes you possess, Mademoiselle Moreau?

I'm not condemning it; I'm just pointing out its disastrous result. I don't dispute it; I'm just saying that it's dangerous. The majority of couples who live freely—"I lead my life and you lead yours"—are doomed to see their ménage wear itself out, which is like saying that they become victims of their own freedom. People are so caught up in the frenzy of freedom, and I understand that. But the freedom fanatics often end up by no longer giving anything, or by giving meanly, and meanness has never brought happiness. "I lead my life and you lead yours. . . ." Bah! I don't know whether woman is a complement of man or man is a complement of woman, but the whole interplay between man and woman living together is indispensable, it's the reason for life, the origin of life. Man and woman are made to cohabit, and to deny the rightness of this cohabitation means going in for the worst kind of racism: that which sets men against women and keeps them in a state of perpetual war.

At this point I would like really to know what you think of marriage, Mademoiselle Moreau.

I still have an adolescent idea of marriage, the same that I had when I was convinced that a man and woman ought to get married in church, for as long as they live, finding again in their spouse the same constancy of affection that they found in father or mother, the same accord, the same complicity without need of explanations or words. Naturally even between father and mother quarrels can arise, but this doesn't alter the fact that they are father and mother and therefore love each other. Marriage is a serious, important thing.

So why haven't you married again then, Mademoiselle Moreau?

Because it's a serious and important thing. Because I have a son of fourteen, a son who has always lived with me, who continues to see his father, with whom I have remained on terms of true and steady friendship. Because I don't feel I want to introduce another man into my son's life—I'm very attached to him, it's only normal. Because I'd have to be very sure indeed that the man was the right man. Because my marriage went wrong. Because my parents' marriage went wrong. Because the setback I suffered from those two broken marriages has disturbed my whole life. Because the risk is too great, and I don't want to face it. Because the things I have said about marriage are part of an ideal, a fantasy, and the reality of my own life is different. I have never wanted to marry and live with a man.

Not even when you married your husband?

Not even when I married my husband. We got married because there was a child on the way. I was young, I had enough money to support a child, enough sense to educate a child; I decided to have the child and go on living with my husband who wasn't my husband, a situation that suited us perfectly well. But there was an outburst of complications, families, friends. "Heavens, how disgraceful! Heavens, how scandalous! Think of the child when he grows up, he'll be called Moreau. What will they say to him at school? They'll say, 'Who's your father, where's your father?' . . ." The doctor who was to help at my confinement was the worst of the lot. And so . . . but it makes an extraordinary story, my marriage. I was married on September 27, 1949, at midday, and my son was born on September 28, 1949, at six in the morning—eighteen hours after the sacred rite. On the other hand I don't think I did wrongly: it's very difficult to raise a child on one's own— almost impossible. I know women who have bravely decided to raise a child on their own, and they've found it very hard.

Now, Mademoiselle Moreau, I have to broach one of those subjects that you so dislike but that other people like so much: Pierre Cardin. I know you don't like talking about it, but it has been said that you were going to get married, and then it was said it had all ended in a breakup.

Breakup? Whenever? Oh, it's incredible! You can't have
any affection or admiration or tender feelings for someone
without journalists embroidering it and inventing stories.
I'm so right always to say that I've no statement to make. Why
a breakup? Because he's gone to New York and I haven't?
He has his work and I have mine; he has to make trips and so
do I. About Cardin . . . I can say this: I've known Cardin
for more than two years and every announcement that has
been made of one kind or another is absolutely false. And I
can say this: that we are very, very close. Oh, naturally people
subscribe to the conventional mythology, and when they see
a well-known person and an actress together, they always
have to say the usual banalities: "They're engaged, they're
going to marry, their friends say they're going to marry. No,
they aren't going to marry, but what's going on? How on
earth, and why? Oh, it's the breakup. I said it couldn't last,
of course it couldn't have lasted. You've seen they've left each
other?" In reality things are both much simpler and much
more complicated. But what can I do? Explain everything?
I'm not the type to give press conferences to say, "I have found
love," or, "I made a mistake, oh, what a disappointment." Far
less do I give press conferences to deny such rubbish as that
I've put money into the Cardin Fashion House. "Obviously,
she's become a shareholder. They stay together out of mutual
interest. Why else do you suppose they stay together?" Imagine
it! And where do I have the money to put into the Cardin
Fashion House? I'm not rich, I never will be because I don't
know how to save money. All I own is an old car I bought
secondhand two years ago, a rented house in Versailles, a country house I bought for my father. I wish I did have money to
invest in the House of Cardin! I'd ask for nothing better. But
just try and explain it. Try and explain that I admire Pierre
because he's a great worker, a man full of ideas and an artist,
that I'm attached to him because he's noble, good, a poet and a
realist at the same time. He lives in the world of Haute Cou-

ture, so hypocritical, so coquettish, yet certain things don't even touch him, he doesn't even notice. . . . In short, we get on together, and that's all there is to it.

You continue to surprise me, Mademoiselle Moreau. Perhaps this comment I've always thought was only attributed to you is really yours: "In these days people take up with each other and drop each other too easily. Pleasure is practiced like a sport, and the easy game of love leads to the dissolution of the feeling of love." Maybe you even believe in true love, Mademoiselle Moreau.

It would be demoralizing not to believe in it. Yes, the comment is my own; they didn't just attribute it to me. But more than in one true love I'd say I believe in many true loves, in true love, that is, in the sense that when you have truly loved someone you go on loving him for the rest of your life. For me it's not possible to forget, and I don't understand people who, when the love is ended, can bury the other person in hatred or oblivion. For me, a man I have loved becomes a kind of brother. Naturally this is considered immoral, and if I say of a man I've loved, "I'm so fond of him, I'm so glad to see him again," they look at me as if I were a monster. But one of the things that has disgusted me ever since I was a child and used to observe the world of adults is the enmity between former lovers or former husbands and wives. Nothing is more stupid than saying: "Oh, that fool man with whom I ruined my life!" "Oh, that idiot woman with whom I lost so much time!" To condemn someone to whom we have been attached means to condemn ourselves. Perhaps this will shock other people, but I've said it before and I'll say it again: I always look on the men I have loved with pleasure and affection, they are all related to me, because not only marrying but also loving a person amounts to forming a new family.

Shock other people, Mademoiselle Moreau? I wonder what's happened to the perverse femme fatale *people talk of; it's more like listening to a lady sergeant in the Salvation Army. Maybe this other comment is yours, too: "The liberty that woman has managed to achieve is turning against her. There are women who have everything they need to be happy, but they aren't because they confuse liberty with license."*

Yes, I said that. Women, today, tend so much to minimize the gift of giving themselves and to belittle the woman who gives herself. . . . In French novels of the last century one often reads this phrase, which I find so right, "I gave myself." Today it's no longer a gift, it's more like abandonment prompted by outside factors such as a pleasant evening, a momentary closeness, holidays, sunshine, whiskey, a movie. . . . And it's curious to see how sound, brave women have such low resistance to experiences of this kind. The episode lays them waste, the aftermath of an act of bravado, and you know why? Because they aren't aware of the theft that is being practiced on them, and, consequently, they are the least loved and respected by men. Seducing isn't what counts. Seducing? . . . You can seduce a man for three hours, after which he won't look at you. What counts is being esteemed, respected.

How moral can you get?

I don't say it to be moral. I say it because I'm very fond of women, I esteem them highly, and I like being with them. Being in the company of a woman is, for me, always an interesting experience, never in the least boring. I have a lot of women friends. I know people don't believe in friendship between women, but I believe in it. I think it is a very modern feeling. Before there was no such thing as friendship between women, there was always competition or enmity between them, but today it exists, even if it doesn't exist to the same extent and in the same degree of complicity as friendship between men. Oh! You look surprised. . . . Don't you have any women friends? Don't you like women?

. . . I like you very much. I'd like to have you for a friend.

Thank you, but I mean women in general.

Let's drop it, Mademoiselle Moreau. And let's talk about

something else; for example, the fact that you have always worked in Europe, never once in America.

They've asked me, but I've never wanted to go. I only went once to America, just for pleasure, with my friend Florence Malraux. California, Florida, New York.... New York terrified me, for two days I stayed locked in my room watching television. I'm no good at traveling, the speed of travel petrifies me. The idea of taking only six hours to get to New York seems abnormal to me. For me traveling is slightly absurd: it strikes me the way those tourists visiting the Louvre who have to see everything in three hours do. And then I'm tied to Europe, to a certain entourage. I'm like cats: I have to get used to a place before I enjoy it; I have to stay in the warmth of the same spot before I understand it. Really, I enjoy myself more by meeting people than by traveling, by reading than by traveling. Isn't meeting a person or reading a book a kind of traveling?

Yes, yes. I know you like mixing with writers, cultured people. In Italy, too, I've been told, you were happier spending your time with intellectuals rather than with movie folk.

It isn't that I don't like or don't value actors, the more so as we are all more or less the same. It's that I enjoy myself more with intellectuals. I like laughing, having fun, arguing. And this is easier with intellectuals than with actors. Naturally there are exceptions in this, too. Orson Welles, for example, I like very much: with his enormous gusts of laughter, his enormous rages, his enormous enjoyment in living, his enormous interest in everything, in women, men, anger, drunkenness, light, darkness. I liked Fellini, too: such an extraordinary liar that he's certainly not far from his own truth. Nothing is more like truth than a lie, don't you find? However, in Italy I met some extraordinary people, *charmant:* Vittorini, Piovene, Moravia.

But once, if I'm not mistaken, you were to have dined with Moravia, and you didn't go.

Maybe; it's possible. I often forget things. It appears that it's a Freudian thing: when you forget to go somewhere, it's because you don't want to go there. However, in Milan I have a great many friends, and not only writers. In Milan I made *La Notte*, you know. Heavens, I don't even want to speak about that film. It was such a nightmare . . . such misery. . . . The only two people who would speak to each other were myself and Mastroianni. . . . I was wretched . . . I had to take sedatives, sleeping pills. And in short, quite apart from so many other things I don't ever want to mention, I've never looked as ugly as I did in that movie. Ugh!

I suppose you rightfully bear a grudge.

Heavens, no! I've forgotten it. I can't even say I forgive; I forget, in spite of myself. When someone plays me a lousy trick, I promise myself I'll bear a grudge against him. But then I see the person, and I forget. This and one other thing are part of the good side of my nature. The other thing is that when I'm sad, I hide in a corner and wait until it's over. I used to do it even as a child. As a child! As a child! How many times have I said that.

Yet it certainly can't be said that you're obsessed with growing older. As far as I know, you're one of the very few actresses who have never concealed their ages.

No. I was born in 1928, and it has never entered my mind to rub out the date on my passport. After the little shock of going from twenty-nine to thirty, I haven't cared. Today it's so easy to remain young and beautiful: you only have to take care of your body, and I take great care of mine. And then, even if you do conceal your age, there's always someone who'll make you older. Goodness knows why, a successful woman is always made older than she is. It must be her constant presence, all the talk about her, that makes people say a successful woman is older than she is. "She began, let's see, in such and such a year, I was so old, so that makes her nearly forty, or fifty, or sixty." The hell with them! Sorry. Well, what do you conclude?

This, Mademoiselle Moreau: either you are what you are, in which case you're an exceptional woman, or else you are quite the opposite, in which case you're an exceptional actress. Either way, the conclusion is in your favor.

Paris, May, 1963

MARY HEMINGWAY

My Husband Hemingway

She is small and slim and nervous, and most of the time she wears slacks. So, from a distance, you would say she is a boy, not a woman in her early fifties. Her face is sharp, as pointed as the beak of a stork, and has the mysterious beauty of things seasoned by storms, its lines engraved by the wind, the sun, a tragic dawn of seven years ago. Her eyes are firm, without illusions. Her lips are hard, with no lipstick. Her movements are sudden, sometimes masculine. Look at her as she sinks her fists in her pockets and raises her head to tell you how she doesn't like women and idiots and those who shake hands weakly. She is the widow of Ernest Hemingway, the woman with whom he lived during the last seventeen years of his life, until that dawn when he shot himself with a rifle. Hemingway loved her and admired her. He tenderly called her Miss Mary, as they do in the South. In the fall of 1956 he wrote: "Miss Mary is durable. She is also brave, charming, witty, exciting to look at, a pleasure to be with and a good wife. She is also an excellent fisher-woman, a fair wing shot, a strong swimmer, a really good cook, a good judge of wine, an excellent gardener, an amateur astronomer, a student of art, political economy, Swahili, French and Italian and can run a boat or a household in Spanish. She can also sing well with an accurate and true voice, knows more generals, admirals, air marshals, politicians, and important persons than I know dead company commanders, former battalion commanders. . . . When she is away, the Finca is as empty as the emptiest bottle she ever ordered removed and I live in a vacuum that is as lonely as a radio tube when the batteries are dead and there is no current to plug into."

You feel rather uneasy about facing her after reading such an avowal of love. And as you ring her door bell, you wonder, worried, how it will go; she was a journalist, too, and she doesn't speak much to journalists. Months ago there was that trial with Hotchner, author of the book on Hemingway that she tried to prevent being published. No one was able to steal a statement, a judgment from her: she defends her silence as well as her solitude. She lives alone. You'll notice that her apartment door is locked more than once and that there is also a safety catch, though the doorman downstairs protects her well. Many people have been trying to see her all these years, trying to rummage in that July dawn. The sun had just risen, she slept, the shot woke her. "Then what did you do, Miss Mary?" "Was he already dead when you found him, Miss Mary?" "Suicide or accident, Miss Mary?" "And what about the manuscripts, Miss Mary?" After all, she is the one who decides whether or not to publish the manuscripts he left; she is the testamentary executrix. We who were swayed so much by his way of writing, of living, we who wish to read him again, we would like to know everything as much as she would like to keep silent. In all honesty, I don't know why she consented to this interview, why last night she said, "All right, tomorrow at 2:00 P.M." We'd already met last night, with friends, over a drink. We spoke about literature, the same old things, and when the ice broke, she showed me the apartment. It's a penthouse in Manhattan, kitchen, living room, guest room, bedroom, the shelter of a woman who looks at the future coldly, because her life is still in the past. In the bedroom, over a bureau, there is his photograph that she likes best: a very young Hemingway—he resembles Clark Gable—black moustache and white teeth, proudly showing two deer horns. Near that photo is the note he wrote for her birthday, three months before that dawn. It begins: "To my kitten." In the corridor there is the skin of the lion she killed during a safari. No, not the one after which he wrote *Green Hills of Africa*. In the guest room there are two leopard skins, the very beautiful one that she bagged and the ugly one that he bagged. They often joked about this; he was happy to have a wife who shot well, and he had been her teacher. In the living room there is the stuffed head of a deer and the paintings she was able to take away from Cuba, with the help of Fidel Castro. What a story. What a pity she obliged me to swear I wouldn't write it because she wants to write it herself. And then, near the desk where she works, his last photograph, preciously framed. And this time it is Hemingway in his sixties, with a large beard; he resembles a patriarch. She always knew him with his beard. He had it because he suffered from a skin trouble that was made worse by shaving; his skin was so delicate.

Here we are, the door has been unlocked, it opens, her firm hand shakes my hand, her face, seasoned by storms, smiles kindly. Is she perhaps trying to disguise a shyness? Softly she thanks me for the flowers; she immediately sets them in a vase. Her fingers are delicate now; she moves them as a geisha would. Is this perhaps the real Miss Mary? In three hours, when our conversation will be over, we'll go out in the rain. She'll seem almost sweet, almost tender. And so we'll go walking, out in the rain, as women who can be friends beyond their different experiences, their different ages. Now let's listen to her—my tape recorder is speeding—I interrupt her as little as possible. It's an afternoon in New York, and Hemingway observes us from his frame, a little ironical, maybe indulgent. Miss Mary is sitting on the floor. Her voice is severe, and her hair is short, very blond.

ORIANA FALLACI: *How strange, Miss Mary, to find you living in New York, a city Hemingway hated so much that he wouldn't ever stop here long.*

MARY HEMINGWAY: I hate it, too. This filthy, noisy city. Why do I stay then? Well . . . publishers, lawyers, notaries, solitude. You know, it's easier to live in a place where we were never together. This isn't really my home. My real home is still the one in Cuba, though it doesn't belong to me anymore—such a lovely house. Have you read Moravia's article? He describes it so well. The only thing I don't understand is his being surprised to find it Anglo-Saxon. After all that is what Ernest and I were, two Americans of Anglo-Saxon stock, weren't we? My house . . . look at this picture, this broken step at the front. Ernest never wanted to fix it because wild flowers grew in the cracks. This side was my bedroom, Ernest's the other. But he never slept there, he slept with me. We shared that room for sixteen years, and he used to say, "It is always here you come back, wherever you go." Sometimes I dream of going back, then I wake up and say no. You know, I would go into the living room, see his armchair, wait for him to walk in and sit down. . . . I would go into the library, see his desk, wait for him to come in and sit before it. . . . I couldn't stand it, you know? I don't feel the same way for the house in Ketchum. Oh, no, not because he died there. The fact that he killed himself there doesn't make me dislike it. I like it, I feel such a loyalty for the house in Ketchum. I don't know how to explain it any other way: loyalty is the right word. So I can go back to Ketchum—I often go back—we had happy days there, too, you know. But we didn't stay long there and . . .

Forgive me for interrupting, Miss Mary. But you've just said, "That he killed himself there." To my knowledge, that is the first time you've admitted Hemingway's suicide. Until now,

*and against all evidence, you've always maintained his death
was accidental.*

No, he shot himself. Shot himself. Just that and nothing
else. For a long time I refused to admit it even to myself, it's
true. I don't know what happened in my subconscious. I mean,
I've never discussed it with a psychiatrist, but I suppose it had
something to do with self-defense. It's just like what happens
when someone hits you and you instinctively tighten your
muscles to lessen the pain, you cover your face, or you hold
your arms around your body. I defended myself like that, by
pretending it had been an accident. Admitting the truth
would've snapped my nerves, split open my brain. But I soon
realized it was stupid to go on pretending and believing it to
have been an accident—absolutely stupid. Lots of people, like
you, say that his death was coherent, that he wasn't a man to
succumb to disease, to die in his bed. I don't know how to answer that. Losing him has cast me in such darkness, an endless
tunnel, and only now I am attempting to escape from it. But
Ernest's sister once said, "If Ernest thought that was the best
thing to do, then he was right to do it." Well, for me it's too
difficult to say such a thing; I miss him so desperately. Yet I
agree because I wouldn't like to see him alive but sick, insecure, and unhappy. . . . What for? Only to have him with
me? How selfish it would be. Yes, if Ernest thought that was
the right thing to do, I must accept it. Without thinking of
how lonely he left me, without crying with the regret that I
wasn't able to stop him. He was sick and desperate, and we
cannot judge the behavior of a sick and desperate man. In his
condition, probably, I too would've ignored the sorrow I was
about to inflict, I too would've ignored the idea of leaving him
alone. You know, there is a kind of loneliness much worse than
my present one. His. And writers are lonely persons, even when
they love and are loved.

Miss Mary, you say he was sick. What sickness?

When he went to the Mayo Clinic, in the winter of 1961,

his blood pressure was very high. But his real trouble was a serious, very serious, breakdown. He was so depressed. I cannot even say when he started to feel so depressed. I am unable to fix the time. Nor can I truthfully say that he thought of suicide. You saw the note he wrote on my birthday, three months before. Does it look the note of a man who is thinking of suicide? Of course, I remember some episodes during his illness . . . there were a few manifestations during the last days . . . but I don't want to speak of them because I don't think the public should be told about them. A writer doesn't belong to the public, only his writing does. Unlike a prima donna or an actress, he has a right to privacy if he wants it. And Ernest did want it. He used to say that everyone has a right to some privacy, especially where illness is involved. That's why I am against Mr. Hotchner's book, apart from the many inaccuracies it contains. No one should be authorized to tell the dissolution of a man, even less to tell it for money or sensationalism. Such protection should be made part of man's civil rights, of human dignity; people should be prohibited from writing about others' intimate lives. And I insist in my fight, I go on with my lawyers, and I don't care about the publicity that I make for Mr. Hotchner doing this. It is my duty to defend the dignity of my husband as I can until I can no longer, it's a matter of principle. Look at the many books printed on Kennedy. Do you think it's right, each time a famous man dies, to jump on him and rob his secrets?

All the same, Miss Mary, there is one question I must ask you. It has been said and repeated on several sides that in his last years, or in his last months at least, Hemingway found himself unable to write anymore, and that that is why he killed himself. Is that true?

No, it isn't true. It is a total and absurd fabrication. Ernest committed suicide on July 2, 1961; at the very least, the very least, he worked up to spring, 1961. I can tell you for sure that he even went on working at the Mayo Clinic, where he stayed till March, 1961. He was working at *The Movable Feast*. Before that he was working at *A Dangerous Summer*, an enormous work on *corridas*, a very good book. *Life* magazine, where a few extracts were published, had persuaded him to write it, and for some time he put aside *The Movable Feast* and wrote *A Dangerous Summer*. He wrote approximately one hundred and fifty thousand words—stupendous pages. How silly to say he couldn't write any longer. Right up to the end he went on writing: even in Ketchum, after leaving the Mayo Clinic. In Ketchum he got up at six every morning, as he had always done, and went on working until late in the afternoon, when daylight failed. It was his working method, I have never seen him do any writing at night. Sometimes he got up at dawn. That morning, I remember, I woke up about six for a glass of water, and he was already up. He always went early to bed so he could get up early . . . and because of that I wasn't surprised he was up already. . . . I went back to sleep. . . . I used to get up later than he, at seven. . . . Yes, the shot woke me up. . . . Yes, when I found him he was already dead . . . very dead. What were we talking about?

About the manuscripts, Miss Mary. There is a great curiosity as to the books Hemingway left and you are to publish.

He left forty pounds of manuscripts. Ernest wrote a lot, writing was his life, but he was never in a hurry to publish. When he had finished a novel or a story, he would lock it up in his safe-deposit box at the Bank of Havana and leave it there, sometimes for years. At times he would say he was not eager to publish absolutely everything he had ever written, and his publishers would beg in vain for a manuscript. Why should he listen to them? He had enough money to live in the way he liked; that is, writing for love, not out of necessity, going fishing, walking, hunting, traveling. That's why it is such a burden, believe me, to be his testamentary executrix and decide whether to publish or not. When he wrote his good will, in 1955, I didn't imagine the responsibility that I would have one day. In fact until now I have only released one book: *The Movable Feast*. I made up my mind because I knew he wanted to publish it fairly soon and because Malcolm Cowley, the prominent critic, suggested I shouldn't wait too long. There remains another novel, maybe two. I mean *A Dangerous Summer* and one set in the Caribbean. Then there are many short stories. The next to appear will almost certainly be the one set in the Caribbean. I am working on it with the publishers. Of course I ask their advice, also that of Ernest's friends, especially on the cuts he would have made. Before handing over his work to the publishers, Ernest used to delete far more than he added —at the second reading, too. I know it because I used to copy out all his work, whether he wrote it by hand or typed. Yes, sometimes there were pages almost untouched, sometimes instead pages full of corrections. He corrected by hand, in that rounded handwriting of his. You have seen it.

There is a story, Miss Mary, on the way you regained possession of those manuscripts, a story that has never been told before.

Yes. Shortly after Ernest's death, let us say very shortly after, I had a phone call in Ketchum from the Cuban government asking me whether I would consent to donate our home in Cuba as a museum. In exchange I would be allowed to remove all the papers from the Bank and my personal belongings. I accepted. At the time I was so grief-stricken I didn't care about giving up the house; once the real essence of life is lost, what do objects matter? Besides, what I really cared for was to regain the manuscripts; they could take all the rest. The rest was all there: we had left without packing a thing, even a pile of unopened letters. We wanted to be back before winter, and this is what we were going to do when Ernest got sick with the sickness that killed him—I mean, that made him kill himself. We had left to go to Ketchum in July, 1960. We wanted to stay there for a while, then go shooting in the north, then go back to Cuba. . . . I returned to Cuba alone, after that phone call, to hand over the house in exchange for those forty pounds of precious papers. I also took a few personal things, my jewelry, the little I have ever owned, two paintings, twenty-five books, not many if you consider how large our library was; Ernest used to receive in Cuba all the newly published books. Finally I took all the letters and the jotted-down notes. Ernest never threw away a letter or any bit of written paper. In 1938, when we moved from Key West to Cuba, he carted along a roomful of notes and mail. I shall donate those papers to the Kennedy Library when it opens. This, briefly, is the story behind the manuscripts. Of course, I wouldn't have obtained a thing if Fidel himself hadn't intervened. But that's something I'll write myself.

Pity. But tell me, Miss Mary, did Hemingway and Fidel Castro know each other?

They met only once, at a fishing competition that Ernest had started years before. Fidel entered this time and won; he caught the most fish. And since it was Ernest who distributed the prizes, he found himself awarding one to Fidel. They didn't talk much together, eight or ten minutes, let's say. And I cannot repeat the exact words because although I know Spanish, I didn't understand all. When he is not making political speeches, Fidel's voice is soft and low, and Ernest's voice too was soft and low. However, I remember they talked all the time about fishing: rods and hooks and the best weather to catch this and that. . . . I also remember that Fidel kept protesting he wasn't a great fisherman, he had just been lucky this time. After that they never met again, but I know they liked each other—a reciprocal respect. Fidel once said that he had learned his guerrilla tactics from the Spanish translation of *For Whom the Bell Tolls*, and I once found a postcard on which Ernest had written: "The Cuban revolution was a historical necessity." The revolution didn't change our life in Cuba, partly because nobody could accuse us of exploiting the people: we always spent so much money there. . . . No, I am not sorry to have given up the house, the only thing I am really unhappy about is that they have put our boat "Pilar" on land, in the middle of the Finca. A boat must live on the water, not on land. She'll die, grounded like that, even if Gregorio watches her well. Gregorio was our sailor, now he looks after the museum. How I would like to see him again. I would like to see them all again: the people of La Floridita and the fishermen who used to tell us stories when we went to La Floridita. . . .

This may sound unpleasant, but I must tell you, Miss Mary. Years ago a rumor was going around in Europe, and it said that the adventure of The Old Man and the Sea *had really happened to a fisherman who told it to Hemingway in exchange for a boat. But, according to the rumor, Hemingway never bought him the boat.*

Yes, I know. But do you really think Ernest spent his time swapping boats for stories? Ernest and I always heard similar stories. There isn't a fisherman in Cuba who hasn't his own personal epic of a struggle with an outsize fish to relate. And when the book appeared, each of them thought it was his own story retold. Some time ago I had a call from Miami, the Immigration Office, I think. "Do you know anyone called Anselmo?" they asked. "Yes, I do know an Anselmo. An old man of ninety-six, a good boy," I answered. "Well, he has left Cuba, and he wants to enter America, and he's telling everybody he's the old man of the book." "If it makes him happy to believe it, don't disappoint him," I said. But the rumor you mentioned had someone else at its center. I don't remember his name, but I know he had given the news to a Havana newspaper for a few dollars, ten or so. When they heard about it, the other fishermen brought him to our house and made him eat his words in front of a tape recorder. I still have the tape. "Come on," they said, "if that's your story, tell it again. We want to hear when you told Papa that story, and where, and how." And he admitted the fabrication.

I wonder, Miss Mary, if Hemingway ever saw the movie based on The Old Man and the Sea.

Don't let us speak about movies based on Ernest's books. Of all of them there was only one that he liked, based on a short story, *The Killers,* with Burt Lancaster and Ava Gardner. The others . . . you know, very often he wouldn't even go to see them; he would send me instead. For instance, he sent me to *A Farewell to Arms,* yes, with that actress, what's her name, Jennifer Jones. Sooner or later they all reached Cuba, and each time he refused to see them. But he saw *The Sun Also Rises,* this time we went to see it together. Well . . . Ernest couldn't understand why they had shot it in Mexico instead of Spain. The bulls were as small as this coffee table, and there wasn't a single Spanish-looking face. Ernest, such a stickler for precision, kept on repeating, "Look at those faces. Do they look Spanish, do they?" When these things happened, he used to leave in such a temper. He would say, "Let's go and have a drink to forget that f . . ." As for *The Old Man and the Sea,* one cannot say that Mr. Tracy looks like a hungry Cuban fisherman. Mr. Tracy had promised to slim a bit, but he didn't. And the picture itself . . . Ernest had even given Viertel some help with the parts concerning fishing; Viertel, who wrote the script, knew nothing about fishing. I mean he helped with advice, not writing; Ernest never agreed to work on the movie. He liked writing books, only books. He often quoted a passage from Cyril Connolly: "All excursions into journalism, broadcasting, propaganda and writing for the films, however grandiose, are doomed to disappointment. To put of our best into these forms is another folly, since thereby we condemn good ideas, as well as bad, to oblivion. It is in the nature of such work not to last, so it should never be undertaken. . . ."

And yet, he had been a journalist, too. So had you. Weren't you both working for magazines when you first met?

Yes. In 1944 in London. I was working for the *Time-Life-*

Fortune group, Ernest was working for *Collier's*. We were both war correspondents. Friends introduced us in a restaurant, the day before the Normandy landings. I liked him at once because I found him amusing, but I cannot truthfully say it was love at first sight for me. Not so Ernest; seven days later he asked me to marry him—in front of everybody: "I want you to marry me, so I'm offering myself in marriage." I answered, "Don't be silly." We hardly knew each other, and I even wondered whether he was joking. He wasn't. He was such an impulsive man. He knew that I was married; he was married, too. We both got divorced, and we were married eighteen months later. But of course we were together all the time during those eighteen months, in London and then Paris. Ernest went there ahead, he entered Paris with the Allies. I joined him a few days later and stayed there to write about French politics.

I have always wondered, Miss Mary, about the frightening complex that could develop from being a journalist, a woman who writes, and a person married to a great writer. It is no surprise that you gave up your career when you married him.

Let's say I changed my job; being Ernest's wife was such a full-time job. Of course, I hesitated before deciding to marry him; I loved my profession. But once I made up my mind I felt no regrets, though my new life was so different and quiet in comparison with the turbulent one I used to lead. In Cuba, you know, we lived very simply: very few dinners, very few parties, and from time to time a long journey. Africa, Italy, Spain, Peru. No, the complex you mention I never developed. Once in a while I still wrote for magazines, it helped me to escape from the daily routine of housekeeping. Ernest approved, he liked my writing. Of course, he also liked a wife who was a wife before anything else, but I *was* that kind of wife —which is fairly rare in America. You see, here wives are so seldom gentle with their husbands, so rarely admiring. All their stupid talks on equality! Equality, what does it mean? What's the use for it? I've said it before, and I'll always repeat it: women are second-class citizens, and not only biologically. A female's first duty is to bear children and rear them; with the exception of a few freshwater fish, all animals follow this basic rule. Usually I don't like women, I admit it. I always feel like shouting at them, "Go and do something. Have success in something instead of talking and talking about equality!" Equality! I didn't want to be Ernest's equal, I wanted him to be the master, to be stronger and cleverer than I, to remember constantly how big he was and how small I was. . . . I know I don't look very feminine: no makeup, always slacks. . . . But I am feminine, and he knew it. I got used to slacks because he preferred them. Well, to be exact, what he really preferred was shorts. "Shorts and shirt," he used to say, "that's how I like you." And I obeyed.

What about him, Miss Mary? How did he look at women? How did he like them? How did he behave with them?

Ernest was a real male, and in women he looked first of all for a beautiful face, shapely legs, rounded bosom. I mean, to the things that could give him pleasure. I don't believe Ernest gave one minute of his attention to woman's equality and women who speak of woman's equality. Yet he was difficult to please; physical beauty wasn't enough for him. When asked what he liked in women, he said that a woman should have personality, strength, courage, common sense, wit, wisdom, and the ability to hold a conversation. . . . In other words, he liked beautiful women, but they never lasted long in his interest if they were brainless and couldn't understand what he spoke about. I remember in Paris, one day, oh, she was really a fantastically beautiful girl. Ernest had asked her out to lunch, and he was very excited, so I said to him, "Why don't you go alone? You'll enjoy yourself much more." He went off alone, and after lunch he came back. I was writing a letter. I looked up and murmured, "I hope you had a nice time, Papa." He answered, "What hell kind of enjoyment might one find with such a nitwit?"

Were you jealous, Miss Mary?

Seldom, very seldom. What use is there in being jealous with such a man? Besides being talented and famous, he was so attractive, so handsome. With Ernest, at the most, you could say to yourself, "Gosh, I wish he were not so happy, so excited, when he looks at that girl." Jealousy is a waste of time with men. If a man doesn't feel free, he will shake himself free. You see, Ernest didn't know what jealousy means; he took it as a compliment that people should look at his wife and admire her. Maybe it was because he knew he ran no risks, I was so devoted to him. And how could I have been otherwise? I had everything, in every sense. He was quite a husband, quite a man, that man Hemingway. Of course we quarreled sometimes. We'd begin with a mere discussion on some little ridiculous thing and end by shouting, then sulking. But it never lasted more than half an hour, never. During that half an hour he would call me Mary instead of Miss Mary, and I would call him Ernest instead of Papa; nothing more. I used to call him Papa, he hated anyone to call him Ernest. He considered it a bourgeois name, stupid, expressionless, and without imagination. I don't know if you follow me. Ernest in English is pronounced more or less like "earnest," and "earnest" means steady, conscientious, zealous: attributes he would never apply to people he liked. Neither would I. An earnest man sounds so straitlaced, buttoned, mealy-mouthed. You suppose him pious, never damned. Yet, since he is dead, I call him Ernest. I cannot call him Papa.

And apart from those quarrels, how was your life in Cuba? I cannot imagine, Miss Mary, a quiet Hemingway going fishing and writing at fixed hours.

And instead that was just what it was like, during all the seventeen years that we lived together. If he wasn't writing, which happened rarely, he went fishing or swimming in the pool. He would swim half a mile at one go, and he got cross because I could swim a mile. After the swim we'd lunch. He was a gourmet, not a gourmand; I mean, he liked food, but he didn't eat much. He got more of his nourishment from drinking: at lunch there were always two bottles of wine on the table, one for him and one for me. After lunch he used to read. He would read four or five books at the same time, and he read in English, in Spanish, in Italian, in French. I don't know if you follow me: he would read a chapter or two on fishing, for instance, then a chapter or two of a novel, then a chapter or two of a history book, let's say the American Civil War. He liked to read thrillers, too, one of his favorite authors was Georges Simenon. He always said, "That man really can write!" Ah! He was such a reader! He could read even in the boat when we were out fishing. And when we went on that safari in Africa, he took fifty books with him. He practically never stopped reading, except when he was shooting. And then he used to read in bed after dinner. He went to bed very early, sometimes immediately after dinner. And in bed, when I joined him, we used to read poetry out loud. I read it to him, or he read it to me. He liked poetry, and he liked to read it out loud. He liked music, too, and he listened to it a lot. We had a fine collection of records in Cuba: Bach, Beethoven, Debussy, and jazz, too— he liked New Orleans jazz and Fats Waller. It was such a quiet life. Many people came to see him, sometimes too many at a time, and then he would complain because his work was interrupted. Or because they were idiots. More often, however, he was pleased to see them. He was so sociable, the type of man who enjoys staying with people, and each time he took them for drinks to La Floridita, where he had a good laugh. He didn't get cross even when they followed it up by asking which of the books he had written he liked best. He answered: *"All Quiet on the Western Front"*—Remarque's book.

And the visit of Mikoyan? Didn't Mikoyan come once?

Yes, he had been visiting Fidel Castro, and he called to ask if he could come. Ernest said yes, certainly. So he came, and most of all he wanted to tell Ernest there was a sum in the Russian State Bank, from his Russian copyrights, equivalent to one hundred and fifty thousand dollars in rubles. "The Russians have been reading you for years," said Mikoyan. Then he added that they were studying how to manage to convert the rubles into dollars and pay them in America, although this was against the law. In socialist countries, you know, an author's copyright fees cannot be transferred and must be spent on the spot. "I hope that very soon you'll be able to receive ten thousand dollars a year," Mikoyan added. And Ernest gave him such a chic answer. Oh, very chic! He said, "I'll be happy to accept when you grant the same treatment to all American writers." After Ernest's death I asked for that money, or rather I proposed going there to spend it. But they answered that the sum credited to Ernest could not be credited to his widow, and that there were only three thousand out of the one hundred and fifty thousand. Pity, I liked the idea of going to Russia. Ernest always refused to go there. I never understood why, I still wonder. Maybe because of the language he didn't know and because he was so uninterested in politics. Among the wide circle of his acquaintances I cannot recall a single politician. In any case, now he is dead, what do I care about Russia?

You are very lonely, aren't you, Miss Mary?

Totally lonely. My husband's sons are scattered around the world—one in Africa, one in Miami, one in San Francisco—and I never had any children of my own. . . . How sad not to have been able to bring a miniature Ernest into this world. I longed so much for a child. And so did he. In 1946, a year after we were married, I became pregnant. Ernest was so happy, he hoped it would be a girl. He had always wanted a daughter. But the child was never born, we lost it during a trip to Wyoming. The greatest loss in my life, except the death of Ernest. Yes, I am alone. Alone with attorneys, publishers, lawyers, alone with the responsibility of Ernest's books, alone with my loneliness. To fill my days, I have started writing one, too: a sort of autobiography, the story of a woman born in north

Minnesota; a girl who chooses a newspaper work and goes to
Chicago, then to London for the *Daily Express*, then to Paris,
then to London again; there she meets Ernest Hemingway and
marries him; she settles with him in Cuba. . . . I write without
worrying about chronology, up to now I have put down forty
thousand words on our African safari. The next work will be
Ernest's return to Spain. After the Civil War he would not go
back, saying he would do so when all his friends in prison had
been set free. In 1953 all his friends had been freed, so he went
back there. He made new friends on that occasion: Ordoñez,
for instance. Ernest admired his peasant wisdom, his courage.
Ernest sought wisdom and courage wherever he went.

*Have you ever thought of marrying again, Miss Mary? Do
you feel you could?*

I don't think so. First of all, where would I find a man like
Ernest? Life with anyone else would be nothing but endless
comparison. Besides, who would like to have a wife who spends
most of her time putting her previous husband's papers in
order, seeing to the publishing of his books, writing about him,
talking continuously of him? Mine is a different destiny, but I
don't weep. I don't. Only that first morning I wept, when I
found him, and I couldn't get over, and . . . no more. Tears
are nothing but self-pity, and self-pity is a waste of time.

Durable Miss Mary, so Hemingway wrote.

Do you know what he meant by durable?

Yes, I think so. Resistant, lasting. . . .

Durable means something that lasts because it wants to last,
not because it was built to last. A scrap of iron exposed to the
wind and the rain and the sun is not durable because it needs
no effort to be so. But a spider's web is durable. It looks so
frail, but it resists the fiercest storms and winds and rains. . . .
In the garden of our house in Cuba there were always lots of
spiders' webs, and one obviously thinks they'll be swept away
by every storm. Tropical storms are ruthless in their violence,
they destroy trees and roads and houses. But they don't destroy

spiders' webs. Spiders' webs wave in the wind, letting the rain-drops through their mesh, and when the storm is over one always finds them in the same place, practically untouched.

New York, March, 1966

DEAN MARTIN

A Very Happy Man

He is probably one of the most complicated men Americans have
ever fallen in love with, and the extraordinary fact is that they
don't know it. They think he's simple, elementary, easy. They
identify him with the image of the happy citizen who has everything that represents paradise on earth: a handsome body, a beautiful wife, seven children, two grandchildren, an expensive house
with a swimming pool and a tennis court, money in the bank,
worldwide popularity. They see him as a very fine person touched
only by a few glamorous faults—the reputation of a drinker, a
woman chaser, a swinger—and nobody will say a word against
him. Many will portray him as a combination of Humphrey Bogart and Cary Grant—generous, gentle—what each of us would
like to be at one time or another of his life. They say: Maybe
there is something wrong about him secretly, but I have never
seen it, and I've never found a guy that I liked better. It's all true,
but that is not all, because he is much more—and much less. For
instance, he is not a drinker at all, not a swinger, and infinitely
more interesting than they believe. So be careful when you lift the
lid of the pot and look at what boils inside. The unexpected ingredients might confuse a bit. The man is a dilemma.

Says Jeannie, his wife for nineteen years: "I don't know him.
The important thing to say about my husband is that I don't
understand him. Nobody can; there is something in him that is
unreachable. You might find occasions when you think he's reach-
able, but the procedure is so painful that you get tired of trying
and give up. I couldn't even tell you why he married me. I suppose
it was because of my blue-eyed-blond college-girl look, I was the
symbol of something he thought he wouldn't get. All I can tell you
is that he took me home, and he put me in a shell without realizing
that I was proud to be Mrs. Dean Martin, but I wasn't about to
give up being Jeanne Martin. He's bossy. It has been tough. There

159

have been battles. At times, I've tried to skip from him, only to find out that I am happiest with him, that I love him as the first day. He is 100 per cent man. I am not supposed to be an authority on men, I am an amateur student, yet I adore all men between eight and eighty years old, and Dean Martin covers the range between eight- and eighty-year-old men."

What unexpected ingredients make up this man who sometimes is eight years old, sometimes eighty, and, according to his birthdate, fifty?

First of all, there is his aloofness, his shyness, particularly in front of women. "Oh, he does, he does intimidate me," Jeannie says. "I can't be at my best with him, I can't shine. With him, I feel as you feel when a man you madly admire pats you on the head and kisses you on the forehead. He's a man of few words, but with women he's a man of no words. You see, he never made me doubt his fidelity. I don't believe there is a woman of twenty who can take him from me. He doesn't care to stay with women. And my opinion is that he doesn't have a tremendous amount of respect for them, he's too much of a man's man."

Barbara Rush, one of his few women friends, says: "I think Dean hasn't much to say to a woman. I think a woman to him is soft and cuddly and pink, and he hasn't much time to waste on them. As for the modern aggressive woman, he doesn't even recognize her. I would be very surprised to hear about any adventures of Dean because I've seen many women in love with Dean, you have no idea how many, and he's always behaved with great kindness toward them, great patience, but also with a sort of detachment and maybe embarrassment. They simply aren't very attractive to him. He prefers men because he can talk with them, play cards, box, and say rough words."

Second, his vulnerability and goodness. He's only apparently rugged, imperturbable. Inside his heart and mind he is a knot of uncertainties, amazements, and confusions; he's being strangled by them. A wrong word, a wrong gesture can wound him forever. He hasn't yet forgotten the humiliation he suffered when he was rejected as a Dago or overshadowed by Jerry Lewis. And the scars are still there, very visible, easily inflamed. Would you expect this champion of calm to have an ulcer? Well, he has one, and he got it,

I'm convinced, because he hasn't yet realized that evil is normal on this planet and that most people don't share his capability for love. He would give his life for a friend. Look how devoted he is to Frank Sinatra, look how he was with Montgomery Clift when they did *The Young Lions*. He took care of him as a father takes care of his child, he defended him with his teeth. He's a man who can cry without feeling ashamed. He is also a real Christian, though not very well trained to wear crosses.

Third, his lack of curiosity and vivacity. His passions are all beneath this surface. Excitement and novelties don't thrill him.

"Dean isn't unpredictable," says Jeannie. "He's very predictable. He has made a pattern of his future, and he follows it stubbornly, with a total lack of curiosity. His eyes get darker when he's interested, but they get darker so rarely. He can talk on a subject, but talking and caring are two different things. What he sincerely cares for, after his work, is golf. Golf is his real, honest love. He plays it every single morning, for hours, for years, with the same three men: two are real estate men, one is in automobiles. Why this golf thing, I don't know. He's an athlete, all right. While playing golf, he can stay with men in the open air, all right. But the deepest reason, I believe, is that he doesn't enjoy other things very much. He doesn't read, he prefers television and watches it constantly until the late late show. The less provocative the program, the better."

Her judgment seems rather severe, but many confirm it. A couple of his friends have told me that the abstract doesn't excite him, only reality: what is here and now. In a peculiar way, you would guess that he isn't terribly ambitious; the most he wants is to be relaxed. Consider two more of Barbara's observations: "It's revealing that Dean plays golf, because golf takes a great deal of patience. . . ." "People are constantly discovering Dean. Did-you-see-Dean-in-that-picture? Isn't it extraordinary? they say. The fact is that Dean never acts as someone who's able to do things, so they're surprised to see that he is able to do things."

And finally, his Italianism. To define an Italian is as impossible as to define an American. But should I be forced to give a face and a soul to the Italian of the common people as he has been produced by centuries of foreign occupation, Catholicism, hard work, little bread, and blind traditions, I would choose the face and the soul of Dino Crocetti, alias Dean Martin, when he speaks his bad English and waves his ugly-beautiful peasant hands. Such a type reflects a noble cliché: the man with his feet on the earth, yet sentimental; with no cultural curiosity, yet much knowledge in his blood; respecter of men, not of women, yet most respectful of his wife and mother; individualistic; secretly nationalistic; above all, very practical and profoundly wise. For instance, send him to war. Once there, he will fight like a lion, he will die as a hero. But to avoid such an inconsiderate end, he will devise any stratagem.

Like that cliché of the common Italian, he does not enjoy politics. When he reads the newspapers, he goes straight to the sports page. His family is sacred to him in an old-fashioned way. At home, he's the master. Parents are something never to be abandoned, always to be protected when they are old. Children must obey. Besides, he's religious. He believes that the good will go to paradise with the angels, and the evil will go to hell with devils. He accepts legal authorities. He doesn't trust progress, machinery, automation. He trusts sophistication even less, whether it is intellectual or social or aesthetic. Happiness for him means avoiding boring complications, then aging in comfort earned through a success that was to him a continuous surprise. And wherever he might go with his dreams, with his changes, he will always belong—naïvely, proudly, courageously—to the land his parents came from. I even wonder if Dino Crocetti, alias Dean Martin, spoke so much with me, and so openly, because I am Italian and began our conversation as I did.

ORIANA FALLACI: *You know, Dino, I feel sort of strange speaking English with you because I cannot help seeing you as an Italian.*

DEAN MARTIN: Well, until I was five years old, all I spoke was Italian. Then I went to school and was on the road a lot, and I forgot it till I came out here and met people like Frank Sinatra and Vic Damone and Nicky Conte. And kiddingly we would start talkin' Italian 'cause we didn't want others to listen to what we were talkin' about. I also used to get into conversations with Sinatra's father, who spoke Italian all the time with my father. They got together, and I was sittin' with them. But mine isn't really Italian. It's a dialect from Abruzzi, and I speak it badly. I don't speak good English, either. When Jerry Lewis and I were big, we used to go to parties, and everybody thought I was big-headed and stuck up, and I wasn't. It was just 'cause I didn't know how to speak good English, so I used to keep my mouth shut. I used to say "ain't" all the time, and "dese" and "dems," and I didn't know how to hold a conversation. Now, I've reverted to "dese" and "dems" on TV, and I'm a big hit 'cause I talk bad English. Yeah, it's a crazy world.

Do you feel Italian, Dino, or don't you?

I tell you how much I feel Italian. Three years ago, on my birthday, Frank and I were at the Polo Lounge over here. We were with six other people, mindin' our business, and we were a little loud. When we were goin' out the door, there is a couple of guys, and one of 'em says, "There goes the two loud Dagos." Well, Frank got there one split second ahead of me, and he hit one guy, I hit the other, and we picked 'em up and threw 'em against the wall. The cops came. We said we didn't know who did it and walked out. But we did, yeah. And I did, another time. When my father talked broken English, a couple of people said somethin'. I picked 'em right up off the floor and said,

"You aren't gonna say somethin' about a guy who can't talk English well 'cause he's been a barber all his life on thirty dollars a week." When it happens, I just hit 'em and throw 'em out, wherever I am. In the past, I've been rejected a lot by prominent people who say, "Well, he's Italian." But I always would punch the guy right in the mouth for this. Even when I was workin' onstage, and somebody would say Dago or greaseball, I would jump right on the table—which is why I couldn't get a lot of jobs: they'd say, "He's a hotheaded Italian." The only one who can call me Dago is Frank. I call him Dago, too. With anybody else, there's a fight, 'cause I never call anybody Chinaman or Jew, so why should they call that to me?

Do you mean you have been humiliated for this, Dino?

Sure! Many times! Oh, it still happens, 'cause everybody knows the Mafia is Italian. I hate to go into that, but it's the truth. Anytime somethin' happens, they blame it on the Mafia even if the Mafia had nothin' to do. So I get angry. 'Cause I'm proud to be Italian, very. I love every bit of bein' Italian, and I don't think of the Mafia; I think of Christopher Columbus, and Michelangelo, and Marconi, and Toscanini, and Fermi, and all those great people who gave much to my country, America. Italians are so talented. Just take the singers here; 90 per cent are Italian. Take Tony Bennett, Frankie Avalon, Frankie Laine, Perry Como, and Mario Lanza, rest in peace, and Vic and Frank. 'Cause they sing from here, from the heart, the stomach, not the throat. Anybody can sing from the throat, but then you just say words. And then, when I get angry with those who talk about the Mafia, I think of my father, who came all alone from Abruzzi to Steubenville, Ohio, to find his brother and his hope. He was so young, nineteen or so, and he didn't even know his brother's address. And he was just walkin' down the street, and he recognized Joe, and he said, "Are you Joe, *tu sei Giuseppe?*" And Joe said, "Yes, *sì*. Are you Gaetano, *tu sei Gaetano?*" And he said "Yes, *sì*, I am Gaetano, I am your brother."

Dino, what do you think about the American Italian Anti-Defamation League?

I don't know what to say. I'm not in politics like Frank. I don't attach too much to that, I confess. The best anti-defamation for me is my father. See, these emigrated Italians were not skilled workers like pharmacists or lawyers, but they knew how to work hard. My father did, too. He worked hard as a barber, and he got his own barbershop, and then a beauty salon, and so he gave us a beautiful home, and a car, and good food, and good Christmases, and we never were poor, my brother and I. 'Cause my Pop had guts. My Mom, too. She was Italian, too. Her name was Angela Barra, and think of the guts she had. She was in a convent. She met my father and fell in love at first sight. She left the convent, and she married him two weeks later. He couldn't speak English, and she couldn't speak Italian 'cause she was born in New Cumberland, West Virginia. They just died, you know? Six months apart, this year. First, Mom. She got that bone thing, and she got smaller and smaller, and she said, laughin,' "I'm gonna whip this thing if it kills me, Dino." Then my father. It was his heart, and, also, he was takin' pills because of Mom's death. What a terrible blow. You know? The two of 'em. Almost together. And I loved 'em so. I had got 'em a beautiful house in Inglewood, and I got 'em everythin' they wanted in the world. My mother had diamonds, a fur coat. My father had a car and money. And you give 'em all this, and they die. Oh, they always wanted what I wanted.

What did you want, Dino?

Simple: to come to California and to make movies. Oh, yeah! I knew someday I would get here, though I didn't know how. And my aunts, they said to my Mom and Pop, "Your son's gonna be a gangster. He's gonna die in the electric chair." And my Mom said, "You're crazy. My son's gonna be a star." She knew, and I knew. When a Bing Crosby movie ever came to Steubenville, I would stay there all day and watch. And that's how I learned to sing, 'cause it's true I don't read a note. I don't.

I learned from Crosby, and so did Sinatra and Perry Como. We all started imitatin' him; he was the teacher for all of us. See, when I was a croupier, there was a café called Walker's Café. And every night after work, I used to go there and sing a song like Bing Crosby. It was for singin' that I quit school and worked in a gas station. Then I became a boxer.

Did you ever regret quitting school?

Never. You can learn a lot more doin' the life that I did than sittin' at a desk. I mean, I wouldn't say to the children, "Stop school." But for me, it was good. I liked boxin'. Wanna see some scars from fightin'? See this cut here on the lip? And these over the eyebrows? The teeth were pushed in. That's why I wear caps now. My nose was flat from fightin'. Everybody says, "He had his nose fixed." No, I had my nose straightened; it's different. And all my fingers are broken from fightin', see. Look. . . . Well, they aren't very nice. I mean, I don't look so good when you look at me. But I don't care now.

You look as a man must look. Dino, what else could you be if you hadn't become a singer, an actor, a performer?

I'd be a croupier. What else could I be? I don't know anythin' else, and I loved bein' a croupier. More than a boxer. See, Steubenville was a small town of steel mills and coal mines, but it was called Little Reno at that time. Every corner had a gamblin' house. You could walk down the street and see the crap tables, the roulette wheels. I sold cigars and cigarettes in the poolroom, and I went in the back to practice with the chips, the cards, and so they let me become a dealer though I was sixteen. I was tall and strong and looked twenty. And I talked to my Mom and Pop and said, "I'm not a gambler, Mom and Pop. I deal, I work." Then I brought 'em down to see me, and they let me do it. And about twenty-three or so, I was a damn good dealer. 'Cause I never cheated, never.

But you also like to gamble, don't you?

Oh, yeah! 'Cause I know how to gamble. It's complicated, but I know how to do it, and I will not be *taken*. I will never be cheated, 'cause I know how to cheat, though I don't. And I know how to win more times than I lose. You listen to me: the only way you can win is to take your money and leave. The only way. And whenever I lost, I would leave. Once you lose, you seldom win it back. You gotta leave and come back. You gotta leave and come back another day. Do you like Vegas? I love Vegas. But I stopped gamblin'. Just stopped. One day, like that. Two years ago, I walked into a casino, and I wanted to play a little blackjack, and there were mobs of people, and they started runnin' over for autographs, and I lost the desire to gamble. Besides, gamblin' meant money to me, and I don't need money anymore. Of course, you know that I didn't always have it like this. When I left Steubenville and went to work with an orchestra in Cleveland, I made maybe forty or fifty a week. And I had two children. And I had to work in a gas station in the afternoon to pay bills. And then I had three children to take care of, and then four. I was very poor. When I went to New York to get a job in a nightclub, I couldn't get it, and I had to drive a cab.

Is that the reason you hate New York?

Yeah. I starved in New York, and I was humiliated, and I hated every moment of it, and I never go back to New York. Last time, I was forced to go back for that golf award. I arrived in the afternoon, and I left in the night. Straight back to Los Angeles, without sleepin'. You don't live in New York, you exist. Nobody helps you in New York, you don't get a hello in New York. Besides, New York's full of elevators, and I hate elevators, a physical fear. Each time I take an elevator, I get stuck. Once in Cincinnati, Frank said, "Come on, it will not happen." I went, and it happened. I'm like an idiot in an elevator. Especially those where you push the button, no elevator boy. You are like in a casket. I don't believe in elevators. I don't even believe in television. And those rockets, oh! Do you believe these guys gonna go to the moon? What for? I don't like it.

What else are you afraid of, apart from elevators?

Nothin' else. The war, perhaps; I hate it. But the elevators are worse. Success kills fears. Even the fear of dyin'. I'm not afraid to die. If the Good Lord up there says I'm gonna die, well, I'm gonna die.

Do you believe in God that much, Dino?

Oh! So very much! Oh! Every night—I still have never missed a night without prayin'. And I have my Saint Christopher, and when I get on the airline, I cross myself and pray to Him. I don't get on my knees, I pray in bed. Oh, yes, I believe in God. I don't understand too many things. For example, when a baby comes from a lady, who's gonna make this thing with the ears and the nose and the mouth and the eyes? Who? God does. And when people die, what do they say? "God help me," they say. 'Cause who they gonna turn to? To Henry Ford? Naw, they're gonna turn to God. He's the one who put 'em here and takes 'em away. See, I'm a Catholic, like everybody in this family. And I care about it, though I go to church only when I feel like goin'. I remember when President Kennedy, rest in peace, was shot. I ran to my car, and I went down to church, and I lit a candle at the altar, and I prayed. And I said to God, "Please, don't let him die." You know, sometimes I say to myself, "You don't go to church on Sunday. You only go when you need things. What are you? A sort of hypocrite?" But when your mother dies, and your father dies, or a friend dies, what do you do if not pray?

Is a friend as important to you as one of your parents, Dino?

Oh, yeah, sure! You can always find money, but you cannot find a friend very easily, right? For example, Frank's my friend. Some time ago, he called and said he had a bad throat. I say, "I'll be right there." Got an airplane, did two shows for him. Then I flew right back, very happy. Three days later, he calls me again and says, "My throat is gone again." I flew back and did two more shows, very happy. Oh, there was another friend very dear to me: Montgomery Clift, rest in peace. I did *The Young Lions* with him, and nobody wanted him around, nobody would eat with him. So I took him to dinner, or I would have a drink with him, or I would put him to bed 'cause he was always on pills, you know. He was such a sad, sad man, and he was like a boy, so unhappy and rejected, and so I'd say, "If you don't want him, you don't want me." And we'd leave the party. But first I'd spit in their faces for him.

You don't feel that strongly about women, do you, Dino? I mean, you respect men more than women, don't you?

Oh, yeah! I mean, I also have some women friends. Ursula Andress, for instance, and Shirley MacLaine and Barbara Rush. What a lovely lady, Barbara. Nothin' fake, nothin' put-on like high-class, etc. But apart from these ladies, I'm more relaxed with men—with Frank, with Vic Damone, Nicky Conte, Tony Bennett, Henry Silver, all Italians—'cause men are down-to-earth and more honest, and I can get a repartee with them, have fun. Women instead are crazy, crazy, crazy, and they're flighty, and they are always lookin' for somethin', and they always tell you how good they are. And I don't want to hear how good they are, as I don't want to talk shop. I mean movies.

Let's talk shop, Dino. I mean your work. It's all your life, isn't it?

Oh, I enjoy it so much because it's so easy for me, so spontaneous. I mean, bein' an actor. For me, it is like singin'. I do it with my body, my heart. Why do you think I split with Jerry? 'Cause I was doin' nothin', and I was eatin' my heart out. I sang a song and never got to finish the song. The camera would go over him doin' funny things, then it would come back to me when I'd finished. Everythin' was Jerry Lewis, Jerry Lewis, and I was a straight man. I was an idiot in every picture. And I was makin' a lot of money, you know, but money isn't all, is it, and I knew I could do so much better. And I proved it. Not to the public, not to the country or the world. To myself, to my wife. When I said to Jeannie, "I quit with Jerry," she said, "Wow." And she gave me the biggest kiss I ever had. And the lawyers said, "You can't break this team up." And I said,

"Oh, yes, I can. Watch me." And my own lawyer said, "You're crazy." And I said, "Yeah, but I'm walkin' out, I'm through." And Jerry calls me and says, "Let's go on." And I say, "You go to . . . you . . ." And I hang up. And everybody says, "Oh, that poor Martin, he's gonna die." And for the first year, I did die. Then my friend Frank gave me the role in *Some Came Running*. Two of the greatest turnin' points in my career were: first, meetin' Jerry Lewis; second, leavin' Jerry Lewis. I became a real actor because of these two things. And for me, it isn't work, it is fun. Honestly. I don't understand these movie actors who come home and say they're so tired, it has been such a tough day. What's so tough? They do a scene, and if it isn't right, they do it again. And they give you a seat to sit on if you're tired after one minute of work. What's so hard? Workin' in the steel mills is hard. Standin' on your feet for eight hours as a croupier is hard. Gas station was hard, and boxin', and cab-drivin'. This isn't hard. And it gives much money. You know I've signed the N.B.C. contract for thirty-four millions. God! I am not worth it. What do I do? I do an hour. And out of that hour, I sing maybe ten songs. The rest, I talk. And I make fun of my wife, of my children, of my mother-in-law, of myself, of my drinkin'. People love to hear about my drinkin' or to think that I'm drunk. Like with Phil Harris. In fact, every time there is a joke on TV about drinkin', you may be sure that the name of the drinker is gonna be either Dean Martin or Phil Harris.

Once and forever, Dino, are you that much of a drinker?

I swear I am not. I swear this is my first drink, and it's now eight o'clock in the evenin'. I'll have one more, or two more, then I'll eat dinner and go to sleep. The image is there because when I was with Jerry and I was so unhappy, yes, I used to drink. There was nothin' to do but drink, and I drank, gettin' drunk at times. But no one has ever seen me drunk. I've never been picked up by the cops, as many actors have. I could name you a dozen. You know, these all-American boys who drink like hell, those liars, and are picked up by the cops, but their names never get to the papers. If I had been picked up, be sure, right away it would have been in the paper. Yet they think I am a drunk, and who cares? There's nothin' wrong with drinkin', and I'm not sayin' I don't drink. I love to drink a little. And to make fun of it. 'Cause I'm a very happy man.

And a very lucky one.

Oh, yeah! I have been lucky through my whole life. I never had to kill anybody. I was inducted, and for fourteen months I never left a place called Akron, Ohio, 'cause I got a hernia. I have seven children that I am so proud of. I'm a grandfather at fifty. And I found Jeannie, such a wife. She took my four children from my previous marriage, and she won 'em over, and she was so young. They call her Mom, you know. And we had three others, but she loved 'em like my four. Isn't that fabulous? After my divorce, the court eventually gave me the children, and I think it was the first time in California that a man got the children. 'Cause Good Lord knows that I never did any wrong, and I deserved 'em. But what luck that my Jeannie was there and was such a fine lady. My Jeannie and her blue eyes. I call 'em nazi eyes. Thanks to them, I don't even care givin' my ex-wife twenty-four hundred dollars a month for eighteen years.

You're a grandfather. But how do you keep so young?

Oh, I could give a hundred reasons. That I love life. I think young. I do funny things with kids, like rollin' around the floor with 'em, and they hit me and I hit 'em back. That I take care of myself. Want to see my bathroom? I got a rowboat there. I do two hundred strokes a day. Then I could tell you that unless I work in Vegas, I'm in bed at ten o'clock, and I never go out, maybe party once a month, at home at midnight. Three years ago Jeannie and I had a party on our anniversary, here at home. At midnight I went upstairs and called the police. I said, "I'm a neighbor of the Martins. Will you tell 'em to hold that band down." So they came and stopped the band, and Jeannie came runnin', "Hey, Dino, the cops are here. Some neighbor wants

to stop the party." And I said, "Too bad." Or I could tell you
that I get up at six or seven to play golf. Things like that. But
the real reason is that I'm Italian. Italians are tough; they're
born rugged, they love to work and to love. This makes 'em
look good. Consider my friends: Vic Damone looks beautiful,
and Tony Bennett, and Nick Conte seems thirty-five, and
Frank's so strong. He's a little bald, but that's all. Besides, you
know, I mind my business.

There aren't too many things you care about. Right, Dino?

Well, I like golf. Same as Jeannie likes boatin'. I can't stand
boats. Where am I goin' on a boat? I can only go a hundred feet.
Fish, I don't like to fish. Sail, I don't like to sail. Everybody
says the bow, the stern, let's go to the Pointed End. I don't know
what that is. Well, others like politics. Like Frank. I don't. I
stay out. I might do a show 'cause Frank asks me. I did shows to
help Kennedy, rest in peace. I did for Johnson. But I stay out.
All these actors who go into politics. I go as a gag on the stage
when I say, "I only would become governor if all the drunks
voted for me." And I have fun with Ronald Reagan. I know
him since twenty years, and he knows that Frank and I were for
Governor Brown. We raised two millions for Brown. So I say to
Ronnie, "I know you're the Governor, but if you want a small
little part, just playin' an Indian, in my next picture, just call
me." My relationships with the politicians are these. Take
Bobby. I mean, Bobby Kennedy. Sometimes he stops here, and
we go down to his sister's house at the beach, and there we
would sing. Man, how bad he sings. Old college songs, that's all
he knows. With that voice, the worst voice in the whole world.
So I say to him, "I didn't ever go to high school; how am I
gonna tolerate your college songs with that voice?" And he
laughs, 'cause he's a cute guy. And I like him, and would he be
a candidate! I would work for him, and I would pray for him to
win. But I like Reagan, too, see, and I like Johnson, too. He
made a couple of mistakes. But do you know what a terrible job
that is, this Vietnam thing, with his hands tied up? And they

insult him continuously, and this bird, and that bird, Lady Bird. You see, I'm a simple man.

Oh, no! You seem simple, but I find you a very complicated man.

Well, see, I'm shy. Always been. See, if I walk into a party, I sort of go into a corner, 'cause I don't know what to say to people. "How's the weather?" they ask. Who cares about the weather? Just give me a drink, and I'll sit in a corner lookin' for someone I know. I hate small talk. I'm an honest guy who doesn't bother anybody and nobody bothers him. All I want at fifty is a piece of land with lots of cattle. And I'll get it. 'Cause I want to live there and be a cowboy and hustle cattle, round up the cattle, and see the sun that rises in those beautiful colors, and the sun that sets while you meditate. And then go to sleep, just like an old man. And what else do you need in life?

Los Angeles, August, 1967

DUCHESS OF ALBA

The Duchess

It took me nearly twelve days to gain admittance to the most breathtaking palace in Spain and to the presence of Cayetana, Duchess of Alba: last descendant of the lady of the same name whom Goya painted as naked as an egg, to the grave scandal of those proper people for whom peasant women may be painted in the nude but not duchesses—they should wear pajamas. I was admitted, finally, because I had let the Duchess know that if she made me wait one day more, I would write her off and choose another duchess. The Duchess is always very pleased to have newspaper articles about her, and photographs, too.

The Duchess (and she isn't only a Duchess she's also Marchioness, Countess, Baroness, Viscountess, and a whole lot of other things) was in the seventh month of her tenth pregnancy, she was wearing a smock, and her hair was so back-combed that you couldn't tell where her scalp ended and her hair, which is fair, began. Like the royal personages of whom she speaks, she was so, so sweet, and so, so nice, and she was burdened with the care of saying as little as possible. In fact, though we spent nearly four hours together, when I played back all the tapes, I discovered that she had spoken for no more than thirty minutes. When added to this is the fact that the Duchess' voice is a whisper—and I wasn't able to decipher a lot of the whispers—I conclude that she spoke even less.

The Duchess was also burdened with another care: denying the story, which by now is history, that her antecedent and namesake was Goya's mistress. The word "mistress" filled her with horror. The fact that I spoke it with ease and frequency made her wretchedly uncomfortable. How, how could I think that her ancestor Cayetana could have slept with a painter who, apart from anything else, was forty years older than she? Uselessly I pointed out that forty years more, forty years less, are of no importance in what are generally reckoned great love stories. In any case, that painter wasn't a house painter, his name was Goya, for heaven's sake. The Duchess sighed, groaned, suffered. And she denied it as urgently as a spokesman for Buckingham Palace would deny the flirtations of Prince Charles or Princess Anne. In fact, I don't understand why she's so keen on painting, telling me that her greatest passion is painting, and that she even has a studio in the palace attic. It's true that her paintings—I saw them—are not much like the paintings of Goya. They are, how shall I say it, very, very modern, and very, very ugly.

The Duchess was also kept busy denying her enmity with Franco, an enmity, besides, that runs counter to the family tradition: her relations and her husband's relations fought in the Falange. (But nieces and nephews don't necessarily hold the same opinions as their aunts and uncles.) On the topic that some wicked little spirit always makes me raise when I'm in Spain she did indeed make one thing plain: she is fiercely monarchist. No one doubts it; many kings both with thrones and without are her grandfathers or cousins, or at the least her in-laws. Her blood is bluer than the bluest blood on earth. Meeting her in front of an elevator, Elizabeth of England would have to let her go first. It's true that she talks about this without giving it any importance and that she associates with all kinds: movie stars, dancers, bullfighters.

The Duchess is to my mind a very complex woman. She says she doesn't go shooting because she can't bear to kill little birds, yet, herself a lady bullfighter, she adores watching bulls being killed. She says she isn't rich, yet her collection of masterpieces is beyond price, and furthermore she owns fifty castles and I don't know how much land and how much ready cash. She tells you how much she loves her paintings, which had me fainting away with ecstasy, and yet she doesn't even look at them. For fear that a wisp of smoke might damage them, I didn't even dare to light a cigarette. "What on earth are you worrying about?" the Duchess finally said. "Smoke, smoke. I always smoke in here." Maybe it's because the Duchess is so, so sweet, so, so nice. At any rate, the Duchess doesn't like me; I don't like the Duchess.

ORIANA FALLACI: *Let me recover my breath, Duchess. No, no: with all due respect, not on your account. Notwithstanding the fact that your blood is bluer than ink and through your veins flows the blood of Mary Stuart, the Empress Eugenia de Montijo, and the Cayetana painted I don't know how many times naked or clothed by Goya himself. . . . Notwithstanding the fact that, as I was saying, you are so gentle and fair and frightened: you wouldn't even do away with a Bombay pariah. It's just that it isn't every day one does an interview in a drawing room with a Fra Angelico, a Perugino, a Titian, a Bellini, a Rubens, three Andrea del Sartos, and a Fra Bartolomeo, not to mention the Goyas hanging in the next room. It almost seems sacrilegious to have a tape recorder in here, to drink gin fizz, smoke. . . . Is it really all right if we smoke? Won't it damage anything? What does it feel like to live in an art gallery?*

CAYETANA D'ALBA: Really I'm so used to these paintings I don't see them anymore. I mean, I know they're here, but I don't stop to look at them, they don't make any impression on me anymore. The ones in the Prado or the Uffizi or the Louvre make much more of an impression on me. We Albas, you know, grew up among masterpieces; for centuries my family has collected fine painting. Did you see that Titian of the Duke of Alba fighting for Charles V, in the Italian room? And that other Rubens, of the Duke of Alba when he was younger?

Yes, yes. But how many paintings are there altogether? A hundred? Two hundred? Three hundred?

I don't know. I've never counted them. You know, I have so many homes with paintings like these. I have the palace in Seville, for example. There there are a lot of fifteenth-century paintings. Then there's the Salamanca palace. There's also . . .

I understand. And aren't you afraid they might be stolen?

In our country paintings even get stolen from art galleries. Here, if I'm not mistaken, it would be easier.

Oh, no! Spaniards never steal. Spaniards are a special people in every way, and they do not steal. Here, in front of the Liria palace, for example, there's a policeman on duty all night. But I'm always asking him: What are you standing here for? To admire the facade?

It's a very handsome facade. And a very handsome palace inside it, too: those sculptures from the fifth century B.C., *in the entrance . . . those Canova statues on the staircase . . . that Greek Venus . . . and then the tapestries, the collection of armor . . . apart from the fact that it's a huge place. How many rooms are there, Duchess?*

I don't know. I've never counted them. The reception rooms, the ones that are open to the public on Sundays, number twenty-four, I think. No, twenty-five. No, twenty-six. Then there are the apartments . . . I don't know. The children's rooms . . . I don't know. The servants' quarters . . . I don't know. I'd have to look it up in some book or other.

But you were born here, if I'm not mistaken. How can you possibly not know?

Yes, yes. I was born here. And I stayed here until the Civil War. When the Civil War broke out, we went to Seville, and then they sent me to boarding school in Switzerland and France. After that, England. My father was ambassador in London, during the Civil War. But my cousins and my uncles fought, and so did my husband. He was a volunteer, only fifteen years old. He lost two brothers, I lost an uncle.

Not with the revolutionaries, I suppose. With Franco, I suppose.

Yes, yes. Oh, the Reds confiscated the palace and bombed it, too. When we came back, it was quite destroyed, all broken. We had to rebuild the facade. Only the paintings were in safety. We'd put them in a safe place sometime before. You understand?

I understand. Certainly you are one of the richest women in the world, if not the richest. Apart from these paintings, which are worth millions, one has only to think of your palaces, your fifty castles strewn all over Spain, your lands and estates.

Oh, no. There are the castles, of course, but they're all in ruins, useful only for making the view prettier. The palaces and the land . . . well, my mother was an only child, and so when she died—I was only four—she left her entire family patrimony to me, for I, too, am an only child. The same thing happened when my father died. But I can't be said to be the richest woman in the world. Types like Rockefeller or Patino or Niarchos are much richer. I promise you I'm not an eighteenth as rich as they are, in spite of the paintings, you know how it is. Motor industries and oil fields are worth much more than my Goyas, my Titians, my Rubens.

And your jewels? I once read, I can't remember where, that when you were married, you were wearing seven hundred thousand dollars' worth of jewels—not bad for just one person, a fourteen-year-old what's more. You were fourteen, weren't you, when you were married?

I do have a few jewels, the family jewels. But I don't know what they're worth, I really couldn't tell you. I never bothered about it. Oh, all this talk about money. I find it *affreuse*, disgusting, hateful. I hate money, I never bother about money. What use is money, so long as you have enough to live well? The necessities. What's the use of having more?

No use. No use at all. There are even proverbs that say that money is no use, it doesn't buy happiness or love or peace of mind or the Kingdom of Heaven. The Evangelist says so, too: "Blessed are the poor for theirs is the Kingdom of Heaven." Are you religious?

Oh, yes. Very.

In fact, I have read that among your privileges is that of nominating the priests of three hundred parishes in Spain: a nominal right, of course, but still a right all the same, which

*you inherited along with all your many titles. You won't deny
you're the most titled woman in the world.*

That yes, that might well be so. But I'd rather you said it. I
have sixty-three titles, maybe more.

*And the one you like most is the title of your celebrated fore-
bear: the Cayetana d'Alba, whose name you use although your
full name is Maria de Rosaria Cayetana Stuart, eighteenth
Duchess of Alba. Let's talk about the Cayetana d'Alba a little,
before we start on your titles. You seem so different from her.
That portrait by Goya that I saw in the next room shows a
dark-haired woman, passionate, without any shyness. And indeed, from what they say, she was no saint. . . .*

Oh, that poor woman! Why is everyone forever talking about
her, slighting her. I don't understand. It was all of five generations ago, or rather six, seven, I don't know, ten, and they still
go on slighting her.

To be called Goya's mistress isn't exactly a slight.

Mistress? What can you mean? Goya was in love with her,
obsessed with her; that much is child's knowledge. Cayetana
was a very beautiful woman, popular, passionate. Everyone
was in love with her. But she in love with Goya! There might
have been friendship, sympathy, affection. . . .

*Excuse me, Duchess, but how would you know? You weren't
there. And the story of their love has never been doubted in
nearly two centuries.*

But there's nothing to prove it, nothing! Not a single letter,
nothing. And then—*mon Dieu!*—an age difference of forty
years and more! He was already seventy when he met her, she
was in her twenties. How frightful!

*As far as that goes, you know, the history of great love affairs
offers us indisputable examples. There are times when age
doesn't count. You don't ask a person for his birth certificate
before you love him. Just think, it was right here in Madrid
that Peron married a woman forty-five years his junior. And*

then, the "Maja desnuda." . . . This morning I went to the Prado to look at it again and . . .

And you'll have seen that it isn't the Duchess of Alba at all. Even her figure is different. The "Maja" is short, stocky, it was clearly some country wench. You wouldn't want to compare her with the tall, slender woman you saw in the other room? And then again, it was clearly a girl of about sixteen. But at that time the Duchess of Alba was over thirty.

As far as that goes, there are women of thirty who keep their looks quite well. You are one of them, Duchess. . . . And then her face is identical to the one in there.

I've said no. We have never even had that painting in our possession. And we have never had it in our possession because it has nothing to do with any of our forebears. I say so again, once and for all.

As you like. We don't want to quarrel about it. Tell me, rather, whether it is true that when you married your husband, Luis de Sottomayor, you passed your title on to him the same way as a husband passes his on to his wife. It seems strange in a country such as Spain, where women count for little.

The title musn't be allowed to become extinct. In the absence of male heirs the title goes to the female. And when the female marries, she can give her title to her husband, like a surname.

And your other titles? Of course, I don't mean you to tell me all of them. But if you happen to remember a dozen, or even just five or six. . . .

I know them nearly all, all really. Duchess of Alba, of Berwick, of Liria, of Xerica, of Arjona, of Huescar, of Olivares, of Ija, of Aliaga, of Montesa . . .

Fine, thank you. You don't have to say them all.

. . . Marchioness of Carpio, of la Algaba, of Coria de Eliche, of la Mota, of Moya, of Oyera, of San Leonardo, of Sarria, of

Tarazona, of Villanueva del Fresno, of Barcarrota, of Villanueva del Rio . . .

Yes, yes. That's fine, thank you. I think that's enough.

. . . Countess of Lemos, of Lerin, of Miranda, of Castanar, of Monterrey, of Osorno, of Siruela, of Andrada de Ayala, of Casarrubios del Monte, of Valdefuente, of Valdepevos, of Fertiduena, of Galvez, of Los Gelves, of San Esteban de Gormaz, of Santa Cruz de la Sierra, of Navarra . . .

Listen, that's enough. Truly. I believe you. I promise.

. . . and then I also have an Italian title: Countess of Modica. And then other things such as Algadeza dell' Alcazar di Siviglia, Grandeza di Spagna, twenty of that one. It's just that in my family we have always had great generals or great ministers, and so they were given titles. People sometimes ask me if they matter a great deal to me. Well, I can't say either that they do matter or don't matter. They were given to me, that's all, and I don't feel ashamed of them.

Quite right. Eh, yes. Certainly when one thinks that these days nobody loses his head over the aristocracy anymore and even its decay is submerged in total indifference. . . .

Listen, I'm a modern woman who doesn't think herself at all different from women who don't have titles; this aristocracy doesn't weigh on me. I just think that aristocracy imposes greater duties. People always expect us not to make mistakes, to be better than other people, to behave with greater responsibility, to near perfection. . . .

Excuse me, won't you, but it seems to me that these days nobody expects a thing of the aristocracy. What is one supposed to expect of a count or a marquis? We live in an age of science, progress, an age when men will go to the moon and even kings have to go around on bicycles if they want people to put up with them. The monarchies have nearly all fallen, there are few left now. Incidentally, you must certainly be a monarchist?

Sentimentally monarchist. If it were up to me . . . *Mon Dieu,* no, I don't want to talk about this. Don't make me talk politics.

I cannot, I don't wish to, I shouldn't. Don't ask me this thing because I shan't answer you.

I won't ask you. Please, don't be so alarmed. Let's change the subject. You are related to the English royal family through the Stuarts and James II. Do you know Elizabeth and Margaret?

I have seen Elizabeth at receptions. I've known Margaret since we were children and I was living in London. You know, children's parties. We would drink orange juice, play musical statues, and when it was time to go home, they would give us a balloon on a string. No, I didn't go to Margaret's wedding. Margaret . . . very sweet, very nice.

But you went to Fabiola's wedding. Fabiola is Spanish; I'm sure you can tell me more about her. I know you were at boarding school together in Switzerland.

Yes, years and years ago. Then we lost touch, partly because I married. Her marriage took us completely by surprise. We didn't know the first thing about it. She had never even hinted . . . that she even knew Baudouin. A fairy tale. Fabiola . . . such a good person. Very sweet, very nice.

And Juanito? I know that you're close friends, that you see each other very often. Your private apartments are full of photographs of Juanito inscribed "To Cayetana."

Yes. Oh, yes. Juanito . . . very sweet, very nice.

And Sofia? You know his wife Sofia very well, too, I understand.

Yes. Oh, yes. Sofia . . . very sweet, very nice.

And the Savoys? I understand that Umberto often comes to stay with you. And Maria Pia too. And Maria Gabriella. If I'm not mistaken, it was you who took Maria Gabriella to Seville to take part in the pageant for the inauguration of the equestrian feria, when Maria Gabriella met Peralta. Wasn't she staying with you?

Yes. Oh, yes. Umberto . . . very sweet, very nice. And Maria Pia, very sweet, very nice. And Maria Gabriella, very sweet,

very nice, and so cultured, too, so beautiful, such artistic feeling. She had a great success, she understands Spain so well.
Maria Beatrice I don't know. What is she like?

Very sweet, very nice.

And Constantine's fiancée?

Very sweet, very nice.

Oh, yes. They're all so sweet, so nice,

All.

Soraya too.

Soraya too.

And Margarita too, Simeone's wife. I know her well.

Margarita too.

Maria José too. Frederick of the Hellenes too.

They too, they too. Tell me, Duchess, your company is, after
all, requested more than that of any other woman in Europe.
There isn't a marriage you aren't invited to, there isn't a cruise
you aren't pressed to join, and engagements, and funerals.
Life is one long holiday for you.

Yes. Oh, yes. Umberto . . . very sweet, always. I met so
many people during my childhood and my adolescence, in
Czechoslovakia, too, and Hungary—in those days there weren't
the Communists. There are so many people that now I don't
want to meet anymore. And then I don't mix only with the
aristocracy, you know. I mix with painters, actors, bullfighters,
writers, directors. For example, I know Cocteau very well, such
a nice man, and Salvador Dali, he's *simpático*, too, and Ava
Gardner, she's very *simpático*, and Orson Welles, he's very
simpático, too. And Hemingway was very *simpático*. And Ordoñez is very *simpático*, and so is Dominguin. Of course, I
admire Ordoñez more for his art, but Dominguin is very
simpático, too. And then I take an interest in the Red Cross, the
work of the Salesians, and a boarding school with a thousand
children, and the week of the poor—you know, when you go
around the poor districts and ask the poor what they need.

Admirable. Truly admirable. I have here the list your secre-

tary gave me. You're patroness of the hospitals of Ampudia, Toro, Penaranda, Belmonte, the Opera Pia del Carpio, the Dominican convent of Loeches, and even president of the regional center of the Blood Transfusion Service. But how do you manage to do so much?

Considering I have four children to take care of. And soon I'll have five, I'm in my seventh month. I adore children. I take all that God sends me. If I hadn't lost five, by now I'd have nine. I love children and animals. I could never go shooting.

But you can fight bulls. I know you're a good bullfighter.

Not exactly a bullfighter, a *rejoneadora*. *Rejoneadores* are the ones who fight on horseback. I used to do it when I was younger; I learned with Conchita Citron. But I didn't do it in the plazas, for the public. I used to do it in the country, for friends. Yes, I know what you're thinking: that a bull, too, is an animal. But it's an animal that one can kill. Manolete killed them. I knew Manolete very well, what an extraordinary person: aristocratic, tragic, he was unlike anyone else.

Listen, Duchess, if you had had to work for a living . . . or better, if you had to work for a living, what would you do? I'm just asking for fun of course.

Mon Dieu, interior decorating, or rather, no, painting. I adore painting. Have you seen my studio? I paint at least four days a week. In these days aristocrats have to show that they can do what others do, apart from the fact that painting is my true passion.

Yes, I saw your studio in the attic. What lovely colors. Abstract-synthetic painting, I believe it's been called. Something completely different from Goya's painting. And . . . do you sell?

And how. At high prices, too.

And . . . tell me, Duchess, what else can you do with the same skill? What else could you do if you had to work for a living? I'm only asking for fun of course.

I dance flamenco well. I've been dancing it since I was a

child, I adore flamenco. Flamenco is good for the muscles, gives elasticity to your movements. You need to be healthy to dance flamenco.

And what does the Duke of Alba, your husband, think about it?

Oh! My husband is quite different. He's interested in the countryside, the olives, the cows, the corn, and he's also a member of the Academy of Fine Arts.

I know he is very close to the King, Juanito's father, his counselor or something of the sort.

Would you like to see my library? There's even Christopher Columbus' shipboard journal and the letters of Mary of England. Students often come to study them. Why are you looking at me like that?

I'm not looking at you, Duchess. I'm just thinking how far we have come from the day when your great-great-great-grand-father they called the Great used to terrify the Flemish people, and parents would tell their children: "If you aren't good, the Duke of Alba will come and eat you up."

Far, very far. I've disappointed you, haven't I?

No, no, Duchess, how can you say such a thing? You are so sweet, so nice. It has been an unforgettable conversation.

Madrid, February, 1963

FEDERICO FELLINI

Famous Italian Director

I have known Fellini for many years; to be precise, ever since I met him in New York for the American première of his movie *The Nights of Cabiria*, at which time we became good friends. In fact, we often used to go to eat steaks at Jack's or roast chestnuts in Times Square, where you could also do target shooting. Then, from time to time, he would turn up at the apartment I shared in Greenwich Village with a girl called Priscilla to ask for a cup of coffee. The homely brew would alleviate, though I never understood why, his nostalgia for his homeland and his misery at his separation from his wife Giulietta. He would come in frantically massaging his knee, "My knee always hurts when I'm sad. Giulietta! I want Giulietta!" And Priscilla would come running to have a look at him as I'd have gone running to have a look at Greta Garbo. Needless to say, in those days there was nothing of Greta Garbo about Fellini, he wasn't the monument he is today. He used to call me *Pallina*, Little Ball. He made us call him *Pallino*, sometimes *Pallone*, Big Ball. He would go in for innocent extravagances such as weeping in the bar of the Plaza Hotel because the critic of the *New York Times* had given him a bad review, or playing the hero. He used to go around with a gangster's moll, and every day the gangster would call him at his hotel, saying, "I will kill you." He didn't understand English and would reply, "Very well, very well," so adding to his heroic reputation. His reputation lasted until I explained to him what "I will kill you" meant. Within half an hour Fellini was on board a plane making for Rome.

He used to do other things too, such as wandering around Wall Street at night, casing the banks like a robber, arousing the suspicions of the world's most suspicious police, so that finally they asked to see his papers, arrested him because he wasn't carrying any, and shut him up for the night in a cell. He spent his time shouting the only English sentence he knew: "I am Federico Fel-

187

lini, famous Italian director." At six in the morning an Italian-American policeman who had seen *La Strada* I don't know how many times said, "If you really are Fellini, come out and whistle the theme music of *La Strada*." Fellini came out and in a thin whistle—he can't distinguish a march from a minuet—struggled through the entire soundtrack. A triumph. With affectionate punches in the stomach that were to keep him on a diet of consommé for the next two weeks, the policemen apologized and took him back to his hotel with an escort of motorcycles, saluting him with a blare of horns that could be heard as far away as Harlem. In those days Fellini was truly *simpatico*, and I liked him very much.

When I approached him for this interview, he was a little less so, although he greeted me, as was his wont, by swinging me off my feet in a passionate hug, pinching and squeezing me from my neck to my knees, swearing that if he wasn't already married to Giulietta he would immediately have married me. "Come to think of it, why weren't we in love in New York? Ah, how cruel of you not to have given yourself to me." And he pretended to have forgotten, of course, that not once during the course of our escapades in New York had he shown me the slightest sign of romance, that never had he made a single adulterous suggestion to distract us from our respective flirtations. He had made *La Dolce Vita*, a movie for which he had been compared with Shakespeare, he was about to present *8½*, a movie that was being talked about as if it were the *Divine Comedy*. And, while not actually admitting it, he was fully aware of the glory that surrounded him: he thrust out his jaw rather like Mussolini, his eyes were serious, one knew that one could no longer call him *Pallino* or *Pallone*. Besides, once the hugging was over, he made it clear to me almost immediately. He had agreed to see me, he said, only because it was me; he had very little time, and the only way he could grant the interview was by doing it as he ate. That was why he had invited me to the restaurant we were then entering.

I tried to talk him out of such an awful plan. The tape recorder was electric, and there was no electric outlet, or if there was, it wasn't near our table. My complaints were all to no avail. Either we did it in the restaurant while we ate or nowhere else and never again. So I looked for a table next to a plug, made room for the tape recorder among the plates and the glasses and the hors d'oeuvres platter, and started the interview, which, since we were constantly interrupted by innumerable telephone calls, proceeded as smoothly as a lame man running, against the clatter and noise of forks, glasses, and vulgar chewing. When I played back the tape, phrases came out like this: "With this movie I am trying to say . . . Do you want the ham or the salami? I'll take the salami. People who talk about metaphysical dialectics . . . No, I don't want any pasta, it's too fattening. A steak without salt, that's what I'll have. . . . It's so stupid to shut one's eyes to the mystery." . . . Crack! Clink! Clink! . . . "The silence that surrounds you and becomes a gleam of light . . . french fries! Why aren't you having any french fries?" Without a doubt it would all have to be done again. And sighing, groaning, Fellini said all right. Seeing it was for me, he would come to my hotel next day at ten. "But we shan't be quiet in the hotel, Federico." "Yes, we shall. I'll come up to your room."

My room in the Excelsior wasn't exactly a large one, and a double bed almost filled it. Knowing the way a bed can seduce Federico Fellini, I mean to sleep of course, I asked the manager for a suite with a sitting room: "I am expecting Fellini." "Fellini, Miss Fallaci? Oh! But of course! Yes, yes!" And they gave me the suite in which the Shah of Persia and Soraya had stayed, with a sitting room that was more like a ballroom. Thither I removed, at hideous expense, and at half-past nine the following morning I was all ready to receive him, with cigarettes on one table, flowers on another, a waiter ready to bring us coffee—"Signor Fellini likes it strong and hot, please remember." I felt like a seducer waiting to reveal the marvels of sex to his latest victim, all that was missing was a little violin music. But ten o'clock came and of Fellini never a trace. Eleven o'clock came and went, then midday, one o'clock, two o'clock, but from Fellini never a word. The telephone rang when it was past three-thirty and I was swallowing, along with my mortification, some tea and cookies. "Little treasure, little love, little Oriana, baby, I've been trying to ring you since this morning to tell you I'll be late. But where are you, where do you keep going, why do you never stay in the hotel? Never mind, I forgive you, and I'll be with you at five, not a moment later."

Quite convinced, I replaced the receiver. He was a liar, but he would come. I went down to get a breath of fresh air. "And Fellini?" the hall porter inquired with an indefinable smile. "He'll be here at five," I replied grandly. But five o'clock came, and Fellini didn't. Nor did he come at six, nor at seven, nor at eight, and as darkness descended on the sitting room where Reza Pahlevi had stayed and on my disappointed expectations, on my crushed prestige, on the ever more irritating impatience of my editor, who kept calling from Milan, saying, "Well, how far have we got? Well, has he come?" the telephone rang like a liberator. "Little treasure, little love, little Oriana, baby . . ." An unforeseen complication had prevented him, physically prevented him, from coming to see me. He was pained, embarrassed, but I knew he was a man with a thousand things on his hands. To anyone else he would have said, "Forget it." It was quite something that he wasn't refusing altogether, that he was only putting it off. However, he would see me that very evening at eleven o'clock at the private showing of the movie in Via Margutta. "Listen, Federico, I'm already late with this, at least two days late, my editor is angry, the pages are being kept open, listen Federico . . ." "Ah! How dare you doubt my word?!? How could you think I wouldn't come?!? It's insulting, wicked. . . ."

So there I am, at eleven o'clock at night, waiting with my tape recorder in a doorway on Via Margutta for Federico Fellini, famous Italian director. I know he won't come at eleven, but I wait for him. I know he won't even come at midnight, but I wait for him. I know he won't come at one o'clock either, but I wait for him. In the projection room the movie began an hour ago, an hour and a half, two, two and a half hours ago, it's over, the people are coming out, stopping for refreshments, the refreshments are over, too, the people are going away, somebody closes the big door. I move onto the sidewalk, I go on waiting, with my eyes closing, my legs giving way. Pestered by young punks, I go on waiting, until a taxi comes by, and I get in it. By now it's half-past one in the morning. On my way in I tell the hotel porter to book me on the first flight to Milan. In my room I drop exhausted onto my bed. I fall asleep instantly. I wake up at the sound of the telephone. A mellifluous voice sings: "Little treasure, little love, little Oriana, baby, why didn't you come?!" "Because I'm going," I tell him. "I had to pack my bags. My plane takes off at eight in the morning." "But that's my plane! I'm leaving at eight, too! Isn't that extraordinary? Isn't that convenient? We'll talk in the plane." Needless to say, he missed the plane. Oh, he had his ticket, and a seat reservation too. That was his flight all right, columnists and photographers were waiting for him in Milan, his producer had sent his Cadillac and driver to meet him so he wouldn't get lost. But he missed the plane all the same. And when it landed at Linate, the photographers came running to the steps, and coming down the steps were myself, two Americans from Oklahoma, four Frenchmen from Nîmes, and two Lombardian industrialists who dealt in chemical fertilizers and suchlike. Fellini arrived at midday, and a friend conveyed my message of welcome: that he could go to hell and stay there—providing they'd accept him, which was doubtful.

Italians and Chinese, Norwegians and Chileans, Mexicans and Frenchmen, Indians and Greenlanders, people of the world, remember this. You musn't send Federico Fellini to hell because Federico Fellini gets angry, he gets as angry as a wild beast and telephones you to heap insults on your grandfather, your mother, your aunt, your grandmother, your in-laws, your nephews, your cousins, and to remind you that he is a great director, an artist, a very great artist, and that by virtue of this he can miss all the appointments he wants, miss all the planes he wants—in fact, the planes would do well to wait for him, because one waits for Federico Fellini, we are all born to wait for Federico Fellini, etc. I was at the newspaper office when he telephoned, and he was shouting so loudly that everyone could hear him reminding me that Federico Fellini was a great director, an artist, a very great artist, bellowing in a voice that would have frightened to death the gangster who had frightened him to death, insulting me, whilst I imagined his Mussolini-like jaw, his saliva covering the telephone like dew, his big face sweaty with anger and horror at the blasphemy I had dared to commit. I tried to turn aside his insults with *politesse*, to explain to him what I thought of him at that moment. He didn't hear me, he wasn't listening. And while everyone was laughing and passing comments on his yells, I gently replaced the receiver.

Then began a crisis, for he isn't a bad man, I swear. It was his misfortune to have such good luck, that's all. Not even Saint Anthony could resist the scourge of so much good fortune, and it aroused the Emilian violence that lurked beneath that peaceful cat-like appearance. But afterward he is very, very sorry, to the point of tears. He is ready to call on a hundred people to tell you that his heart is rent with anguish, that he loves you as he loves Giulietta, that he's always loved you, that he'll love you as long as he lives—until, like someone hypnotized or sleepwalking, you find yourself getting into the Cadillac he has sent to fetch you, driving along the road thinking that it has been your fault and not his at all, entering the elevator wondering how he will ever forgive you, and finally opening the door of his hotel room looking like Judas after selling Christ. Here you find him stretched out like Ibn Saud on a bed, blissfully purring, saying in that mellifluous voice, "Little treasure, little love, little Oriana, baby . . ." Then you are clasped in a grim hug and begin to listen to him throughout a still grimmer evening.

Fellini wanted to read over the interview that follows, and he read it over three times, each time making various corrections to his answers, adding new opinions, making last minute reversals. This is the least genuine interview in the book, every single sentence in it has been revised and re-revised. The Napoleonic Code and the American Constitution assuredly cost less effort than this precious document.

I used to be truly fond of Federico Fellini. Since our tragic encounter I'm a lot less fond. To be exact, I am no longer fond of him. That is, I don't like him at all. Glory is a heavy burden, a murdering poison, and to bear it is an art. And to have that art is rare.

ORIANA FALLACI: *So then let us brace ourselves, Signor Fellini, and let us discuss Federico Fellini, just for a change. I know you find it hard: you are so withdrawing, so secretive, so modest. But it is our duty to discuss him, for the sake of the nation, too. It won't be long now before the story of your life and the meaning of your art become subjects taught in every state school, like mathematics, geography, religion. Haven't the textbooks already been written?* Federico Fellini, The Story of Federico Fellini, The Mystery of Fellini. . . . *Not even about Giuseppe Verdi has so much been written. But then you are the Giuseppe Verdi of today. You even look alike, especially the hat. No, please, why are you hiding your hat? Giuseppe Verdi used to wear one just like it: black, broad-brimmed. . . .*

FEDERICO FELLINI: Nasty liar. Rude little bitch.

Why? Verdi was great, too, you know. The opening nights of his operas were exactly like your film premières. I believe that only over La Traviata *have the Italians ever made the fuss they did over your* 8½, *with seats booked months in advance, the ladies in new dresses, the critics plaiting laurel wreaths. . . .*

Oh yes. . . . As if *The White Sheik* hadn't been a howling failure, and *Il Bidone* hadn't been given an icy reception, and *La Strada* hadn't been greeted with ridicule and insults. And *La Dolce Vita?* Do you suppose it had nothing but praise and admiration? Eh, kid?

Heavens. In Milan somebody spat. In Rome the police intervened. But even Verdi had vegetables and raw eggs thrown at him from time to time. Signor Fellini! You aren't worried by any chance? Forgive me, but seeing you so placidly stretched out on the bed, looking like a pussy cat, you seemed so calm. . . .

I am, very calm. After all, I've done what I meant to do. I managed not to worry too much about whether or not people

will like the movie. The waiting doesn't leave me cold, obviously. But it doesn't affect me in the way you might think.
The anguish and the trepidation I feel are the same as when I
made my first movie. I mean that my previous successes don't
make me a nervous wreck with thinking, "Help, now they'll
expect me to do a triple somersault." It isn't being presumptuous when I tell you that my sole anxiety comes from fear
that the movie may be misunderstood, certainly not from the
thought that people might expect more from me than I can
give. Why should I worry about disappointing people who
watch me as if I were a chorus girl who has to go one step
higher each time and flaunt more and more ostrich feathers?

*Signor Fellini, let's look each other straight in the eyes. For
a man who couldn't care less you've made quite a stir. All that
mystery about the plot so that people die of curiosity, that
playing hide-and-seek with the journalists, that saying nothing
even to the actors about the parts they're playing, in short, all
that secrecy. . . .*

Oh, yes? Everyone pays the price of the world he lives in;
it's the cinema that translates everything into vulgar terms.
My little treasure, I'd be good enough at inventing stories if
I had to and if I wanted to fall back on publicity. If I haven't
talked about my movie, it's because I didn't know what to say
about it; I still don't know what to say about it. It isn't the
kind of movie with a plot you can relate. When people ask
me to tell them the plot, I shrug my shoulders and say, "Well,
imagine that one evening you meet a friend who is in a con-
fidential mood, and this friend disjointedly and confusedly tells
you about what he does, what he dreams, about his childhood
memories, his emotional entanglements, his professional
doubts. You sit there listening, and at the end you have been
listening to a human being. And maybe then you too feel like
starting to tell him about something. . . ." Understand? It's
a confused, chaotic snatch of talk, a confession made with
abandon, at times even unbearable. . . .

Yes, in fact there's something Proustian about it. Proust translated into pure cinema.

Proust? Could be! I'm very ignorant. . . . Disgraceful, eh? One healthy, vast, solid, thick-skinned ignorance. I don't know anything about anything. And that's not only true of books. It's true of films, too.

I know, I know. The only movies you go to see are Federico Fellini's. Never anyone else's, isn't that true?

It is so true that I have the courage to admit it. I can never get myself organized for the ritual that going to a show entails: leaving the house, getting into the car, sitting down among so many people, staying there to be tickled by collective emotions. If I do leave home to go to the movies or the theater, you can be sure that on the way there I'll see something that interests me more. And then if I do see someone else's movie and I realize that he has done something that I wanted to do . . . I don't like it. Of course I've seen Chaplin's films. What a fabulous artist! But for people in their forties like me, Chaplin belongs to the mythology of our lifetime: father, mother, schoolteacher, priest, Chaplin. Chaplin . . . I met him once in Paris. He had seen *La Strada;* in a low voice he complimented me, I think. He struck me as very, very small, with two tiny, tiny hands. I couldn't understand his French, he couldn't understand my English. I felt ill-at-ease, over-awed. . . .

Let's forget about Chaplin, we're here for Fellini. The main character in 8½ . . .

You saw it? Did you like it?

Of course I liked it. But what a sad movie. All those old people, all those priests, that atmosphere of decay and death. . . . Even the living are dead, in that movie.

Then you haven't understood much, it isn't a sad movie. It's a gentle, dawn-like movie, melancholy, if anything. But melancholy is a very noble state of mind, the most nourishing and the most fertile. . . .

If it makes you happy, let's just say I didn't understand much.

Little treasure, are you hungry? Are you thirsty? Do you want to lie down for a bit?

I'm not hungry, I'm not thirsty, and I don't in the least want to lie down. Please, let me go on. As I was saying, the main character in the movie is forty-three, is a director, and is Federico Fellini. Even if you have called him Guido Anselmi. . . .

Are you sure you don't want anything? Coffee?

I don't want a thing. Please, Signor Fellini, leave my tape recorder alone. If you keep on fiddling with it, you'll break it. Why do you want to break it? By now everyone knows that your movie is autobiographical anyway, blatantly, indisputably autobiographical. Even Guido Anselmi's hat is identical to yours. Even the way he flings his coat over his shoulders, the way he walks, smiles. Leave my tape recorder alone. Even . . .

But he's a failure that director, he's failing. Oh, baby! Do I strike you as a failure, me? Guido Anselmi is forty-three like myself, all right, but he could equally well be forty-one or forty-seven or thirty-five like that other great director. "At the noon of our mortal life I found myself inside a gloomy wood having lost the path that leads straight ahead." He's a man lost in a dense dark wood. . . .

. . . even the same capacity for telling lies. "You lie like you breathe," his wife says to him, not that the resemblance shows you in a very good light. The sketch is merciless: "Hypocritical and cowardly buffoon." "Feeble, weak-willed, and mystifying." "Presumptuous, unsure and a cheat." "A type who's fond of nobody." And, finally, that terrible admission, "I have absolutely nothing to say but I say it just the same."

All right, all right. What does it prove? It certainly doesn't prove that the movie is autobiographical, in the usual sense. And even if it were? I don't want to give the audience an interpretation based on anecdotes and autobiography; on the level of simple autobiography the movie would become merely a useless, boring, narcissistic exhibition.

Perhaps it is. A splendid, shameless, narcissistic bit of chatter.

I'm sorry, but I don't think that's what it is. It's the story of a man like so many others: the story of a man who has reached the point of stagnation, a total blockage that is choking him. I hope that after the first few hundred feet the spectator forgets that Guido is a director, that is, someone who does an unusual job, and recognizes in Guido his own fears, his own doubts, his own ill manners, cowardice, ambiguity, hypocrisies: all things that are the same in a director and in a respectable lawyer and family man.

Look, Signor Fellini, the respectable lawyer might recognize himself in Guido all right, but the fact remains that Guido is Fellini. Come on, it's like a last will and testament, that movie, a final reckoning—leaving aside the fact that making a final reckoning of one's life at the age of forty-three seems to me to be rather too early.

Why? Better to make it early than late, when there's no longer time to change anything. At forty-three it's not a bit too soon to make a reckoning of one's own life. That's exactly why the movie did me so much good. I feel somehow liberated, now, and with a great urge to work. The movie—*8½*—is like my last will and testament, you're right, and yet I don't feel drained. On the contrary, it enriched me. If it were up to me, I'd start making another tomorrow morning. Honestly. And of course if they say, "How clever, Fellini, what talent," it gives me a lot of pleasure. But it isn't compliments I'm looking for with *8½*. I want . . . I want this feeling of liberation to communicate itself to anyone who goes to see it, so that after seeing it people should feel more free, should have a presentiment of something joyful. . . .

Good Lord, Signor Fellini, don't try to tell me you care about the people who go to see your movie. If there's a man who

couldn't care less about his neighbor and is devoid of evangeli-
cal spirit, it's you. Let's drop it, for goodness' sake, and concen-
trate on the important admission: the reckoning you make in
8½ is a reckoning of your own life and not of some imaginary
person.

Ugh, what a little pest. What do you want me to say. So many
things . . . of course . . . are true. What happens in the movie
has happened to me to a certain extent. . . . There was a
moment when I no longer knew what to do, could no longer
remember a thing. I would work with Flajano, Pinelli, Rondi,
without any conviction. I had the Saraghina episode, the one
about the cardinal. But they were isolated things, floating
in the void, and I could no longer remember a thing, honestly.
The production team used to stand there, looking at me with
imploring, suspicious eyes, and I had a strong desire to say
to the producer, "Let's drop it, let's forget about making this
movie." Then it appeared to me that my bewilderment was
perhaps an invitation, help from some invisible collaborator
who was saying to me: "Tell the truth, tell about this." And
so I got the idea of making a movie about a director who wants
to make a movie and can no longer remember what it is about.
Yes, Guido Anselmi is only experiencing what I also partly
experienced in this movie. And the conclusion, if you can call
it a conclusion, is this: we must never strain ourselves trying to
understand, but try to feel, with abandon. We must accept ourselves for what we are: this is what I am, and this is what I'm
content to be. I want to stop building myths around myself, I want to see myself as I am: a liar, incoherent, hypocritical, cowardly. . . . I want to have done with making problems
out of life; I want to put myself in a position where I can love
life, where I can love everything. I'm still talking about Guido,
of course. . . . And after all Saint Augustine said the same thing,
"Love, and do what you want." Well, he didn't put it like that
exactly, but more or less. . . .

Coming from someone who hasn't read anything, a quote from Saint Augustine is pretty good.

It's just that sometimes I happen to go into a bookshop and open a book, and my glance falls on a page that says something like that. Then, maybe I don't even understand this bit my eye catches, immediately. . . .

Liar. Tell me rather why you didn't after all choose Laurence Olivier for the part of Federico, sorry, of Guido. He would have been perfect.

Laurence Olivier . . . an Englishman, a Knight, a very great actor. How can one? It's too much. I needed an Italian, a friend who would humbly accept being a kind of respectful shadow, who wouldn't put himself forward overmuch. So I took Mastroianni. I already knew him, and he was very, very good: so allusive, discreet, likable, unlikable, tender, overbearing. He's there, and he isn't there. Perfect.

It's true, you become fond of the actors you use. And Giulietta? Did you lose her on the way, Giulietta?

I have a couple of movies in mind that derive from *8½* like pears from a pear tree. Giulietta will also be in the next one. For me Giulietta is a character who evokes a world where nothing is faded or tepid. I shall take up that character with fresh willingness, fresh imagination. I shall make these two movies in Italy. . . . They keep on inviting me to go to America, offering me dizzy sums, but why should I go anywhere else? I don't need any outside stimulus. My own land, my own countryside, the people I know are still enough to stimulate me. What would I go to New York or Bangkok for? I'm the worst traveler; when I travel, everything becomes a kaleidoscope of colors and sounds, I don't understand a thing. All I bring back is some little item that is either useless or heartrending. And then how can one throw oneself into one's travels if one has to keep sending back news to those who are left behind and finally has to come back oneself? I'd like to go to

Egypt, maybe, or to India. But I think about it while I'm sitting down. My place is in Catholic Italy.

Yes, in your heart you are an incurable Catholic, or, at least, very much more tied to Catholicism than people think. One can tell as much from 8½; the ecclesiastical authorities have found nothing to fault in it.

Do you know any Italian who is completely lay-minded? I don't. How could we be? We've had it in our blood, Catholicism, for centuries. How long? Our attempt to free ourselves of it is a necessary and most noble attempt, which we all should make. But it shows that the bruise exists, obviously. If the object against which we revolt doesn't exist, why should we rebel against it? Guido is the victim of a medieval Catholicism that tends to humiliate man rather than to restore him to his divine stature, to his dignity. The same Catholicism has filled mental homes and hospitals and cemeteries with suicides, has monstrously brought forth an unhappy humanity, separating the spirit from the body although they are one and the same thing. In short, Guido's enemy is the degenerate Catholicism that Pope John is fighting in such a heroic and marvelous way. Did you like the episode of the child and Saraghina?

It is indisputably the finest in the movie, the punishment of the child especially. Those ice-cold, pitiless priests. I felt I was looking at some of Goya's drawings again: the Inquisition, the martyrdom of the witch. . . . So much the more pathetic in that the witch, in this case, was a child. Was it you, that child?

I never went to that kind of boarding school, but one summer I went to a Salesian convent, and it was more or less like that. You know, education based on the mortification of the body, being rapped over frost-bitten hands, how it hurts, being forced to kneel on hard corn, how it hurts, that feeling of being perpetually judged by God. . . . You think you're alone, they keep telling you, but God is watching you, He's always watching you. You know, to a child these are real wounds, and it's hard to recover from them. No, I can't cut out of my life the memory of churches, nuns, priests, voices from the pulpit, voices from the confessional, funerals. . . . But what Italian can do without this backcloth, this choreography?

And yet, in spite of this merciless, terrifying education, you can still pray. Isn't that so?

Certainly. Don't you pray? Prayer is a conversation with yourself, with the most secret, most genuine, most mysterious part of yourself. And whenever you turn to it, there's always the chance that something good will come out of it because you're asking help of what's most precious, most virgin in you. . . . God, let's drop it, some things sound ridiculous when you talk about them. I only wanted to say that I don't understand how anyone can fail to pray, can fail to be fascinated by the mystery. It's so stupid to shut one's eyes to the mystery, so inhuman, an animal attitude. The mystery of everything . . . the silence that surrounds you and becomes a gleam of light. . . . Oriana! What are you making me say?

Nothing. You're the one who's talking. And you know whom you remind me of when you talk like this? Ingmar Bergman. It's incredible how much you have in common, you and Bergman: you so Latin, Bergman so Nordic, you so full-blooded, Bergman so ascetic. Apart from the similarities in your movies—there are similarities, don't you think?—you are alike in that he, too, can never do anything out of his own country, he, too, is a sinner obsessed by sin. . . .

Bergman, yes: I've seen one of his movies, *The Face.* I liked it very very much. Bergman is the greatest author in the cinema today.

Next to Fellini? Before Fellini? Or along with Fellini?

You wretch, how should I know? How can I say? For me he's a brother. He has what a man who speaks to others should have, the mantle of the prophet, and on his head is the tall hat with the clown's spangles. That's it. Bergman has both: the mantle and the spangles.

And Federico Fellini?

Hmm. Perhaps I have less mantle and more spangles.

Interesting. When I interviewed Bergman, he also talked to me at length about you. He wanted to know heaps of things, how you live and how you talk. . . .

And you told him the usual bullshit—God knows what you told him. My lies mixed up with yours. . . . God! I'd like to meet him, Bergman. So far we have only written to each other. There's a nice irresponsible producer who wanted to make a movie in three parts, with me, Bergman, and Kurosawa, that extraordinary director of *The Seven Samurai*. He asked me to write to Bergman, to whom incidentally I had always sent my greetings through Swedish journalists. So I wrote him: "Dear Bergman, I admire you so much and love you like a young brother. There's this producer who wants to do this thing. In my opinion it's a rather nutty project, but just because it's mad, it might be worth trying." Bergman wrote me a very beautiful letter in which he said that he would be delighted to do this thing, but in fact so far he hasn't done anything.

Another of Bergman's characteristics is that he doesn't give a rap for what critics write about him, but in this respect you aren't alike. I know that you take quite a bit of notice of certain reviews that use difficult words ending in "ism" and "asm" and are full of dialectics, ethics, aesthetics. . . . For instance, have a look at this article.

What's this man talking about? What's he driving at? He can't have understood my movies, even though he does like them, I'm sure of it. And to put it plainly I'm sorry he likes them. I have a limited vocabulary, words like these make me feel uncomfortable. It's true the cinema, apart from five or six comforting exceptions, gets the criticism it deserves: it's a young, disjointed art. Everyone writes criticism in a bookish sense, never humanistically, but what do I care? I'm not one of those who goes running to the newsagent's to find out what such and such a critic has said—incidentally, what did Marotta say about *8½?* I'm always glad to read good reviews. I know perfectly well that negative criticism can be constructive, too, but the only kind I understand is the maternal sort, all little kisses, cuddles, flattering little words. . . .

In point of fact, in your movie, that bore who won't give you any little kisses ends up hanged by the neck. How often have you dreamed of hanging people who don't tell you how good you are, Signor Fellini?

Very often. Blunt criticism is to my mind very dangerous, because it kills spontaneity.

I wonder what you could have done if the cinema didn't exist. Suppose you'd been born when the cinema didn't exist? In you the borderline between fantasy and reality is so fluid.

What could I have done? I really don't know. Write, no. Writing is an ascetic discipline; a writer must be surrounded by solitude, silence, I could never get used to that. I'd certainly have devoted myself to something connected with show business, or else I'd have tried to invent films. I like movies because in them you express yourself while you are living, you tell about a journey while you are making it. I am extremely lucky in this, too: I was led by the hand into the only job in which I could fulfill myself in the most joyful, immediate way. . . .

I certainly can't imagine a Fellini hiding himself away, a solitary thinker. We journalists have invented the deification of movie directors, but this deification suits few others as much as it does you. You always need to be on a stage, in the limelight, with an orchestra playing a little march for you.

There might be this element of vanity in me. On the other hand, plays are acted with the footlights on. Let me tell you, I'm a very shy person. Yes, I am, even though you hoot with laughter and don't believe me; I'm really shy. And I'm glad I am because I don't believe there can exist an artist who isn't shy; shyness is a fount of extraordinary wealth. An artist consists of complexes.

*And that other kind of wealth? That common earthly kind,
a lovely bank account? By now you're a rich man.*

No, no, a thousand times no. My little treasure, how many
times do I have to tell you that I am not the producer of *La
Dolce Vita?* You know, I don't care about money. It has its
uses, that's all. What would I do with a villa with a swimming pool? What matters is to have no debts.

*Listen, Signor Fellini, the cardinal in 8½ says something
chillingly true: "No one comes into the world to be happy."
Are you happy? Or at least satisfied?*

Happy? Ah . . . yes . . . I'm glad to be in the world, glad to
be among people. I'm interested in what happens to me, I do
my work gladly, the more so since it never even seems like
work to me. Satisfied? . . . Ah . . . I hope I have never been completely satisfied, because that would be the end. Things have
turned out very well for me, of course. But they've turned out
the way they had to turn out.

*You mean that you think it's only right and fair that you
should have had the success you've had? You mean that you
have no doubts about the legitimacy of your success? You mean
that you don't consider with any modesty the fact that you are
exalted as "the most important film phenomenon of our time"?
That, in short, you consider sacred the triumph of* La Dolce
Vita, *the Greta Garbo-like veneration that surrounds you, the
fact that one newspaper advertisement is enough to bring out
hordes of madmen to offer you dying grandmothers, paralytic
aunts, and virtuous wives for your movies?*

How can I say to what degree this is fair or unfair? I have my
doubts while I am working, and they are the doubts of everyone who creates, who invents. Afterward, when the movie is
finished, I can never make myself objective, adopt an impartial
attitude. It's as if you invited me to talk about my life, about
a love affair, about an adventure, about a journey. How should
I judge it? No! I don't judge, I simply say it was necessary to
me. Everything that has happened to us, good or ill, has been

necessary. *La Dolce Vita* is a movie I made years and years ago. It was harder for me to free myself of it because it was a kind of monster, it kept on growing. Whether its success is justified, I don't know. Obviously the movie had a charge that justified so much emotion. As for the dying grandmothers and the paralytic aunts they offer me for my movies . . . I'm a romantic, I always like to see life in a fantasy key, so I could say that the cinema is a siren of infinite seductive power, and that this is why they give me their dying grandmothers. Instead, I like to think that people bring them to me to help me make a movie. Take that!

What a sublime diplomat. What a heavenly hoaxer. That's no answer. Recently, if I remember rightly, we two had a violent clash on the telephone as a result of which I shall no longer call you tu. *And that time you did give me an answer, I reminded you that journalists have always treated you with esteem and affection, and you answered that journalists had always given you the treatment you deserve because you are Federico Fellini and a great artist.*

Dirty liar. Rude little bitch.

Maestro, words like these will have to be deleted from the textbooks when grade school children study the life of Giuseppe Verdi, sorry, Federico Fellini.

Milan, February, 1963

EL CORDOBÉS

Story of a Bullfighter

He was an ugly, starving, filthy child, without father or mother. The youngest of five children, he had come into the world in Andalusia, and in the midst of the Civil War: May, 1936, remember? He couldn't even write his own name, Manuel Benitez, he couldn't count one two three four five. By day he looked after other folks' pigs, and by night he stole chickens, oranges. His only amusement was on the bull farm, practicing with the *muleta*, for which his guardians would beat him across the shoulders and the chest until he fainted. He was the living symbol, in those days, of a despairing, illiterate, defeated Spain. Today he is the most famous, well-loved, venerated, adulated, exalted man you can meet there. He is adored by the rich and the poor, the stupid and the intelligent, the ignorant and the cultured. His popularity is such that it has shattered that of any other bullfighter. You can't walk down the street with him without being assaulted by a delirious crowd. His movies (he makes movies, too) make millions. A brand of wine is called El Cordobés, its label bearing a photograph of him in his suit of lights. Generalissimo Franco invites him to dinner and to go shooting; the ministers and heads of the Falange come to pay homage to him; aristocratic ladies count it a point of honor to make love for at least one night with him: this idol who has a long, slender body covered with scars and a face that to some looks like the face of James Dean, to others of Sinatra, but to me looks just like the face of a bricklayer, like the faces of those bricklayers with dry, sunburned cheeks crossed with little lines that always harbor a little cement and dust. Besides, wasn't he in fact a bricklayer when, tired of being hungry, he wanted to emigrate and look for fresh hope in France?

The idol has dozens of farms, hundreds of bulls, six cars, and even a private airplane. He earns twenty-eight thousand dollars for every bull he faces, which makes it fifty-six thousand for every bullfight. He doesn't know that there is a queen in England, a president in Italy; he is afraid to compromise himself by saying that twenty years ago a world war broke out; and it isn't so long since he thought the sun went round the earth. Culture to him is an insidious snare by which wicked people propose to do him harm, condemn him to hunger again, and his advisers defend him shrewdly from any such danger: "He would lose his own personality if he learned." And he, lazy like all children, obeys. He buys lined and squared notepads, but then he leaves them blank. He makes appointments with the priest who maintains that he is teaching him, but then he doesn't turn up. In the silence of a primitive spirit, in the darkness of a lively mind, he continues to risk his life for the bloodthirsty. *Hombre*, have you ever seen a madman kneeling and laughing and skipping around in front of a bull as if the bull were a toy, a cloth teddy bear? His suicidal courage is his real wealth, apart from money, and he wastes it in the bull ring, not even suspecting that a light in that darkness, a voice in that silence, would transform him suddenly into a great man, a kind of El Cid, a national flag. In point of fact, there is no doubt that he has a disconcerting personality, that he's the greatest character given to Spain in recent years. Hemingway, if he had known him, would have been hopelessly fascinated by him, would have dedicated goodness knows what book to him—provided he could have spoken with him, which is almost impossible.

You realize it as soon as you meet him, on his farm—luxurious villa and swimming pool—outside Cordova, where he appears surrounded by his court of *banderilleros*, priests, lawyers, in-laws, guitarists, *cuadrillas*, photographers, chauffeurs, Frenchmen wanting to write his biography, a brunette just picked up in Granada, whither tomorrow, by when he'll have had enough of her, she will be returned, in time for another to take her place. His court flatters and exploits him, he wallows happily in it all, and, seen from behind, he strikes you as a charming and irritating young layabout. But then you see him facing you, and, facing you, he is someone who knows what he wants, has paid dearly for what he has, with a price that cost him all his illusions. That tumbling lock of coarse, fair hair, for example, isn't tumbling by accident; he disarranges it that way to give himself a *genre*. He doesn't wear that white sombrero by chance; he has put it on so that he can be spotted from afar. Those smiling white teeth, that smile of a wild animal that cannot be caged, doesn't merely reflect an animal-like sexuality; he smiles so on purpose to win you over from the first moment. At table, where he's invited you to sit without grasping who you might be (the priest in the place of honor, you on the priest's right-hand, himself next to you to nudge you when the priest is thanking Our Lord for the food: "Say grace with the priest. Why aren't you saying grace with the priest?"), he immediately starts calling you by your Christian name, not because he calls everyone by his Christian name, but to make you his friend, put you on his side: you could be useful to him. He hasn't grasped who you are, what you do, what you're after, but he's grasped that you're a foreigner, therefore dangerous but maybe useful, and, "Look at this picture of me with Caudillo, I'm a great admirer of his." For him the world goes no further than Spain, Mexico, where he knows only the arenas, and Paris, where he knows only the night spots (he goes there from time to time and brings back with him some lady thirsting after violent emotions, but he sends her back after a week, as he will the brunette he picked up in Granada). For him the rest of the terrestrial globe is a desert. The past doesn't count, or if it does count, it's to remind him that he's been in prison once and doesn't want to go there again. Who would think that he's interested in the heavens, though not the heavens of the priests, the heavens of man, the journey to the moon and to other planets, those sputnik things, and that he's jealous of those what-do-you-call-them, that's it, astronauts. When you tell him that his suit of lights embroidered in gold and silver weighs as much as an astronaut's spacesuit, his eyes shine with pride. His eyes are intelligent, and he is intelligent, too, in his silence and his darkness: to escape from this interview he kept me moving for three days, on his farms, among his bulls, shooting in his woods, drinking in his *cuevas*. Silent, or speaking Andalusian so I couldn't understand him, or Spanish to tell me that some people scare him more than an angry bull. Why? *"Porque tu empleas las palabras como los cuernos del toro—y no soy tonto"*: "Because you use words like the horns of a bull—I am not stupid."

On the day he finally made up his mind to talk to me he subjected me, rather by way of vendetta, to a wild gymkhana in a

Land-Rover, from which I still thank God I survived. Seated behind the steering wheel, with myself and the *espada* boy alongside and a terrorized *cuadrilla* behind, he hurtled that truck up and down hills, hurled it down precipitous slopes, made passes at trees, missing them by no more than a fraction of an inch, plowed through hens, hedges, daisies, stopped to shoot at a pheasant or a rabbit, and finally sank it in a field of mud and stones, destroying the lot: springs, wheels, engine, a Land-Rover worth some three thousand dollars. Then he climbed onto the roof and with cupped hands yelled for them to bring him a horse, two horses, five horses. On horseback he set off to find a fighting cow; on horseback he took us to a clearing, to work the cow with the cape—for his own pleasure or for ours, either way my only safety lay in a tree behind which I could hide in difficult moments. He worked the cow for so long that the moment came when, exhausted, she fell forward onto her nose, breaking both her jaws and becoming an atrocious, useless fountain of blood: the very symbol of today's Spain. So then the *banderilleros* tied her to the tree to kill her, and he himself suddenly calmed down, like a child who has broken a plaything and is about to cry over it. *"Vámonos,"* he said roughly, dejectedly.

ORIANA FALLACI: *That poor creature tied to a tree like a man about to be shot, with her jaws broken, her nose streaming with blood. Listen, she's still crying. What a tragic job yours is, Manuel. What on earth makes anyone become a bullfighter? Money, ambition, what?*

EL CORDOBÉS: When a man's poor, he's hungry for everything, not only for bread. And so he becomes a bullfighter for so many reasons together, you see, from necessity, from ambition. My father died when I was a year old, my mother died soon after. I was the youngest of five small children, and the one who did best out of us all, see, was the one taken by my grandmother, who had a bit of land. My sisters all went into domestic service; I used to plow or mind pigs for other folk. Hungry, see, always hungry. And when this happens to you, you think how grand it would be if you could buy yourself a whole ham, see, and hang it up in the window and cut a slice off it whenever you wanted. And then you think how grand it would be to be somebody instead of nobody, somebody maybe like Manolete, who's even been given a statue in a square in Cordova, all because of the bulls. It's grand, see. It's grand when the papers talk about you and people recognize you in the street, recognize you out of millions of people. They don't recognize the other millions, but you they do: it's fantastic. So is having so much money. Money's grand too because with it you can buy whatever you want, and you can buy an apartment for each of your sisters so that they don't have to work for other people anymore, and as well as an apartment you can buy them a car and a TV too. There, she's stopped crying. Maybe they've killed her. Look, it hurts me to see an animal die, I can't even kill a hen. Once, when I was hungry, I stole a hen, and I killed it. But I was shaking all over as I killed it, and as I killed it, I turned my head away and didn't feel hungry anymore. Have they killed her?

Yes, they've killed her. Now they're taking her away with the tractor.

She was a good cow, she was. She fought well. I respected her, and I still respect her because she died at her work, see, just like I might or the horse might. It's true, see, that we come into the world to work and to die, all of us, men, animals, and the bull, too. When he enters the arena, he realizes he's come into the world to work and to die. I know when he realizes it because he fights hard to defend himself, and then I'm sorry to kill him, see, and I ask the spectators for permission to spare his life. Yes, it's a tragic job, mine. But when you're fifteen years old and you've been working other folks' fields for ten years and dreaming of being somebody and owning a whole ham, that's tragic too, see? When I got tired of working in the fields, I went to Madrid and became a laborer. I was paid thirty pesetas a day, which isn't much when you're working nine hours a day and they take twenty-five pesetas off you for a bed at night. All you've got left is five pesetas, which isn't even enough to pay your train fare home if you want it, and so you have to travel on the roof of the train. You know how you travel on the roof of a train? You jump onto the first car, and when they catch you, you escape, jumping from car to car, but against the wind, so the wind doesn't knock you under. And as you escape, you know what you think? You think of bulls; that is, you think that since you have to run such risks, you might as well risk your life against bulls. And, anyway, if your life's wretched enough, you have to take risks, don't you? So you get off the train and find a *muleta*, and you start making passes with the first cow you see and then with another and then with another, until you've learned. That's how I learned; nobody taught me. I didn't even go to the bullfights because I didn't have the money to pay for the ticket. You can never get in without paying, see. I tried it, but it's hopeless. Have they taken her away with the tractor?

Yes, they've taken her away. Now they're loading her onto the truck.

She was a brave cow, see, she didn't deserve to come to such a bad end. Not that her life's worth the life of a man, the life of a man is more precious than the life of a cow or a bull, even if the man's wicked. Still, the life of a cow or bull is precious too, inasmuch as he risks it, don't you think? A lot of men, you see, get tired of minding other folks' pigs, you see, and they choose other jobs like playing soccer or boxing. I don't like soccer, and I don't understand boxing: I don't understand two men hurting each other, punching each other, and people yelling for them to hurt each other more. The bull is a wild animal, and in a bullfight the man is pitting himself against the wild animal; the animal has strength, but the man has brain. But a man is a man, and how can anything pit itself against a man? Two men hitting each other like that—bam! bam! bam!—and afterward their faces all disfigured, noses broken, I don't know, it strikes me as all very boorish. Rather than do that I went on working as a laborer, and in fact I was just about to emigrate to France, to work in the vineyards or as a laborer, when my fortunes took a sudden turn for the better. Have they loaded her onto the truck?

Yes, she's on. Now they're taking her away. Don't think about it anymore, Manuel.

Because, you see, I never went to school. It's barely a year since I learned to read and write. It was a year ago that I took on that teacher who used to follow me everywhere, see, and he used to teach me words and numbers and stuff. Now the priest teaches me. I go to him nearly every day, whenever I can anyhow. And he corrects my spelling mistakes and other mistakes—for example, you might write two words joined together and they should be separate words, or you might write two separate words and they should be joined together—and then multiplication, division, and yesterday he gave me a poem to read. It was the first time I'd ever read a poem, see, and it had such an effect on me that it made the hairs on the back of my hand stand up, like when the bull's charging me. I was trembling more than if the bull had got me, because the poem was so beautiful, see, so strong, and it said things that are true, see.

What did it say, Manuel?

Hombre, I can't remember it exactly, but it was about a poor man whose wife has died. The judge comes to seize everything he has, and he says, listen to what he says: "Come in, judge, sir, come in everyone. Don't worry, don't be afraid, judge, sir. If you'd come the day before yesterday, I'd have crushed you against the door, judge, sir, but today's she's dead! Take the furniture, take it all. There's no money here, I spent it on food for her and on medicines that didn't do any good. What's left only upsets me. Take the bags of corn and the sickles and this bit of stuff, what would I do with it anyway? . . ." And then he says, listen to what he says: "But watch out, judge, sir, if anyone dares to touch this bed where she died, this bed where I loved her when we were both healthy, the bed where her body lay. . . ." You know, it still makes me shiver.

Listen, Manuel, doesn't it make you angry to think that until now you never knew how to read or write, aren't you sorry? And weren't you sorry before, Manuel?

No, because I didn't know there was such a thing as school. And when you don't know a thing's there, you don't want it, do you? I used to work and eat, eat and work, and so I thought I had everything there was to be had. Then one day I heard about this school. But how I saw it was that it was something very big, so big, impossible, that I knew it wasn't for me, and so I didn't want it. Do you understand me? And I'm not sorry now, either, not because I'm not the only one who doesn't know—there are thousands and thousands and thousands who don't know, and at least now I'm managing as best I can, all things considered. Angry, why? For me to get angry I have to be really insulted, by something really offensive, and poverty isn't offensive. I've been poor, and now I'm not anymore, now I have everything I want, the most of the most. I have farms and clothes and six cars, and now I have an airplane, too. I wanted to be the first bullfighter in the world to have an airplane for getting from one bullfight to another and so on, and also because I like flying very much. You see things from far off, and you just sit back and rest and suddenly you're there, see. I used to dream of having one, and now I've bought that, too. I bought it from a North American in Los Angeles, it's a seven-seater Piper. It's not very big, but still it's an airplane, with a pilot who pilots her for me until I've learned to pilot her myself. And so why should I feel angry?

Listen, Manuel, now that you have your airplane and six cars and so many farms and so many things and so much money, are you learning the things you couldn't learn when you were a child?

The trouble is I don't have time. You see, I have so many things to do, the bullfights, the traveling, business, raising cows and bulls, my own pigs, and then I make movies, and then I go home and the house is always full of people. I'm never alone, how can you learn things if you're never alone?

So you try to spend some time alone?

But I don't like being alone, I've been alone plenty. I like having people around, who come and go and make a noise and talk, I like that better than learning, understand? Any learning I do is done with the priest, and that's enough, isn't it? Enough.

No, it's not enough, Manuel. What does the priest teach you, Manuel?

I told you what he teaches me, all those things he teaches me, and then religion and then general culture, history, geography, stuff about today, yesterday, etc.

Do you know, for example, that there was a world war twenty years ago?

Listen, I don't want you to ask me any questions about politics, understand?

But this isn't a question about politics, Manuel. It's a question about history. There was a great war, twenty years ago: Do you know about it or don't you?

I know, I've heard about it, but it wasn't my doing.

But there's nothing wrong with knowing about it, Manuel. You don't get sent to hell just for knowing. It's the same as if I asked you the name of the Queen of England. What's her name?

There, you see, you're starting on politics again, you see? I don't want to talk about this sort of thing, understand? I don't know about these things. I know about bulls, and that's all, understand?

But it isn't prohibited to know the name of the Queen of England, Manuel. Since in England they have a queen, and her name is . . .

I don't want to know! Now you're making me angry, and I'll go away.

All right then, Manuel. Let's make our peace. But you must tell me what the priest teaches you, apart from religion and numbers and spelling.

He explains things to me. For example, I ask him about the things I like most, and he explains them to me.

And what are the things you like most?

Well . . . it may sound silly . . . because, you see, they're things nobody ever talks about, nobody, I don't know why, but they're fantastic things, see, wonderful, more wonderful than bulls, than anything . . . they're . . . they're things about the sky, astronomical things. I mean, do you know that the earth turns around the sun, and also that around the sun other planets like the earth are turning, and that we can go to them? Of course you know, you do, and you know about the moon and how to get there, but not me. And so I asked the priest, and he explained to me about these sputniks that go and take photographs that they send straight down to us on earth. When there are enough photographs, they'll send up a man. Isn't that fantastic, tell me? Look, I'll tell you something, I don't like danger for danger's sake; for example, I don't understand people who do parachute jumps for the fun of it. If it was necessary for something, for someone, I'd jump, too, but for nothing, like that, just for the sake of jumping, no, never. But to go up, you understand, right up, with those sputnik things, I'd go up myself at once, see. It's truly extraordinary, just think, to be put in a rocket and sent up to the moon. What men! Is it true that you know them?

Yes, it's true.

Listen then, when you see them, couldn't you ask if they need anyone, me, say? I don't know, if they needed someone for something difficult or dangerous that the others don't want to have a go at, couldn't you tell them: look, there's my friend Manolo who's a bullfighter, and he'd be glad to go? At once, at once, at once, even if it means dying. If you could tell them! Look, I'll admit something to you, I wouldn't leave the bulls for anything in the world, not for a woman or anything—if they take the bulls from me, I'll be like a bird that can't fly because they've cut off his wings—but to go in those things, up there, up to the moon, I'd even leave the bulls, I swear to you, even the bulls. I'd leave everything, will you tell them?

All right. I'll tell them. But aren't you afraid, Manuel?

Of course I'm afraid. I'm afraid like anyone else. Don't take any notice of the way I laugh in the arena; I laugh because I'm always laughing, it's my character. I'm always pleased even if the bull's a bad one, but I'm afraid all the same. You know you can die of fear in the arena? Look, it's easier to die of fear than *cornadas.* Your heart bursts when the bull's running at you with those pointed knives on his head. Last year when I had that ugly wound and it looked as if I'd die, I was more dead of fear than wounds. One horn had already been into me once, see, and I'd fallen down, and the bull was driving the other horn in. I felt it probing my insides, probing deeper and deeper, and my fear was stronger than the pain. The heart was going out of me along with the blood. Life is everything, isn't it? Even if it's an ignorant life, it's the only life you have. If you only have four hens, to others they're only four hens but to you they're everything, and you don't part with them easily, do you? I'd like to live a hundred and fifty years, I would. But seeing we have to die . . . I mean, it's idiotic to die falling off a roof, but not going to the moon, for that you'd die even at twenty-eight. There are so many ways of dying. My father died because a eucalyptus fell on him and . . .

I'd heard that he died during the Civil War.

It's not true! A eucalyptus fell on him and broke his leg. And because he had diabetes, he got gangrene. So they amputated his leg, and he died. I know that. It was a sad death, my father was a waiter in Palma del Rio, and he was poor and hadn't seen anything: it was a sad death. But on the moon it wouldn't be a sad death because it would be a courageous thing, and what I like best in people is courage, there's nothing in the world I respect like courage, see, and . . .

What kind of courage, Manuel?

What do you mean, "What kind of courage, Manuel?" Courage. The courage to face up to the bull, the courage to go up in those sputnik things. What other kinds of courage are there?

There's the courage that isn't physical courage, the courage they call moral courage.

I don't understand.

The courage to say no because you're convinced it's right to say no even if it costs you your job, for example.

I don't understand. You're talking about things I don't know, I haven't heard about. You say things that are too difficult for me. You ask questions that are too complicated. And

I don't know how to answer your complicated questions. What were you saying?

It doesn't matter, Manuel, it doesn't matter.

But it does matter! I want to understand, I do. Ah, I get it! You mean the courage to say I've been in prison?

That's it, yes. That, too.

But that isn't courage. What courage do you need to say a thing that's true? A thing that's true is true: period. You say it: period. And since it's true and you say it, what's courage got to do with it?

Have you been in prison, Manuel?

Hombre! I'll say I have. I'll say! Plenty of times!

Because you used to steal, Manuel?

Hombre! I'll say I used to steal! I'll say! Plenty of times! Oranges and hens, bread and potatoes. For example, I'd go out with a sack. And I'd go into someone's orange grove and fill the sack with oranges, and then I'd sell them. Or else I'd go up to a hen coop and steal the hens, but it wasn't really stealing, would you say? When you steal from hunger, it isn't really stealing. Not that I enjoyed stealing, you know; it used to trouble me. And then you're always afraid they'll nab you, but I was the only man in the family, my brother was at my grand-mother's, and I could hardly send my sisters Carmelita and Angelita out stealing, could I? And someone had to steal, didn't they? But that wasn't why I went to prison. I went to prison because I used to jump into the middle of the arena, I was a *spontaneo.* You know, *spontaneos* are the boys who want to be bullfighters, and so they clamber into the arena to face the bull. It's prohibited by law, see, they arrest you—and how. And the only time they ever put me in jail for stealing, I hadn't stolen a thing, see? That time it was the priest's figs. The fact is that the sergeant of the Civil Guard had it in for me—maybe he couldn't stand me because I didn't have a steady job, and I used to practice my cape work on other people's steers—and so when the priest started shouting, "They've stolen the figs from my fig tree! Oh! They've stolen the figs from my fig tree!" the sergeant picked on me, and they took me to court. Then the sergeant realized that it wasn't me who'd taken the priest's figs, and he said so. But by then the magistrates had me under lock and key, and they didn't want to let me go. So they produced dozens of laws, article this, that, and the other, and stuff that showed I was a vagrant, and they condemned me for vagrancy, article this, that, and the other, and shut me up in prison for three and a half months. For nothing.

And didn't you protest. Don't you want to protest now, talking about it?

Why? Tell me, what good would it have done to protest? When you're poor, what's the use of protesting? Who's going to listen to you? Who'll believe you? You have to be rich before you can protest, and then it's quite different, see, because money's the only way to make yourself understood, see. There's no use making yourself unsociable when they say you've stolen the figs and you know you haven't stolen the figs at all. You only wear yourself out with anger, waste your strength. And if you waste your strength, you get weaker, and then you'll never manage to get rich. I just kept calm, quite calm, and then I came calmly out of prison, and slowly but surely I became a bullfighter and earned my first real money and . . .

What did you buy, Manuel, with the first money you made as a bullfighter?

I bought a big ham. When I started doing bullfights, I used to travel around with a big ham. I'd arrive at the hotel, with my ham, and I'd hang it up in the window, and then I'd cut slices off it. It was grand. It was grand because it was grand to have the money to buy yourself a whole ham and cut off a slice or two whenever you wanted, day or night. It made you happy, proud, I don't know. There are fellows who like traveling around with a ladylove or a friend; I like traveling around with a ham. A ham's better than a ladylove or a friend: it never lets you down, it lets itself get eaten up without a word, and it takes away your hunger. And when it's finished and there's only the bone left, you can buy a new one so that it's like always having the same ham, do you follow me!

Listen, Manuel, what else do you like besides bulls and the moon and ham?

Girls. Women. Women are beautiful, they're beautiful even when they're ugly. I couldn't do without a woman. No, I always have to have a ladylove.

So then why don't you start a family, Manuel?

Hombre! Because I watch out! Look, I was engaged one time, see, when I was young—I was seventeen. She was from Palma del Rio. And she left me. Because I didn't have money or work, and her parents used to say I'd be a good-for-nothing because I wanted to be a bullfighter, she left me. Now if I see her, I greet her and say good morning, good evening, how are you. But at the time it hurt me, see? I never let her see that it hurt me, but it did hurt me, and so you see I'm happy like this, with lots of ladyloves. Every now and then the newspapers give me a fiancée, some Geraldina, some Marchioness or other, or some little French girl, but there's no truth in it, you know. You see, I may be wrong, but I think that when a man's married, he's no longer free to die, not even to die, and so a man couldn't work the bulls close, like I do. And I want to work close to the bulls, you understand? Because, you see, I don't fight bulls from hunger anymore; I've got so much money that it'll last me until I die even if I don't die till I'm eighty, a hundred and fifty. I fight now because, well, the moment always comes when you don't do a thing for money, understand? You have to wait for the moment, which sometimes never comes but sometimes comes, and when it comes, you have to work better than if you were paid for it, see. For example, when that one gored me last year, money didn't have anything to do with it. What did was the fact that I was fighting in Madrid, for the first time, in Madrid where I used to be a laborer. And I could see he was a bad bull, and I said to myself, Manolo, you'll come out of this either dead or in triumph. I came out of it dead even if I didn't subsequently die, thanks to Doctor Fleming and his penicillin.

And why do you make movies, Manuel?

Oh, that. I do it because they pay me. But I don't like it, see. It's too easy, and it's boring, too. Somebody tells you to act like you felt such and such a thing, and you do. Period. He says, "The camera frightens you," and, "You feel the horns? They're into you?" And then I don't even like watching movies, I get bored. I only went twice to the theater to see my own movies. I didn't like them. The theater is like the city, full of noise. And you have to wear a tie; I feel strangled wearing a tie. I like the country because it's what I know and because there there are trees and horses and cows and the air is clean and you don't have to wear a tie.

And the sea? Do you like the sea, Manuel?

Yes, no. No! In the sea there are sharks, and I don't know how to defend myself against sharks, because they don't go for the *muleta*, they don't. They tear a piece out of you, and they're off. And you never know where they're coming from or how or why, and they scare me just like your complicated, difficult questions.

And do you like El Cordobés, Manuel?

Yes, I do. I like him for the way he fights; I like him for the way he throws money away; I like him because of how he used to be hungry; I like him for the way he laughs; I like him for the way he defends himself. He never stops defending himself. I know he always has to defend himself, always, from bulls, from women, from friends, from enemies, from the difficult questions of a dangerous woman. Ask if they've taken away my cow, whether the butcher's come.

They must have taken her away, and the butcher must have come; there's no one left in the yard, Manuel. There's only silence, and it will soon be dark. You'd think they'd all died, along with the cow. But perhaps she isn't dead, Manuel, and perhaps she'll live again.

Near Cordova, April, 1965

SAMMY DAVIS, JR.

The Luck to Be Ugly

The most talked about couple in America lived in a house in New York City, on Ninety-third Street East, halfway between the luxury of Park Avenue and the desolation of Harlem. A mile or so north and you find only whites, a mile or so south and you find only blacks: they lived in that limbo because she was white as white and he was black as black. They married, not caring that she was white and he black, and brought into the world a daughter who was neither white nor black and adopted a son. They went on loving each other, living together, cost what it might. It might have cost him his death at the hands of a criminal or a madman; it had already cost her the contempt of a lot of people. She was Mai Britt; he was Sammy Davis, Jr. The house was elegant; before it stood their Rolls Royce; inside it there triumphed a happiness to us incomprehensible. Mai said, "It's four years now since I made a film, and I have no intention of returning to making films. Being an actress didn't matter to me, I became one by accident. It was all through Mario Soldati, who saw me in Stockholm. But it was only when I met Sammy that I realized that my real vocation was this, being a wife and mother. And what more can I want? When you see my husband, you'll understand that I can't want more: he's such a beautiful man, in every sense. He has a beautiful heart, beautiful courage, a beautiful intelligence. For me everything about him is beautiful, his smile, his expression, his face. Oh, you should see him with his short haircut, he looks like a boy! But he's no boy, he's a real man, a man who lives his life in reality, not waiting for kingdom come, and that's another reason why I like him, I love him, I'll always like him, I'll always love him." Together they were beautiful, what a pity they have parted.

Waiting for me, that November, in the big living room was Mai, with Tracey, their coffee-colored daughter, and Mark, their adopted son, also Negro. "We love children. Whether the world approves or

not, we intend to have lots of children, our own and adopted."
After a while Sammy arrived, the ugliest man I'd ever seen. Perhaps
being next to Mai, who is so beautiful, made him look even uglier,
so small and skinny and twisted, with his huge nose flattened by
punches, his mouth that opens wide like a pink oven, like the
mouth of an ogre, his glass eye (he lost the sight of it in a motor accident many years ago) that always looks in the same direction while
the other looks all around. But a very strange thing happened.
As the minutes, the hours, passed, he grew steadily less ugly, until
he almost wasn't ugly, and then he wasn't ugly at all, and then he
was almost beautiful, and then beautiful: the paradox of Mai. He
was beautiful in his ingenuousness, his honesty, his optimism, the
youthful joy with which he showed me his rich man's house, his
hundred suits, his two hundred pairs of shoes, his three hundred
shirts, his dozens of cameras, gold cuff links, gold watches, gold
rings, gold cigarette holders, gold tie tacks, the absurd and useless
luxury that compensates for his hard life, his youth spent washing
dishes, cleaning out toilets, the humiliations, the disappointed
hopes. But his greatest compensation was the woman he had managed to marry, as in a fairy tale, the tale of the princess and the toad.
The princess falls in love with the toad, and the toad turns into a
gorgeous young man, a miracle for which he pays dearly every day,
for which he will go on paying as long as he lives. So it's plain that
he talked of nothing else, that he was able to talk of nothing else,
it was an obsession. Actor, dancer, singer, convert to the Jewish
faith, friend of the Kennedys, star of movies, plays, and a musical,
Golden Boy, which was reaping success on Broadway, author of a
book entitled *Yes, I Can*, he could have talked about a great many
things. And instead he talked only about one thing; he was obsessed by it. About his compensation. About his fairy tale. About
his love for the blond white woman who was in love with him.
And it is the quality of that love that makes this interview remain
so fresh, so worthy of our continued attention.

ORIANA FALLACI: *On my way to your house, Mr. Davis, I had a very disturbing thought. You have absolutely everything to make you hated by the multitudes of mean-minded and stupid people: you're a Negro, a Jew, married to a beautiful blond. . . . Truly there's no other internationally famous person who contrives to combine so many "sins" into one. And I concluded: goodness, this man must positively enjoy doing battle with the world, irritating people, provoking them, defying them. . . . But do you really enjoy it, Mr. Davis, or does it make you unhappy?*

SAMMY DAVIS, JR.: I don't enjoy it in the least. I've no taste for quarreling. I'm not much of a quarreler, and a lot of years have passed since the day when, as a boy, I realized that you can't spend your life coming to blows with your neighbor. In any case, brawls don't get you anything except a broken nose and an ugly face. I don't want to fight anybody intentionally, on principle. I only want to lead my life according to those standards I believe to be right, and the "sins" that are combined in me aren't aimed at irritating, provoking, defying anyone. They arise out of reality, logic, out of being consistent. I'm a Negro, and that's a reality. I'm a convert to Judaism because in Judaism I found the religious faith I was looking for, the solution to a spiritual crisis that was troubling me, and so that was an act of logic. I married a beautiful blond because I loved her and she loved me, so that was simply being consistent. Nothing else. I never thought, "I'll be a convert to Judaism in order to annoy the Catholics, the Methodists, the Presbyterians, and the rest." I never said, "I want to marry a blond, beautiful white woman." All I ever said was, "I'll marry the woman I fall in love with, and she will bear my children." That's all. Chance or destiny willed it that the woman should be blond, beautiful, and white. Period.

*Not period, seeing you don't enjoy it, you said so. Not period,
seeing it precipitates and redoubles and trebles all the prejudices, the outrage, and the hostility. Not period, seeing . . .*

. . . seeing it makes me unhappy. And it certainly does make
me unhappy. I get hurt easily, and who wouldn't get hurt
in my position? Wouldn't you? You can't even have the faintest
idea; you can go wherever you want, you can, with your white
skin. You can enter any place, you can, with your white skin.
Nobody throws you out of a hotel because you're white. Nobody stops you from entering a restaurant because you're fair.
Nobody! And it isn't very nice, believe me, to go into the El
Morocco with your own wife and see people making faces,
turning their backs on you. It isn't even logical. It's absurd!
Why should they make faces, turn their backs on you? Because
you married a white woman, Sammy, obviously. And why
shouldn't I have married a white woman? Because it's against
the rules, obviously. What rules? *The* rules, Sammy. Rules?
I've never gone by rules set by other people; I've always felt
that they don't count for anything, rules, if your own conscience doesn't want to accept them. So don't tell me I can't play
this piano because it's against the rules; don't tell me I can't
have that Rolls Royce because it's against the rules; don't tell
me I can't marry a white woman because it's against the rules.
If I love her, the white woman, if she loves me, if I can be a
good husband to her and give her what she desires, why can't I
marry her? Because it's never been done before, Sammy, obviously. Ah, yes? It's never been done? Then I'll do it. If the
law of it's-never-been-done were a valid logical, consistent law,
the world wouldn't exist. Progress wouldn't exist. Houses,
ships, the printed word, radio, cars, rockets wouldn't exist!
Fellini's movies wouldn't exist, Ingmar Bergman's movies
wouldn't exist, the window wouldn't exist, nothing would
exist. Who made the first window? Assuredly someone who was
told you can't because it's never-been-done. To which he replied: then I'll do it. And he did it. Not because he enjoyed

doing battle with people, irritating, provoking them. Not to give offense. But because he was within his rights to try. Just as I was within my rights to leave Catholicism for Judaism, to marry Mai. . . .

Sacred rights, Mr. Davis, but I have a question to ask you— an unpleasant question, maybe, and a very serious one. When you married, you and Mai, didn't you think about the responsibility of bringing into the world children who would be neither black nor white? Weren't you at all scared at the thought of imposing too hard a life on your offspring? The world is what it is, Mr. Davis, society is as you know it. It isn't comfortable to be neither black nor white: rejected by the whites because you aren't white, by the Negroes because you aren't black. It presents terrible problems, not belonging to any particular race, finding oneself in the middle. . . .

Problems? No offspring of woman's womb is without problems. You, white and fair as you are, are you without problems? You think maybe you have fewer problems or substantially different problems from a Negro with crinkly hair? Let's have a look at them, these problems. Physical problems? The answer to that one is my daughter Tracey: a beautiful child, exquisitely made, wonderful. Mental problems? It's common knowledge that to mingle races does good, it's common knowledge that pure races always end up producing idiots. Aristocratic families, royal dynasties, have died out because as a result of being pure they bred idiots. This is a genetic law, not a personal point of view; it's true of plants, animals, human beings. And this leaves aside the fact that there's no such thing as a completely pure race; each of us has a drop of blood from some other race, a little drop of Jewish or Arab or Negro or Chinese blood, or whatever. Human, social problems? The world is improving. Believe Sammy, it's improving. Prejudices are growing fewer. What once even the imagination balked at is now beginning to be accepted in reality. Life for Tracey will be much easier than it has been for me, for my wife, for you, for today's adults. I am convinced that Tracey will have fewer problems being half white and half black than you, all white, and myself, all black, have had.

It's comforting and good too that you should be so optimistic, Mr. Davis. But are you sure you're not living in a world of hopes and dreams rather than of cruel realities?

Ah! I live in the most tangible reality, believe me. I know very well that I could be killed for the choice I've made, that anyone might take a shot at me: that's a reality too. But I'm an optimist, and I also know that those who'd like to shoot at me constitute a mad minority; the majority is composed of good folk, decent folk. If this weren't so, we'd still be living in caves and eating each other like fish, snakes. I'm optimistic, yes, and I have my own reasons for being so. I'm optimistic because when I met this woman, I said to myself no, she can't love me, there's no future in it, Sammy, don't even think about it, you're ugly, you're black, you've only got one eye, you've got a broken nose, and she looks like a fairy. Come on, Sammy, come on! And then I discovered that she loved me, that there was a future in it even though I was black and ugly and had only one eye and a broken nose. I'm optimistic because everyone said, "All right, but even so you can't marry." But we did. I'm optimistic because they said, "All right, you've done it, but it can't last." But it is lasting, and it'll go on lasting. This doesn't mean I'm saying, "Go ahead, baby, marry a Negro yourself, bring a baby into the world who's neither white nor black." No, I'm only saying that I've done it and it worked for me. It showed I was right, and that makes me optimistic.

But you're in a privileged position, Mr. Davis. You're famous, you're popular, you're rich, surrounded by admirers. Like Duke Ellington, Louis Armstrong, Harry Belafonte, Sidney Poitier, you can do things other people can't. People will always more easily accept rebellion, affirmations of principle, audacities from someone who is someone. When all is said and done, yours isn't a typical case. In the El Morocco they

*might make faces, turn their backs on you, but the doors of
the El Morocco are open to you.*

I never open a door, I never let anyone open a door to me,
unless I'm sure, confident, that the door will stay open for
whoever follows me. I never enter a club that won't admit other
Negroes. I never enter a restaurant that won't admit other
Negroes. I never work in a theater or a movie that doesn't give
work to other Negroes, because I can't forget that if I'm admitted, it's because others entered before me, because they
opened those doors, one by one, little by little, so that I can
open them a little wider. And so I must see to it that after me
another will open them a little wider still, until they are flung
wide open. In short, the fact that many doors are open to
Sammy Davis, Jr., means that the same doors are open to
others. James Baldwin would never have started writing books
if Richard Wright hadn't written them before him. I would
never have succeeded if other Negro actors and singers hadn't
succeeded before me. A Negro, you see, whatever he's doing, a
Negro never does it just for himself. He always does it both
for himself and for the others of his race, even though he
might not be aware of it. And I know, my wife knows, that by
getting married we have contributed something. I know, she
knows, that we have contributed something by bringing
Tracey into the world, and we are proud of it. You see, look,
take my musical comedy on Broadway, *Golden Boy.* I'm proud
to be on Broadway, I feel ten feet tall. When I think of it, my
goodness, I can feel both my eyes. Las Vegas, Hollywood, London, for me nothing was worth Broadway. But I know that
being on Broadway doesn't help only me. It helps twenty
Negro boys who are in the show along with the same number of
white boys. It helps to stir the stagnant waters of a theater of
which people ask only gay musicals that raise no problems.
When on Broadway has there ever been seen such real integration? When on Broadway has there ever been shown the love
story of a Negro and a white girl? *Golden Boy* wasn't that

originally, either; it was the story of a Jew who from being a violinist becomes a boxer. Well, now it's the story of a Negro who from being a violinist becomes a boxer and loves a very fair white girl. And people come to see it, every night the theater is full, people are accepting it!

No, Mr. Davis, people come to see, but they don't accept it. People fill the theater for your sake, not for the love story of the Negro and the white girl. For weeks now there have been articles about the "inopportunity" of showing a love story between a Negro and a white girl. People leave the theater making faces, saying, "How about that, what a thing." I quarreled with a friend of mine over it, Mr. Davis, and . . .

Yes, I know. They're the same people who make faces and turn their backs when Mai and I go into the El Morocco: decent, democratic, maybe even cultured Americans. Americans who maintain they're totally in favor of the Civil Rights laws, ready to defend the theory but not to accept the reality, not to recognize that a Negro and a white girl can love each other, marry, bring children into the world. Americans who go lightheartedly to see Tennessee Williams plays, which in the name of art show the most degrading sides of our society, without batting an eyelid. It doesn't mean a thing. I'm sorry for them, sincerely, but it doesn't mean a thing; they're a minority. And even this minority must feel something when I cry to the woman I love: "What color, what color are my hands? No color! No color!" At the bottom of their hearts they themselves must also feel that love has no color, love is simply love. I added those lines myself; *Golden Boy* is me in a way. I know exactly what it means to be involved in a love story of that kind, to feel yourself stared at when you walk down the street, to feel humiliated, knowing that, however things go, you're going to get very hurt. And in any case the central problem of *Golden Boy* isn't that either; it's the problem of a man who, halfway between the worlds of the whites and the Negroes, feels at ease with neither the whites nor the Negroes and rejected by both whites and Negroes.

But that's the problem I meant when I spoke of the responsibility of bringing into the world children who are neither white nor Negro, Mr. Davis. It's the problem . . .

It's not my daughter Tracey's problem.

Isn't it your problem, either, Mr. Davis?

No. No. No. I know a lot of Negroes who can't manage to communicate either with Harlem people or with Park Avenue people, and they're rejected both by Harlem and Park Avenue. But I'm not one of them. They are misfits, and I am not a misfit. They don't get on with either whites or Negroes, while I get on with both whites and Negroes.

There's one thing I've heard said, Mr. Davis: that you prefer being with whites to being with Negroes. Your greatest friends and supporters—Frank Sinatra, Peter Lawford, Danny Kaye, Jack Benny—are white, after all, are they not?

And Sidney Poitier, Harry Belafonte, Duke Ellington are Negroes, are they not? And my great friends? Harry and Sidney belong to my generation, we grew up together, we read books together, together we chose the road we did. No, there's no truth in the idea that more of my friends are whites than Negroes. The fact is that many of my friends are actors, and there are more white actors than Negro actors, in the proportion of a hundred to one, I'd say. Obviously I'm seen more with white people than with Negroes. Obviously I am going to be talked about, publicized, supported by a greater number of whites. So what? I love the Negroes. God knows I love them!

But do the Negroes love you, Mr. Davis? Especially since your marriage to Mai, are you sure the Negroes love you? There's a racism that's never spoken of, Mr. Davis, the racism that Negroes display toward whites or toward Negroes who marry whites. Shall we talk about that, Mr. Davis? Because I haven't quarreled only with . . .

During the electoral campaign I was alongside Bob Kennedy. I was fighting for him because I believed, I do believe, in him, because I was, I am, convinced that he will be a good senator and as good for America as his brother was. Well then, Bobby's last big rally was held in Harlem, the evening before the elections. And I was there, together with Mai, to ask the Negroes to vote for Bobby. Thousands and thousands of Negroes. And . . . well . . . it's ridiculous, it's incredible even, but they applauded me more than Bobby. Yes, the Negroes love me, and since my marriage to Mai they've loved me even more. Their racism . . . but who denies it? Does a white skin maybe give exclusive rights to hatred, contempt, error? Don't you understand that we Negroes have just as many idiot racists sick with fascism as you whites have? As many full of the same fears, the same arrogance as the whites, the same lack of dignity and generosity? Ah, those who belong to the Ku Klux Klan are neither better nor worse than those who belong to the racist Negro Black Muslim movement. They are both extremists, both disgusting, and I reject the one as strongly as I do the other because I believe that the answer to the race issue does not lie in reciprocal hatred, reciprocal contempt. I do not believe the Negro race to be an inferior race, but nor do I believe it to be a superior race, a model race. Quite simply, it's a race like any other: with its geniuses and its imbeciles. God! These things have to be said! We're in 1964, we're no longer in 1925, when an actress would walk around with a leopard on a leash! It has to be said that not only love has no color, hatred and violence have no color either!

Neither more nor less, Mr. Davis. In fact, as I was going to say, I haven't quarreled only with a white friend over Golden Boy, *I've also quarreled with a Negro girl friend of mine. She also twisted her mouth into grimaces, and I asked her why. Wouldn't you marry a white man? And she replied: "No! No! No!"*

I know girls like that, too. One of them is in my company.

A lovely Negro girl who's very intelligent and talented, she can't stand white men, white people, and she'd never marry a white man, she'd never even talk to a white woman. My wife is the only white woman who gets a word or a smile out of her. What should I say to her? She makes me angry and sad, but I console myself with the thought that Negroes of this kind are in the minority. Months ago when there were the Harlem riots, only two thousand Negroes joined in. And there are three million Negroes in Harlem. One mustn't judge the Negroes and the whites by the worst of them. It would be the same as judging Italians by the gangsters with Italian names. When I think about Italians, I don't think of the Al Capones, the Anastasias, the Johnny Dios, the Frank Castellos. I think of the good folk, the vast majority, who come to America in the hope of finding something—a good life, happiness—work hard to get it, and decently and honestly build their families and their fortunes. Or else . . . yes, or else it would be the same as judging the Jews by the grasping moneylenders who have Jewish names. When I think about Jews, I never think of the characters who lend money. I think of the millions of martyred victims of the pogroms, the millions killed in concentration camps, I think of the unhappy people whose religion I have embraced. Or else . . . yes, or else it would be the same as judging racism solely in an American context. When I think about the people who make faces and turn their backs on me, I don't think only of New York and the El Morocco; I think of London, Rome, Paris, Stockholm. Bigotry and prejudice aren't limited only to my country, to my people. My marriage to Mai had a bad reception elsewhere too: in Europe, in Italy. . . .

I don't think so, Mr. Davis, it's not so. In Italy you have been treated very decently. We Italians have many defects, but they do not include making faces at a Negro because he's a Negro. We're not racist.

Ah, no? I read more mean articles in the Italian press, after my marriage to Mai, than I don't know where. I even took proceedings against the weeklies. It isn't at all true to say that there's no racism in Italy. Try asking an Italian: "Would you marry a Negro? Would you let your daughter marry a Negro? Would you bring children into the world with a Negro? In short, would you do what Sammy Davis and Mai Britt have done?" Try it, and then tell me what they answer. Even the nicest, most cultured, most democratic people, even the people who cried out against Goldwater, would in the majority of cases react like your white friend and the Negro girl you know. They'd answer, "No! No! No!" In Italy, in Europe, you can go into any hotel you want, any restaurant you want, certainly, but the feelings that follow you when you walk down the street with your wife who is white are the same. At most, they respect you because you're a success. But this doesn't mean a thing when you deserve it. And I deserve it. Success didn't come to me by chance, I worked thirty-five years of my life to get it. I've washed dishes in kitchens, I've cleaned out toilets, I've emptied trash cans, and I started acting when I was four. When I was four years old, I used to act and sing with my parents. When I was six years old, I was engaged by some other people and left my parents' company, I never even went to school, because of it. I studied by correspondence course, or by reading books, and I sweated plenty, I still sweat plenty today, just as I used to, more than I used to, every night is my first night, every song is my first song, I deserve what I have, I deserve it down to the last drop, so why should people even want to deny this much to me?

Mr. Davis, one question. Do you count yourself a happy man? A lucky man and a happy man?

Of course I'm a happy man! The happiest you'll ever meet. Of course I'm a lucky man! The luckiest man you'll ever meet! What more can I ask than what I have? God has given me everything, everything: money, popularity, family. And he gave me this extraordinary wife, so good, so beautiful. And he not only granted that I should love her but also that she should love me, ugly as I am, with only one eye, and a broken nose, and small too, and black. How can I complain? I can't complain about anything, anything!

Not even about your broken nose, your one eye, your ugliness?

I know I'm dreadfully ugly, one of the ugliest men you could meet, but ugliness, like beauty, is something you must learn how to use. All my life I've resisted the temptation to be a little less ugly, to have my nose fixed, for example. My bone structure is good, my jaw line is good, my cheek bones are good, my body is well proportioned. Maybe, if I'd had my nose fixed, I'd have become almost passable. But what does being passable make you? It makes you mediocre: neither ugly nor handsome. Complete ugliness, utter ugliness, like mine, though, is almost attractive. Yes, yes, I'm convinced that a really ugly man, in the end, seems attractive. A man who is so-so you don't even stop and look at, much less follow. A man like me you see, you stop and look at him, you follow him to go on looking at him, to assure yourself that he really is the ugliest thing you ever saw, and from looking at him so much you know what happens? What happens is that you find something attractive about him, and you like him. Isn't this what happened to Mai? As for my eye, ah, the optician did such an extremely fine job on it that you can't tell the false one from the real. I look more as if I have a squint than as if I'm blind in one eye. Look, my eyelid doesn't even droop, it stands up nice and straight, a masterpiece, and . . . you want to know something? I see much more now that I have only one eye than I used to see before, when I had both. With my one eye I've discovered a lot of things: Judaism, for example. With my one eye I found my wife and married her. With my one eye I have made her the mother of our children: me so black, her so white, me so ugly, her so beautiful. God, isn't she extraordinary, my beautiful wife? Look what a woman! Look! With one eye I got her, with one eye! And it doesn't matter to her at all that I only have one eye, not to her it doesn't.

New York, November, 1964

ALFRED HITCHCOCK

Mr. Chastity

For years I had been wanting to meet Hitchcock. For years I had
been to see every Hitchcock film, read every article about Hitchcock, basked in contemplation of every photograph of Hitchcock:
the one of him hanging by his own tie, the one of him reflected in
a pool of blood, the one of him playing with a skull immersed in a
bathtub. I liked everything about him: his big, Father Christmas
paunch, his twinkling little pig eyes, his blotchy, alcoholic com-
plexion, his mummified corpses, his corpses shut inside wardrobes,
his corpses chopped into pieces and shut inside suitcases, his corpses
temporarily buried beneath beds of roses, his anguished flights, his
crimes, his suspense, those typically English jokes that make even
death ridiculous and even vulgarity elegant. I might be wrong, but
I cannot help laughing at the story about the two actors in the
cemetery watching their friend being lowered into his grave. The
first one says to the other, "How old are you, Charlie?" And
Charlie answers, "Eighty-nine." The first one then observes, "Then
there's no point in your going home, Charlie." I laugh even more
at another one—it's difficult to put it into words, but let's have a
try. A man who has a tapeworm goes to the doctor, who tells him
to come back with an egg and an apple. The man comes back with
the egg and the apple, and the doctor tells him to undress. Then
the doctor inserts the egg and the apple. The treatment continues
for six days: every day the man comes with the egg and the apple,
and the doctor does the same thing with them. On the seventh day
the doctor says to the man, "Today we'll put the egg in and leave
out the apple." Then he puts in the egg, eats up the apple, and
waits, with a hammer in his hand. After a while the tapeworm
peers out and in an irritated little voice asks, "Where's my apple?"
The doctor knocks him over the head with the hammer, and the
tapeworm drops dead. Hitchcock had told the story to a friend of
mine, and I used to tell it to myself when I felt sad. As the sadness

passed, I would mentally kiss his hands. I feel madly grateful to anyone who makes me laugh.

My opportunity to meet him and really kiss his hand came at the Cannes Festival, where Hitchcock was showing *The Birds*, a sinister film about birds that revolt against men and exterminate them by pecking them to death. Hitchcock was coming from Hollywood, and I rushed to Nice airport to greet him. Three hours later I was in his room on the fourth floor of the Carlton Hotel, gazing at him just as my journalist colleague, Veronique Passani, had gazed at Gregory Peck the first time she met him—and she had subsequently managed to marry him. Not that Hitchcock was handsome like Gregory Peck. To be objective, he was decidedly ugly: bloated, purple, a walrus dressed as a man—all that was missing was the moustache. The sweat, copious and oily, was pouring out of all that walrus fat, and he was smoking a dreadfully smelly cigar, which was pleasant only insofar as it obscured him for long moments behind a dense, bluish cloud. But he was Hitchcock, my dearest Hitchcock, my incomparable Hitchcock, and every sentence he spoke would be a pearl of originality and wit. In the same way as we assume that intellectuals are necessarily intelligent, and movie stars necessarily beautiful, and priests necessarily saintly, so I had assumed that Hitchcock was the wittiest man in the world.

He isn't. The full extent of his humor is covered by five or six jokes, two or three macabre tricks, seven or eight lines that he has been repeating for years with the monotony of a phonograph record that's stuck. Every time he opened a subject, in that sonorous voice of his, I foresaw how he would conclude; I had already read it. Moreover, he would make his pronouncements as if he knew it himself: hands folded on his breast, eyes cast up toward the ceiling, like a child reciting a lesson learned by heart. Nor was there anything new about his admission of chastity, of complete lack of interest in sex. Everyone knows that Hitchcock has never known any woman other than his wife, has never desired any woman other than his wife; because he's not interested in women. This doesn't mean that he likes men, for heaven's sake; such deviations are regarded by him with pained and righteous disgust. It only means that for him sex does not exist; it would suit him fine if humanity were born in bottles. Nor, for him, does love exist, that mysterious impulse from which beings and things are born; the only thing that interests him in all creation is the opposite of whatever is born: whatever dies. If he sees a budding rose, his impulse, I am afraid, is to eat it.

With the blindness of all disciples or faithful admirers, I took some time to realize his failings. In fact, our interview began with bursts of laughter and went on with bursts of laughter for a good half-hour. But then the bursts of laughter became short little laughs, the short little laughs became smiles, the smiles grew cold, and at a certain point I discovered that I could no longer raise a laugh, nor could I have done so even if he had tickled the soles of my feet. That was when I realized the most spine-chilling thing about him: his great wickedness. A person who invents horrors for fun, who makes a living frightening people, who talks only about crimes and anguish, can't be really evil, so I thought. He is, though. He really enjoys frightening people, knowing that every now and then somebody dies of a heart attack watching his movies, reading that from time to time a man kills his wife the way a wife is killed in one of his movies. Not knowing all the criminals whose master he has been is sheer torture to him. He would like to know about all such authors, to compliment each one and offer him a cigar. Because he can laugh about death with the wisdom of the sages? No, no. Because he likes death. He likes it the way a gravedigger likes it.

My meeting with Hitchcock spanned two sessions, in the presence of a publicity man who was protecting him as a bitch protects her pups, checking, watch in hand, on the duration in minutes of each interview. Despite my disappointment I still secretly cherished one acute hope: that Mr. Hitchcock would at least have the fervid imagination he is said to have. So I told him what had happened to me in Milan the morning I'd hurried off to meet him. Drunk with sleep, I had lit the gas under the coffee pot but then had forgotten to turn it off and drink the coffee. The vision of the coffee boiling away had only crossed my mind as the train was about to pull out of the station. So I had leaned out of the window, and yelling my address, I had thrown my front door key to a man I'd never seen in my life. Would he please go and turn off the gas for me, or else the house would blow up or burn down. So my key was in the hands of a total stranger. What would happen? What had happened? Had the stranger really contented himself with entering the house, turning off the gas, calling the fire department if the house was burning? Had he cleaned me out? Would he really have left my key at the newspaper office? Would he have kept it for himself? And supposing he left the key at the newspaper office, what assurance did I have that he wouldn't have had a copy made so he could get back inside the house and murder me? All things considered this was a perfect MacGuffin, an extraordinary teaser to be woven into a Hitchcock film.

Hitchcock listened with happy little eyes to the tale of my little drama, but when I put the above questions to him so that he could invent a suspenseful story, he looked at me as a child caught stealing would look, at an utter loss. And he was unable to invent a thing.

ORIANA FALLACI: *I have seen your last movie, Mr. Hitchcock. Yes, the one about the birds who eat humans. Phew! . . . The spectacle of the corpses whose very eyes have been devoured by the birds! . . . The scene of the children in flight, torn to shreds by a cloud of ferocious crows! . . . And to think you seem so innocuous, so innocent, incapable of even imagining such fearful things. Tell me something, Mr. Hitchcock: Why do you always make movies based on terror and crime, full of macabre scenes and anguish? Why do you always want to horrify and terrify us?*

ALFRED HITCHCOCK: Firstly, because if I made any other kind of movies, nobody would believe them. I explained this to Ingrid Bergman, when she asked me the same question: "Obviously, my dear, I could make a film of Cinderella. I'm a professional, good at my job. But if I make Cinderella, people will immediately start looking for the corpse." In the second place, because I'm a philanthropist: I give people what they want. People love being horrified, terrified. Have you never noticed that terror and horror have the same effect on the human species as a caress? Take a three-month-old baby. His mother bends over him and says, "Boo! I'm going to eat you up." The baby cries with fright and then smiles blissfully, while his mother smiles, too. Now take a six-year-old child on a swing. He drives the swing higher and still higher. Why? Because this frightens him and is more fun. Now take an adolescent on a roller coaster. Why does he ride on the roller coaster? Because every bend, every drop, fills him with horror, and this is fun. Now take a man racing in a car and risking death at any moment. Why does he race in a car? Because risking death gives him an exquisite shudder, and that is fun. People would pay, indeed they do pay—consider my movies— to have fun with fear. And lastly . . .

And lastly because, in spite of looking like a nice, innocuous man, you have fun yourself making these movies.

I don't deny it. I admit it. I don't get such a kick out of anything as much as out of imagining a crime. When I'm writing a story and I come to the crime, I think happily: now wouldn't it be nice to have him die like this? And then, even more happily, I think: at this point people will start yelling. It must be because I spent three years studying with the Jesuits. They used to terrify me to death, with everything, and now I'm getting my own back by terrifying other people. And then it must be because I'm English. The English use a lot of imagination over their crimes. They have the most amusing crimes in the world. I remember that adorable case against that adorable Christie, a necrophiliac who had murdered eight women. Concerning the eighth victim there occurred the following dialogue between judge and accused: "So you knocked the woman down in the kitchen, Mr. Christie." "Yes, Your Honour." "There are three steps down into the kitchen." "Yes, Your Honour." "The poor woman fell." "Yes, Your Honour." "And you killed her." "Yes, Your Honour." "And assaulted her, too?" "I believe so, Your Honour." "Before, after, or during death?" "During, Your Honour." Oh, England's fantastic for this kind of thing. Pity that they never managed to conceal the corpse. It's much easier in America. I always suggest the rubbish disposal chute, straight into the incinerator. Or else eating it, but then it has to be tender.

Mr. Hitchcock do you realize that criminals make use of your lessons and your movies? Do you know that, years ago, in Ankara, a journalist killed a diplomat using a revolver concealed inside a camera, exactly as you did in your movie, Special Envoy?

Yes I know. And I was very flattered. Oh, I don't know what I wouldn't give to know about all the times I've been copied. The trouble is that every day someone commits the perfect crime: one that isn't discovered. As the crime isn't discovered, I don't know whether they've copied me. But three years ago, in Los Angeles, some man who had murdered three wives said he'd murdered the third after seeing *Psycho*. The journalists telephoned me: "So now you're happy?" "No," I told them. "He didn't say after which of my films he murdered the second. Maybe he murdered the first after drinking a glass of milk." From the glass of milk to the revolver, how often that's happened.

Of course you fire a revolver like a champion, Mr. Hitchcock, and during the war you were doubtless a very demon.

I've never so much as held a revolver or any other kind of weapon in my hand. I don't even know what a trigger looks like, and I was never in the Army. When World War I broke out, I was too young, thank God. When the World War II broke out, I was too old, thank God. I've never done any shooting. People who go shooting . . . you don't go shooting by any chance?

Well, actually . . . yes.

You're a criminal, irresponsible, heartless woman. My God! I can look at a corpse chopped to bits without batting an eyelid, but I can't bear the sight of a dead bird. Too heartrending. I can't even bear to see them suffer, birds, or get tired. During the making of my movie, in which I used fifteen hundred trained crows, there was a representative of the Royal Society for the Prevention of Cruelty to Animals on the scene at all times, and whenever he said, "That's enough now, Mr. Hitchcock, I think the birds are getting tired," I would stop at once. I have the highest consideration for birds, and, quite apart from the movie, I think it very right they should take their revenge on men that way. For hundreds of centuries birds have been persecuted by men, killed, put in the pot, in the oven, on the spit, used for writing pens, feathers for hats, turned into bloodcurdling stuffed ornaments. . . . Such infamy deserves exemplary punishment.

I see. In other words, your movie has a profound philosophic

*and moral significance: don't do to others what you wouldn't
like done to you.*

Not in the least. If there's one thing I'll never be able to do,
it's turn my collar back to front and play the part of preacher.
When people ask me what I think of movies that administer
philosophic and moral lessons, I say, "Don't you think it's
up to philosophers to teach philosophy and priests to teach
morals?" People don't go to the movies to listen to sermons.
If that were the case, then instead of buying a ticket they'd put
a coin in the collection plate and make the sign of the cross
before taking a seat in the stalls. People go to the movies to
be amused. And they pay a lot to be amused. Morality, you
know, is much less expensive than amusement.

*Yet I know you are very keen on morality, at least on a
certain kind of morality. You have never been divorced, your
life is untouched by scandal, and I know that one day, when
you happened to go with your wife to the Folies Bergère, you
left, saying, "This is a world of perdition."*

No, no. The story didn't go like that, it was much funnier.
I was thirty-one at the time, I'd been married five years, and
I was writing the scenario for a movie about a young couple
who go on a world tour and consequently visit the Folies
Bergère, where, in the interval, the girls also belly dance. Since
I'd never seen this belly dancing and couldn't even imagine
what it would be, I said to my wife, "Let's go to Paris." So we
went to Paris, and while we were there, we went to the Folies
Bergère. The interval came, and I asked a man I took to be the
manager, a fellow in a tuxedo, if we could see some belly dancing. The fellow said, "Come with me," and put us into a taxi.
The taxi immediately made off through winding streets, but
my wife and I were an innocent pair, and we didn't understand.
Then the taxi stopped outside a house that was one of those
houses where . . . well . . . anyway . . . my wife and I had never
been in that kind of place, you see, and so we stood there

watching in horror, you see, while those girls did things that weren't exactly belly dancing, you see, until I exclaimed, "But this is a world of perdition!" I was thirty-one. And I'd never been with any woman other than my wife.

I see. Of course, you'd judge the whole thing very differently today.

Oh no! I'm sixty-four now, and I can swear that I've never known any woman other than my wife—neither before nor since our marriage. When I married, I was a virgin, I promise you, and sex has never interested me much. I don't understand how people can waste so much time over sex: sex is for kids, for movies, a great bore. And since I've always avoided anything boring . . . I remember the day I had to write the screenplay for the movie *From Woman to Woman:* the story of a man who has a mistress in Paris who bangs his head, loses his memory, and starts going with another woman, who gives him a child. Well, I was twenty-three years old, I'd never been with a woman, and I didn't have the slightest idea what a woman did to have a child. I had even less idea what a man did when he was with his mistress in Paris or when he was with another woman who was giving him a child. And so . . .

Now you know, Mr. Hitchcock?

Now I know. I have a daughter of thirty-five and three little grandchildren. Between you and me, I'm a grandfather. Still, when I think that my daughter was born when I was nearly thirty, and it was only then that I realized that babies aren't found under gooseberry bushes. . . . You won't believe it—no one ever believes it, they say it's an act to make myself a character—but until I was twenty-four, I had never tasted a drop of alcohol; until I was twenty-five, I had never smoked a cigar. I was very shy, more shy than I am today. If people told dirty stories, I used to blush like a rose. So my friends would always tell them when I wasn't there, and if I arrived, they'd say, "Silence, Hitchcock's coming." As for my wife, I married her because she asked me to. We'd been traveling around and working together for years, and I'd never so much as touched her little finger.

But why on earth? Don't you like women, Mr. Hitchcock?

Indeed I like them, more than men. In point of fact, I feel less shy with them than with men. For example, I could never talk like this to a man. But I like them to talk to, to dine with, not for sexual reasons. When people ask me, "Mr. Hitchcock, why are the stars in your movies always blonds? Is it because you have a weakness for blonds?" I tell them I don't know, it must be coincidence or the fact that they are ladies; I've thought since I was a child that ladies are blond, my wife is blond. I don't have a weakness for anyone, neither for blonds nor redheads nor brunettes nor sexy women. . . . You know who are the sexiest women, I mean, the most wrapped up in sex? Nordic women. Evidently the cold makes them hot. Consider Englishwomen: they all look like schoolmistresses, but heaven help the poor fellow who finds himself in a taxi with one. At best he'll get out of it minus his clothes.

Forgive my asking, but how do you know these things, Mr. Hitchcock?

What a question! I listen to what people say, I find out about things. Obviously the information is secondhand. Scientists know that if you mix one powder with another powder, you'll be blown up. But they don't have to be blown up in order to know it.

Too right. Your wife must be very grateful to you, Mr. Hitchcock.

I hope she is. Apart from the fact that in thirty-seven years I have never been unfaithful to her, not even in thought, there aren't many husbands like me. Just think: as we only have a daily maid, my wife has to do the cooking. But when she's getting a meal ready, I help her, and after we've eaten, I wash the dishes. I wash them and dry them and put them away.

Well done. If you get divorced, I'll marry you myself.

Thank you, it's always nice to feel one's wanted. But if you marry me, don't be under any illusion. For me a good stew is worth more than a pretty little nose, and the first thing I expect of my wife is to be good at cooking. Are you a good cook? My wife is an excellent cook, and I could die eating. The things that make me happiest in the world are eating, drinking, and sleeping. I sleep like a newborn babe. I drink like a fish, have you seen what a red face I have? And I eat like a pig. Even if it does make me look more and more like a porker myself. Some days ago, walking along in New York, I saw myself reflected in a window, and before I recognized myself, I let out a yell of fright. Then I called to my wife, "Who's that porker on two legs?" I didn't want to believe it when she replied, "It's you, dear."

I imagine you don't often yell with fright. Practiced as you are in frightening other people, fear must be completely unknown to you.

On the contrary. I'm the most fearful and cowardly man you'll ever meet. Every night I lock myself into my room as if there were a madman on the other side of the door, waiting to slit my throat. I'm frightened of everything: burglars, policemen, crowds, darkness, Sundays. . . . Being frightened of Sundays goes back to when I was a child and my parents used to put me to bed at six o'clock so that they could go out and eat in a restaurant. I used to wake up at eight o'clock, my parents weren't there, there was only that dim light, that silence of an empty house. Brrr! It wasn't accidental, when I married, that I said to my wife, "Every Sunday I want a fine dinner with lots of light, lots of people, and lots of noise." Being frightened of policemen started when I was about eleven. I had been on a bus ride as far as the terminal, and I didn't have the money for the return fare. I made my way back on foot and reached home after nine. We used to live in the district of Soho, in London; my father was a poultry dealer. My father opened the door and didn't say a word, not a word of reproof, nothing. He just gave me a note and said, "Take it to Watson." Watson was a policeman, a family friend. He'd no sooner got the note than he shut me in a cell, shouting, "This is what happens to bad boys who get home after nine o'clock." Brrr! It was fifty-three years ago, but every time I see a policeman, I start shaking. And then I'm frightened of people having rows, of violence. I've never had a row with anyone, and I've no idea of how to come to blows. And then I'm frightened of eggs, worse than frightened; they revolt me. That white round thing without any holes, and when you break it, inside there's that yellow thing, round, without any holes. . . . Brrr! Have you ever seen anything more revolting than an egg yolk breaking and spilling its yellow liquid? Blood is jolly, red. But egg yolk is yellow, revolting. I've never tasted it. And then I'm frightened of my own movies. I never go to see them. I don't know how people can bear to watch my movies.

That's rather illogical, Mr. Hitchcock. Come to that, your movies are illogical, too. From the logical point of view, not one of them can stand inspection.

Agreed. But what is logic? There's nothing more stupid than logic. Logic is the result of reasoning, reasoning is the result of experience, and who's to say whether our experiences are the right ones? My dog doesn't understand music, Bach bores him to death. Does that mean my dog is illogical? It only means that his experiences are different from Bach's. I don't attach any importance to logic. None of my movies is based on logic. They are based on suspense, not on logic. Give me a bomb, and Descartes can go boil his head. There's nothing like a good bomb for creating suspense. Suspense, not surprise.

Enlighten me and our readers, Mr. Hitchcock. Explain suspense to us.

Right. Suppose this interview were a scene in a movie. We're sitting here talking, and we don't know that there's a bomb hidden inside your tape recorder. The public doesn't know either, and suddenly the bomb explodes: we're blown to bits.

Surprise, horror of public. But how long does it last, the surprise and the horror? Five seconds, no more. With suspense, however, we're sitting there, and we don't know that there's a bomb hidden inside your tape recorder. But the public knows, and it also knows that it will explode in ten minutes. Obviously the public gets worried, anxious, says, "Why do they sit there talking, those two? Don't they realize there's a bomb hidden inside the tape recorder?" Suspense. But a second before the ten minutes are up, I bend over the tape recorder and say, "Aha! There's a bomb inside here." I pick up the tape recorder and fling it away. End of suspense. The secret is never to let the bomb explode. I had it explode, once, in the hands of a child who had boarded a bus, three minutes after the arranged time, and it was a very grave mistake. I'll never make the same mistake again. People must suffer, sweat, but at the end they must heave a sigh of relief.

· *And do you like suspense, Mr. Hitchcock?*

Far from it. I hate it. I hate it so much that I can't even bear to stay in the kitchen when my wife is making a soufflé. Will it rise? Won't it rise? I bought an oven with a glass door so I could see whether it was rising, but it hasn't helped. I can't bear to wait the necessary eighteen minutes to see if it'll rise.

On the subject of bombs, Mr. Hitchcock. In your movie Notorious *you talked about the atomic bomb, which, if I'm not mistaken, hadn't yet exploded on Hiroshima.*

That's an extraordinary story, I really must tell it to you. Because MacGuffin comes into it, too. Have you got enough tape left?

Yes, there's enough tape. Mac . . . what?

MacGuffin. You must know that when I'm making a movie, the story isn't important to me. What's important is how I tell the story. For example, in a movie about espionage what the spy is looking for isn't important, it's how he looks for it. Yet I have to say what he's looking for. It doesn't matter to me, but it matters a great deal to the public, and most of all it matters to the character in the movie. Why should the character go to so much trouble? Why does the government pay him to go to so much trouble? Is he looking for a bomb, a secret? This secret, this bomb, is for me the MacGuffin, a word that comes from an old Scottish story. Should I tell it to you? Is there enough tape?

Yes, yes. There's enough tape.

Well, two men are traveling in a train, and one says to the other, "What's that parcel on the luggage rack?" "That? It's the MacGuffin," says the other. "And what's the MacGuffin?" asks the first man. "The MacGuffin is a device for catching lions in Scotland," the other replies. "But there aren't any lions in Scotland," says the first man. "Then it isn't the MacGuffin," answers the other. Clear? Logical?

Very clear, very logical.

Well, in 1944, then, I'm making this movie *Notorious*, with Ingrid Bergman. She's going to South America, where some Germans are working on something. Ingrid Bergman is going there because she's a spy and has to find out for the American government what the Nazis are working on. As well as Ingrid Bergman there's Cary Grant, who has to find out the same thing because he's working for the FBI. Naturally Ingrid Bergman and Cary Grant fall in love, and when Ingrid Bergman has to go to bed with a Nazi to find out what it is, Cary Grant is very unhappy. Well, this thing they had to find out, the MacGuffin, I had no idea what it might be, and in the end I decided in favor of the atom bomb. Ingrid Bergman would have gone to South America to find out if the Nazis were preparing the atom bomb there. Naturally I didn't even know what the atom bomb might be. But I knew that uranium existed, that since 1929 the atom had been split, and I had read a book by H. G. Wells called *The Mighty Atom*. So I imagined that sooner or later someone would make the atom bomb. Clear? Logical?

Very clear. Very logical.

Well, I'm making the film with Selznick, and Selznick asks me, "What's Ingrid Bergman looking for in South America?" "She's looking for uranium," I reply. "What's uranium?" he asks me. "It's the thing they use to make the atom bomb," I reply. "What's the atom bomb?" he asks. "A bomb," I say. "It's about Ingrid Bergman, who falls in love with Cary Grant, and since Ingrid Bergman has to go to bed with a Nazi in order to find out if the Nazi has the atom bomb, Cary Grant is very unhappy. The atom bomb is of no importance: it's the MacGuffin." "I still don't like it," he says. And he sells me, Ingrid Bergman, Cary Grant, and the unfinished scenario to R.K.O., for eight hundred thousand dollars and 50 per cent of the profits. But I have to finish the scenario, and as I'm not sure about this uranium and how big an atom bomb is, I put my hat on and go to the California Institute of Technology, where the most important scientist of all is working: Doctor Millikan, director of the Manhattan project. Naturally I don't know he's directing the Manhattan project, I don't even know the Manhattan project exists; I only know that in New Mexico there exists a secret place where everyone goes in and no one comes out—a journalist told me about it. So I go in, "Good day, doctor. How are you?" I shake hands with the doctor, who has a bust of Einstein in a corner of the room, and I ask him, "Doctor, how big would an atom bomb be?" The scene that follows! He jumps up, yelling, "Do you want to be arrested? Do you want to get me arrested, too?" Then he spends an hour explaining to me that it was impossible to make the atom bomb, that the atom bomb never would be made, and that consequently I should not make the atom bomb my MacGuffin. I said all right. But I still had that bottle of uranium in the scenario, a dramatic sequence. I didn't want to give up the uranium, and so I made my MacGuffin the atom bomb anyway, and two years later the bomb exploded on Hiroshima. And the movie made eight million dollars.

Admirable, Mr. Hitchcock. But the main ingredients of your movies don't consist only of suspense and MacGuffin. I'd say your movies also consist of humor, humor mixed with the macabre.

I can't take any credit for that. For the English it's normal to mix humor with the macabre. You know the story about the two ladies at the fair watching a man eat the heads of live rats? Well, in horror one of them says, "Doesn't he ever eat bread with them?" And the one about the famous actor who's been killed by a bomb, do you know it? Well, there's the funeral of this famous actor, and all the actors go to it. As the coffin is being lowered into the grave, a young actor leans over to a very old actor called Charlie and asks, "Charlie, how old are you?" "Eighty-nine," says Charlie. "Then there's no point in your going home," says the young actor. And it goes without saying that, if it was up to me, I wouldn't send any of them home, actors.

I know, you aren't very fond of actors. You've boasted more than once that you have no friends among actors and cinema folk. "Actors," according to you, "are cows."

When they aren't cows, they're children: that's something else I've often said. And everyone knows that there are good children, bad children, and stupid children. The majority of actors, though, are stupid children. They're always quarreling, and they give themselves a lot of airs. The less I see of them, the happier I am. I had much less trouble directing fifteen hundred crows than one single actor. I've always said that Walt Disney has the right idea. His actors are made of paper; when he doesn't like them, he can tear them up. If I went around with actors, how could I possibly live a quiet life in Hollywood, in an old house without a swimming pool? Think of Kim Novak. Not that she isn't an artist, of course; she paints quite nicely and in the second part of *Vertigo*, when she's dark-haired and looks less like Kim Novak, I even managed to get her to act. But the only reason I took Kim Novak was because Vera Miles was pregnant.

That's not much of a compliment to Kim Novak.

Nor for Vera Miles. I ask you! I was offering her a big part, the chance to become a beautiful sophisticated blond, a real actress. We'd have spent a heap of dollars on it, and she has the bad taste to get pregnant. I hate pregnant women, because then they have children.

And Grace Kelly? Sorry, Her Most Serene Highness Princess Grace? What do you say about her?

Grace is better. She's sensitive, disciplined, and very sexy. People think she's cold. Rubbish! She's a volcano covered with snow. I was sorry I couldn't make *Marnie* with her, almost as sorry as she was. She was very keen to do it, you know. In point of fact I wasn't the one to go after her. It was she who came after me: "Hitch, haven't you got a part for me?" "Yes, Grace. The part of a lady robber." "Ah, splendid!" Unfortunately we broke the news at the wrong moment, when Rainier was having trouble with De Gaulle, and so they said she wanted to leave her husband just when he was having trouble with De Gaulle. Who could have expected it? Too bad. I'll use another blond.

But it's strange, Mr. Hitchcock, that you should be so disparaging about actors. To judge by the systematic way you appear in your own movies, one might think you have a smothered regret that you weren't an actor.

That's a custom that I started when I didn't have enough money to pay my actors, and I had to economize by doing walk-ons myself. As a result it became a superstition, and I decided always to put myself in my films: I even put myself in *Lifeboat*, a film that from beginning to end takes place in an open boat in the middle of the sea. It was a bit difficult to justify my appearance on the boat; I resolved the problem like this: one of the actors, William Bendix, finds an old newspaper in the boat. He opens it, and in the middle there's an advertisement for a slimming treatment, with the photograph of a fellow like a porker. The porker is me. Of course, it's clear that I also put myself in because I know people look for me, but I do it at the beginning of the film so that people aren't distracted by looking for me, and I appear briefly because nothing embarrasses me as much as a camera. I wouldn't have liked to be an actor for anything in the world. A criminal lawyer, that's the job I'd have liked. I'd have seen so many dramas and . . .

But, Mr. Hitchcock, aren't you able every now and then to view life as a drama? Haven't you ever by chance been involved in a dramatic situation?

No. Never. Only in movies. I never get involved in dramatic situations. You're the one who's in a dramatic situation.

Why, Mr. Hitchcock?

Because you have to write an article about me. And you don't know anything about me.

That's what you say, Mr. Hitchcock. But I do, Mr. Hitchcock. With all your cordial humor, your nice round face, your nice innocent paunch, you are the most wicked, cruel man I have ever met.

Cannes, May, 1963